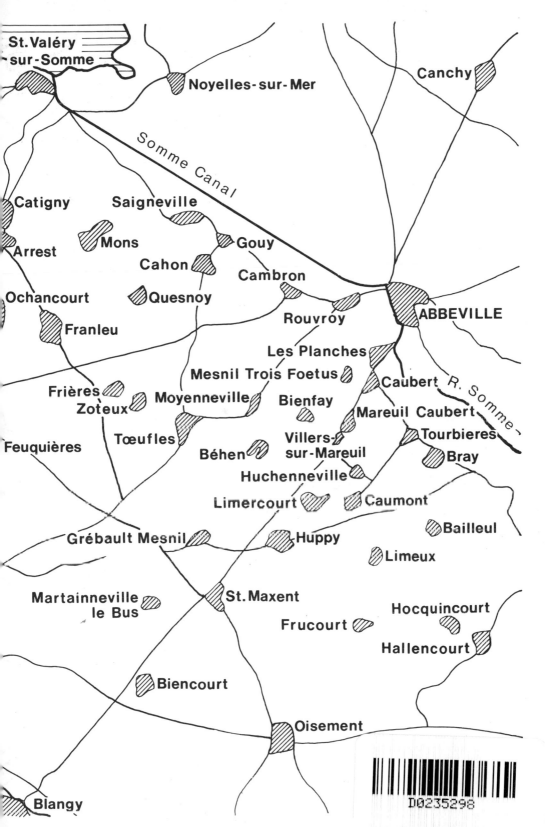

Map 1.   FROM THE SOMME TO THE BRESLE

CHURCHILL'S SACRIFICE
OF
THE HIGHLAND
DIVISION

FRANCE 1940

Major General Victor Fortune DSO.
General Officer Commanding 51st (Highland) Division 1937–40.
(*From a portrait by Fuller in the possession of the family*)

CHURCHILL'S SACRIFICE OF
THE HIGHLAND DIVISION

FRANCE 1940

Saul David

BRASSEY'S
London • Washington

First English edition 1994

UK editorial offices: Brassey's, 33 John Street, London WC1N 2AT
orders: Marston Book Services, PO Box 87, Oxford OX2 0DT

USA orders: Macmillan Publishing Company,
Front and Brown Streets, Riverside, NJ 08075

Distributed in North America to booksellers and wholesalers
by the Macmillan Publishing Company, NY 10022

Saul David has asserted his moral right to be identified as author of this work

Library of Congress Cataloging in Publication Data
available

British Library Cataloguing in Publication Data
A catalogue record for this book is available
from the British Library

ISBN 1–85753–039–X Hardcover

Printed in Great Britain by
Bookcraft (Bath) Limited

For Louise

Dedication

To the proud memory of all who fought with the 51st (Highland) Division in the Battle of France 1940. For the sake of Britain's honour, many gave their lives and many more suffered long years of bitter captivity.

Nemo Me Impune Lacessit

They went with songs to the battle, they were young,
Straight of limb, true of eye, steady and aglow.
They were staunch to the end against odds uncounted,
They fell with their faces to the foe.

They shall grow not old, as we that are left grow old:
Age shall not weary them, nor the years condemn.
At the going down of the sun and in the morning
We will remember them.

LAURENCE BINYON
For the Fallen

Contents

Acknowledgements

My incentive to write about the fate of the 1940 Highland Division was twofold: first, although some of the finest troops in the British Army were involved, the story remains a virtually unknown episode in military history, eclipsed by the earlier 'miracle' of Dunkirk; secondly, it stands out as a tragic example of how the individual soldier suffers needlessly from the miscalculations of his political masters. For both reasons it is a story that deserves to be told.

The plan was to produce a book that would combine the readability and immediacy of vernacular or first-hand accounts with the authority of detailed documentary research. Consequently, I had to spend as much time studying official war diaries, telegrams and reports as I did tracking down surviving members of the Division and the letters, diaries and written accounts of those no longer alive.

My first thank you must go to the scores of former veterans who replied to my initial enquiries, received me into their homes and patiently answered my often ill-informed questions on a subject that, even after 50 years, many still found painful to recall. They are all acknowledged by name at the end of this book in the Author's Note of Appreciation. Many families of former veterans also granted me invaluable assistance and generous hospitality, and I am grateful to them all. I would also like to thank those veterans and relatives who lent me photographs and, in particular, those who gave me permission to quote from unpublished diaries and first-hand accounts: Charles Barker, Andrew Biggar, Bill Bradford, Jimmy Hogarth, Gregor Macdonald, Mrs Katharine McCulloch, Philip Mitford, John Redfern, David Swinburn, Sir Richard Swinburn, Mrs E L Thompson, John Shaw of Tordarroch, Jim Walker. A special word of thanks to Raounill Ogilvie for allowing me to quote from two articles he wrote for the regimental magazine of the Gordon Highlanders and for checking the manuscript of this book for inaccuracies.

The Regimental Headquarters of the Highland Regiments involved in the campaign were exceptionally helpful. My gratitude to all the Regimental Secretaries for answering repeated enquiries and for allowing me access to, and permission to quote from, articles, diaries and other documents held in their museums: Colonel (Retd) Hon WD Arbuthnott MBE, Black Watch; Lieutenant Colonel (Retd) AA Fairrie, Queen's Own Highlanders (Seaforths & Camerons); Major David White and Captain (Retd) C Harrison, Gordon Highlanders; Lieutenant Colonel AW Scott Elliot, Argyll & Sutherland Highlanders. I am especially grateful to Colonel Scott Elliot for permission to use the painting *Fighting Spirit*, hanging in the Argylls' museum, to illustrate the front cover. Thanks are also due to Major General John Hopkinson, Colonel of the Queen's Own Highlanders, Rena McRobbie of the Regimental Headquarters, Argyll and Sutherland Highlanders, JER Macmillan of Regimental Headquarters, The Black Watch and the officials and members of the 2/6th East Surrey St Valéry Association, in particular Charles Bobart, Bill Bampton and Captain Noel Tannock.

Of the institutions that assisted me, I am grateful to the over-worked but ever-willing staff of the Public Record Office, the British Library, the Scottish United Services Museum, and the Imperial War Museum, in particular to James Taylor who was always encouraging and provided me with more than one useful contact.

A number of newspapers published free of charge my appeals to find veterans of the campaign, and I am very grateful: *Daily Record; Eastern Daily Press, Eastern Daily News* (both Norwich); *Edinburgh Daily News; Evening Chronicle* (Newcastle); *The Highland News Group, Inverness Courier, Scotland on Sunday, The Oban Times.*

Acknowledgments for permission to include quotations from *The War in France and Flanders 1939–40* and from documents held at the Public Record Office (both Crown copyright) are made to the Controller of HM Stationery Office; from Commander RF Elkins' *Secret Report* (Crown copyright) to the Trustees of the Imperial War Museum and the Controller of HM Stationery Office; from *The Rommel Papers*, edited by BH Liddell Hart, and *The Turn of the Tide 1939–43*, by Arthur Bryant, to HarperCollins Publishers; from *Return to St Valéry*, by Derek Lang, to Leo Cooper; from *The Fringes of Power*, by John Colville, to Hodder & Stoughton; from *Soldier On*, by Colonel Sir Mike Ansell, to the author; from *The Second World War: Volume II*, by Winston S Churchill, to Cassell; from *In the Thick of the Fight 1939–1945*, by Paul Reynaud, to Macmillan (US); from *Assignment to Catastrophe: Volume I*, by Major General EL Spears to William Heinemann, and *Recalled to Service*, by General Maxime Weygand, to Flammarion (France); and from the 12th June 1990 issue of the *Inverness Courier* to the Editor, John Macdonald.

A first-time author is always a bit of a risk for a publisher, and for this reason I am extremely grateful to the staff at Brassey's for retaining their faith in me despite more than one hiccup. In particular, I would like to thank Jenny Shaw, Caroline Bolton and, of course, my editor Brigadier Bryan Watkins, who was convinced about the viability of this book from the start.

Finally, I owe an incalculable debt of gratitude to my family and to Louise. Without their encouragement and support I would never have been able to give up my job and set out on an odyssey that has taken almost three years to complete.

Callow, June 1994.   SAUL DAVID

List of Plates

(Note: Photographs of individuals all date from before or after 1939–40. Unless credited, all are from private papers. Plates 22, 23 and 24 were all taken either by General Rommel or with his camera and are reproduced by permission of the Imperial War Museum. Ranks shown are those carried during the campaign and decorations shown are either those awarded before 1939 or for services during the campaign or for escapes)

Frontispiece: Major General Victor Fortune DSO
 1. Lieutenant Colonel Harry Swinburn MC
 2. Captain 'Bill' Bradford MBE, The Black Watch
 3. C Company 7th Royal Norfolks at Bizing
 4. Second Lieutenant Johnny Rhodes MC, The Gordon Highlanders and Pierre Boudet (French Army)
 5. At Boencourt. 2nd Seaforths in a fire position
 6. Major CJ Shaw-Mackenzie MBE, The Seaforth Highlanders
 7. Second Lieutenant 'Ran' Ogilvie, The Gordon Highlanders
 8. Second Lieutenants Diarmid Macalister Hall and John Parnell, The Argyll and Sutherland Highlanders
 9. Men of the 4th Black Watch on the Bresle
10. Second Lieutenant 'Ginger' Gall MC, The Gordon Highlanders, gets married
11. Company Quartermaster Sergeant GG Macdonald, The Queen's Own Cameron Highlanders
12. Second Lieutenant Jim Walker, The Royal Norfolk Regiment
13. Second Lieutenant Andrew Biggar MC, Royal Corps of Signals
14. Troop Sergeant Major Jimmy Hogarth DCM, 1st Lothians & Border Yeomanry
15. Private 'Sandy' Russell, The Queen's Own Cameron Highlanders
16. Lance Corporal George McLennan, The Gordon Highlanders
17. Lieutenant Colonel Mike Ansell DSO and officers of the 1st Lothians & Border Yeomanry at an Orders Group
18. Cany-Barville 10 June 1940. Mark VIB Light Tank 'Blue Bonnet' after it had been knocked out
19. A Field Dressing Station on the Somme

List of Maps

1

No Heroes Welcome

Arrive in the fashionable Norman coastal town of St Valéry-en-Caux today, and you are hard pressed to imagine the hell it was for thousands of trapped British soldiers of the 51st (Highland) Division on a June night in 1940, sacrificed by their government as a symbol of Allied unity in the war against Germany.

Little more than a brief interruption in the towering cliffs of the Le Havre peninsula coastline, St Valéry is a secluded spot that appeals to week-enders from Paris. It occurs to few of the Summer visitors who stroll along its seafront that the ground they tread was once blasted by shrapnel and raked by machine-gun fire, as the houses on the seafront burned fiercely; that the narrow, winding streets once rang to the clatter of runaway cavalry horses and panic-stricken soldiers; or that the post-war architecture of the buildings on the east side of the harbour is a legacy of the destruction wrought in 1940. Few will realise that this peaceful, neat seaside retreat once witnessed the last stand of Scotland's most famous fighting division, cut off from the safe haven of Le Havre by a panzer commander destined for greatness. Only the huge granite war memorial to the 51st (Highland) Division, brought from Scotland and raised on the cliff top high above the town in honour of the Highlanders who died, gives a hint to the tragedy.

* * *

In the small hours of 1 September 1939, 56 German divisions rumbled across the Polish frontier. Shortly before midday, two days later, with the expiry of an ultimatum to withdraw, Britain declared war on Germany, and within six hours France had followed suit. Sadly, Britain was wholly unprepared for such an eventuality.

Not until February 1939 had it been decided to send a British Expeditionary Force to France in the event of war. Prior to this the policy had centred around the theme of 'limited liability' – the engagement of only small land forces on the continent whilst the major effort was made on the sea and in the air – and in providing financial assistance for Britain's allies. In December 1937, the Cabinet accepted a paper by Thomas Inskip, Minister for the Co-ordination of Defence, placing strategic objectives in order of priority:

(1)   Protection of the home country against air attack
(2)   Safety of trade routes
(3)   Defence of British territories overseas
(4)   Co-operation in the defence of the territories of any allies we may have in war

The reappraisal of this policy in February 1939 came about because the Chiefs of Staff argued that the security of Britain could not be guaranteed if France was overrun. Hence, they concluded that self-defence 'may have to include a share in the land defence of French territory'.[1]

It was agreed that, if war broke out, four Regular infantry divisions and a mobile division would be immediately despatched to France and that to this end they would be equipped for mobile warfare – as would four divisions of the Territorial Army (TA). It was also decided, in principle, to create a large army of 32 divisions. On 29 March, 1939, just two weeks after Hitler reneged on the Munich Agreement and marched into Czechoslovakia, Mr Leslie Hore-Belisha, the Secretary of State for War, announced the doubling of the TA to provide extra troops, and authorised the resumption of Anglo-French military staff talks. The following month, conscription was introduced for the first time during peace, and agreement was reached with the French that the four Regular infantry divisions would be followed by Territorial divisions as they became 'ready'.

The big problem now was equipping the expanding TA at a time when existing *materiel* was already inadequate. The military establishment had been so long neglected that it was like trying to fit a quart into a pint pot. By the midsummer of 1939, even the four Regular divisions ear-marked for France had only about half of their establishment of anti-tank and anti-aircraft weapons, and about one third of their ammunition.

This neglect had its origins in the revulsion felt by the British people to the massive losses sustained during the First World War, and the desire within the Cabinet to slash spending on defence after the economic catastrophe of four years of fighting. In Autumn 1919 the Cabinet first outlined what came to be known as 'The Ten Year Rule': an agreement that the next year's defence spending estimates would be based on the assumption that there would be no major war for ten years. As a result, in every year from 1919 to 1932 the Army had its Vote for funds cut. It was further undermined by government pronouncements

– anticipating the policy of 'limited liability' – such as that of 1922, which made clear that the Army was responsible for home security and imperial defence, but should not be prepared for major war.[2]

The 'Ten Year Rule' was only dropped in 1931 when the Chiefs of Staff advised the Government that it had brought the military establishment to a dangerously low level of capability. Yet even in the 1930s, as Hitler assumed power and Germany went all out to rearm – expanding her army from 100,000 in 1933 to over two million men by the summer of 1939, despite the limitations imposed by the Treaty of Versailles – expenditure on the British Army was only modestly increased, and only increased at all after 1934. The situation began to improve when a five-year rearmament programme was agreed upon early in 1936, and when the Treasury set up a system of financial 'rationing' to apportion funds to the three Services the following year. Yet the direction of Army spending was as important as its level. In December 1937, ministers agreed a list of priorities for the Army, headed by anti-aircraft defence and trailing with commitments to operations in Europe. Although the Royal Air Force was allowed to order as many planes as industry could assemble by April 1938, the Army had to wait until after the Munich crisis for its 'rationing' to be suspended.

The effect of this neglect upon the Army was farcical, as a Regular officer, who would later fight with the 51st Division, recalls:

> I remember going on manoeuvres in 1938 in Suffolk. As soon as the date was announced, all the field officers, bar one, and most of the senior captains, found that they were unavoidably unable to attend because of engagements elsewhere and all took their leave. I found myself, as a very junior lieutenant, commanding C Company, consisting of myself, the Company Sergeant Major, the Company Quartermaster Sergeant, one other sergeant, four corporals, and about ten Jocks. The ridiculous sight which has always stuck in my mind, as it must have done in the minds of the locals, is of the company in column of route marching along a main road with me at the front, followed by the Company Sergeant Major and a platoon consisting of a sergeant and a Jock carrying a flag, then a long gap filled by the length of a tape held at the other end by another Jock. That was a platoon. As the new light machine-gun, the Bren, had not arrived yet, we had wooden silhouettes and wooden rattles to simulate the sound of them being fired. It's amazing to think that only 15 months before hostilities broke out, a Regular battalion was in this state.

The Territorial battalions of the pre-war 51st Division were no better off as far as equipment was concerned. Bren gun carriers, the new mobile arm of an infantry battalion, were only delivered during the Summer of 1939, leaving little time for training and tactics. Trench mortars, renamed as 3-inch Mortars, had recently been re-issued to the infantry, but bombs were so scarce that firing practice among the battalions of the 51st Division was usually restricted to dry-runs. Some mortar platoons would not loose a live round until they visited a French firing range in early 1940. The smaller, 2-inch Mortar was supposed to be issued to all infantry platoons. In fact, many in the 51st Division did not have their full complement, a number of mortars were without their firing pins, and, worst of all, there were smoke bombs but no high-explosive.

Overall, the weapons possessed by the British Army in 1940 were little advanced from those used in 1918. The infantryman still used the .303 Short Lee-Enfield rifle, with its long knife-edged bayonet, and the Mills grenade. Admittedly, the Lewis light machine-gun had given way to the lighter and more potent .303 Bren gun, but the medium machine-gun was still the .303 Vickers that had performed such yeoman service in the First World War. There was no standard issue of machine-pistols or sub-machine guns, as in the German Army. The .55 Boyes anti-tank rifle was one of the few weapons developed to take account of the changing face of war, yet it was only effective against the most lightly armoured tanks. The 25mm anti-tank gun, intended for brigade anti-tank companies, only began to be issued once the campaign was underway.

In terms of training, the Territorials were at a marked disadvantage to the Regulars. To fulfil his obligations a TA soldier simply had to attend a certain number of drill nights, a week-end camp when he fired his rifle, and two weeks at an annual Summer Camp. If he was present at all these exercises he was paid a bounty of £5. To the professionals, he was a 'week-end' soldier, and this lack of operational training allied to the paucity of his equipment boded badly for the campaign in France. That the Territorial Yeomanry were in the same boat as the infantry is clear from the following anecdote, told by a Warrant Officer of the 1st Lothians and Border Horse, a regiment that was to serve with the 51st Division in France:

> In June '39 I went on the first of the Militia Instructors' War Courses. It was telescoped from three months into a month and was held at the Gunnery school at Lulworth. I got a month off work, and when war broke out I was, at age 20, the only qualified gunnery instructor in the regiment. My Squadron Sergeant Major, Alfie Upton, actually came to me and said, 'Look, will you tutor me up on the guns, I'm not *au fait* with them at all'. That was the .5 Vickers, and the Bren. It shows you the poor state of the British Army at the time. To think that a raw, stupid boy was the only one in the know was unbelievable.

But there was another malaise, spiritual rather than tangible, that was potentially as destructive to military capacity as a lack of training or equipment. The Government's neglect of the Armed Forces in the 1930s had ridden tandem with a policy of appeasing potentially belligerent powers. This had had the effect of stigmatising war in the minds of the people, reducing martial ardour to a low-ebb, and lowering respect for the military, as a young officer in the 1st Gordons recalls:

> I didn't believe that war was possible, being brought up in the shadow of the First World War. I think that was the general feeling. A lot of people say it wasn't but I think that is hindsight. I used to go to London for dances and things, and people would ask me what I did. When I said I was in the Army they would be shocked. 'The Army!' There was a tremendous anti-military feeling. Not in Scotland because the Army has always been very popular there, but certainly in England.

* * *

At the time of its mobilisation, 1 September 1939, the 51st (Highland) Division comprised the usual infantry complement of nine battalions divided into three brigades – numbered 152, 153 and 154. Among these, all five Highland regiments – in order of seniority, The Black Watch, The Seaforth Highlanders, The Queen's Own Cameron Highlanders, The Gordon Highlanders, and The Argyll & Sutherland Highlanders – were represented. Completing the fighting arm of the division were four regiments of artillery and a light reconnaissance of the Royal Armoured Corps. All these troops were backed up by units of the Royal Corps of Signals, the Royal Engineers, the Royal Army Service Corps, the Royal Army Ordnance Corps and the Royal Army Medical Corps.

For the few weeks that the division remained in Scotland, its training was devoted mainly to route marches, drilling and basic weapon training. Because of the initial lack of uniform, some men trained in suits; the rest in service-dress and kilts covered by khaki aprons. In early October, the battalions of the division were moved south to concentrate in and around Aldershot prior to embarkation. Training here became more intense. Specialist platoons, such as the signallers, the anti-aircraftmen, and the Bren-gun carrier crews learned to operate their equipment. For the riflemen, two years of Regular infantry training was compressed into a bare three months: everything from camouflage to map reading, digging to sending messages had to be practised. But there was a basic flaw in all this work: British military strategy and tactics were still based on the primacy of defence which had proved so dominant for most of the First World War. When the British Army, and the French for that matter, was faced with the problems of mobile warfare, it was poorly trained to deal with them. Defensive positions were expected to be held to the last and strategic withdrawals had no place in the Army's training manuals.

* * *

It all began for the Highland Division where it so nearly ended in rescue, at the bustling port of Le Havre – just 30 agonisingly-few miles down the flat Normandy plain from St Valéry. Before the outbreak of war, it was thought that Le Havre was too vulnerable to bombing to be used as a Base Port for the British Expeditionary Force (BEF). But by late September 1939, it was opened to supply ships because its unmatched facilities were needed to help relieve the overloaded lines of communication from France's western ports. The 51st was the first British division to land there at the end of January 1940, having been narrowly pipped by the 48th for the honour of being the first Territorial division to arrive in France.

In strong contrast to the ecstatic welcome given to the arriving troops of the BEF in 1914, the war-weary French were no more than luke-warm in their greetings. No civic reception and no brass band awaited these conquering heroes. Instead, they were hustled to the transit camps near to the quays to be fed, and then sent by rail, usually after a delay of some hours, to the Concentration Area for new arrivals around the towns of Bolbec and Lillebonne, about 15 miles due east. From there they had to march a short distance to their billets in the outlying villages; a miserable experience with France, and the whole of Europe for that matter, suffering the most severe winter anyone could remember since the turn of the century. Living conditions for the officers billeted in houses were just about bearable; not so for the ordinary soldiers in sheds and barns, according to Company Quartermaster Sergeant Gregor Macdonald of the 4th Camerons:

> Our billets would be on a small farm near the town, and although it was snowing hard, we contented ourselves with the thought of a nice dry hayshed or barn. Imagine our feelings when we arrived at a group of broken-down wooden sheds all of which housed lean, hungry cattle, and it was clear that no attempt had been made to clear the sheds out. After much delay we finally contacted the farmer, a filthy unshaven individual who made it clear that we were not welcome. One of our officers spoke fluent French and, after much haggling, the farmer eventually produced a cart of evil-smelling hay, and each man was allowed his ration. It was now dark and our company cooks set up their cookhouse, consisting of four

sheets of corrugated iron. Soon a dixie of M&V [meat and vegetable] rations was heating up on the pressure burner. The farm cattle had been turned out during daylight hours and had churned up the mud round the sheds until it was over the uppers of our army boots and we had permanently wet and frozen feet ... In the evening, the cattle returned to their stalls and were chained a matter of ten feet from where we slept, so we were in constant danger of being spattered in our beds. The flagstones were rough and uneven but when we had cleaned up as well as we could we spread the musty hay and rolled up in our single blanket. We were very tired and soon fell asleep. So ended our first day in France.[3]

When the 51st Division landed in France, the BEF was stationed along a section of the Franco-Belgian border. It comprised just one Territorial and five Regular divisions. The first four Regular formations – the 1st, 2nd, 3rd and 4th Divisions – sent over following the outbreak of war as part of the continental commitment agreed with the French, had been joined by the 5th Division towards the end of October. When the first Territorial division, the 48th, appeared in January the Force was split into I and II Corps, each of three divisions, and the first stage of the development of the BEF was complete. By the end of January the number of British troops in France had reached 222,200.

The next stage in the planned expansion of the Force was the establishment of III Corps, consisting of three Territorial infantry divisions, of which the 51st was the first to embark. The remainder of this corps – the 42nd and 46th Divisions – were scheduled to arrive in France in early February, as was the 50th (Motorised) Division. The 1st Armoured Division would arrive in May and a fourth corps in the late Summer of 1940, at which point the BEF would be divided into two armies, each of six infantry divisions.[4]

On 3 September 1939, command of the BEF had been given to the then Chief of the Imperial General Staff, General The Viscount Gort. His reputation as a fighting soldier with the Grenadier Guards during the First World War was legendary: four times wounded, nine mentions in despatches and decorated with three DSOs, an MC, and finally a VC, won just one month before the end of hostilities. Yet his credentials for leading an army in wartime were limited. Since 1918 he had done mainly staff work, the largest formation he had commanded was only a brigade. He was a soldier's soldier though, and had the advantage of vigorous good health and relative youth for an army commander (he was 53). Indeed, it was soon common knowledge among his troops that he shared their hardships by sleeping on a camp bed in his headquarters and generally shunned the life of luxury that most men of his station enjoyed.

Gort's instructions from the War Office left him very little room for manoeuvre as far as operations independent of the French were concerned. Paragraph two read:

> You will be under the command of the French C-in-C 'North-East Theatre of Operations' [General Georges]. In the pursuit of the common object, the defeat of the enemy, you will carry out loyally any instructions issued by him. At the same time, if any order given by him appears to you to imperil the British Field Force, it is agreed between the British and French Govts that you should be at liberty to appeal to the British Govt before executing that order. . .[5]

This right of appeal, as a last resort, was crucial and ultimately afforded Gort the moral authority to disobey French orders and save the bulk of the BEF by withdrawing it to Dunkirk for evacuation. Unfortunately, the right of appeal did not apply to a divisional commander and this omission would ultimately prove fatal for the 51st (Highland) Division.

Since 1937, the Highland Division had been commanded by Major General Victor Fortune, a Lowlander from the Borders but a man who had commanded the 1st Black Watch in the First World War and was reputed to have been the only officer of the original 1914 battalion who had served throughout without being wounded. His fighting record from that war, capped by the award of a DSO, was enviable, if less illustrious than Gort's. But, like Gort, he was a general after his men's hearts. He understood and got on well with the ordinary soldier and when the division was training in England, he would often appear to talk to the Jocks. At 56-years-old he was by no means over the hill – although older than his army commander – but he would feel every one of those years in the rigours that lay ahead.

The original plan was for III Corps, including the 51st Division, to extend the sector held by the BEF along the Belgian border in a northerly direction. It was postponed for almost two months, while the 51st Division was temporarily stationed in a rear area, because the remaining divisions which were to make up the corps were held back in Britain on standby for a possible expedition to help the Finns in their war with Russia.

By the end of February, the men of the 51st Division were set to work digging an anti-tank ditch in the Corps Reserve Line as part of the system of defences being constructed by the BEF known as 'The Gort Line'. In effect, it was a poor man's extension of the Maginot Line – the massive and elaborate chain of fortresses, enclosed gun positions and tank traps built by the French along their common border with Germany in the 1930s.

Unfortunately, most of the sweat being shed by the BEF was likely to be for nothing as the Allied armies north of the Maginot Line never intended to stand on this defensive position and wait for the enemy. Instead, should the Germans breach Belgian neutrality, the plan was to march into Belgium to the line of the River Dyle and join up with the Belgian Army, to hold the Germans there. The drawback was that the Allies were dependent upon neutral Belgium preparing adequate defences, since no Allied troops were likely to be invited across the Belgian frontier until Germany had *already* invaded. Furthermore, the success of this plan to send the cream of the Allied armies into Belgium depended on the assumption that, as in 1914, Germany would attack with the bulk of its forces marching through Belgium. If Germany aimed her *schwerpunkt* – point of greatest pressure – elsewhere, France and the BEF were in trouble.

But such sceptical strategic overviews were not the domain of the private soldier. If he was told to dig, he didn't ask why and in some cases he enjoyed doing it. Particularly suited to the task were the men of the 7th Argylls. Unlike its sister battalion in the same brigade, the 8th, which was recruited from the rural highlands and islands of Argyllshire, the 7th Battalion was a Highland unit in name only, as it drew many of its men from the industrialised Stirling district. One platoon in particular, the 11th, came from the mining community of Alloa and so its members were used to working with pick and shovel. Their officer, Second Lieutenant Jim Atkinson, recalls that the speed with which they worked was 'astonishing'. The Royal Engineers who were supervising the work were also impressed: they reported that the Jocks of 154 Brigade shifted more earth per hour than Chinese coolies had in the First World War, when the latter had the reputation as the hardest workers.

It was not all work and no play, though. Alcohol was relatively cheap for British servicemen, paid twice as much as their French counterparts, and drinking at the local *estaminet* offered a welcome relief from the boredom of the 'Phoney War'. Corporal Jock Cairns of the 8th Argylls later wrote about one particularly raucous occasion:

> Before we left for the *estaminets*, the CSM briefed us as to our good behaviour. We were to impress our allies, he said. Enjoying the atmosphere of the *estaminet*, but not the quality of the beer, our Company D were quite happy, when the door was pushed open, and the Black Watch of our brigade stormed in ... We experienced our first battle in France, and apparently this was the tradition, as the same occurred between our fathers in the Argylls and the Black Watch in 1914, World War 1. I kept

on thumping away on the piano until hit by a bottle of beer, presumably empty, as no Scot, irrespective of clan, would have wasted beer, not even the mild French type.[6]

* * *

Not all the original troops of the 51st Division were destined to remain. By the end of February, Gort's General Staff had decided to switch certain units for Regular ones in an effort to 'stiffen' the division with professionals. On hearing the news, General Fortune wrote to his corps commander, Lieutenant General Sir Ronald Adam, suggesting two options: either to take from each brigade the junior battalion of the regiment with two battalions in it, or to aim for regimental brigades by retaining the two Seaforth, Gordon, and Argyll battalions and adding their Regular counterparts. In the event neither option was chosen: the first, because there was no Regular Argyll battalion in the BEF; the second, because it would have left the Cameron Highlanders unrepresented in the division.

Instead, the 6th Battalions of Seaforth, Gordons and Black Watch were removed and replaced by their available Regulars. As a result, the 2nd Seaforths, 1st Gordons and 1st Black Watch joined 152, 153 and 154 Brigades respectively. To strengthen the artillery, the 76th and 77th Field Regiments were exchanged for the Regulars of the 17th and 23rd Field Regiments, while the 238th Field Company, Royal Engineers changed over with the Regular 26th Field Company. Fortune had got his way, in that the Highland unity of the infantry was maintained, but his expressed hope that the changes would be temporary – he suggested three to six months – never got the chance to be put to the test before being overtaken by events.[7]

* * *

In September 1939, it had been decided by the War Office that kilts, the traditional Highland battle attire that had given rise to the First World War nickname 'The Ladies from Hell', were not suited to the increased mechanisation of modern warfare, and afforded no practical protection against gas attack. Accordingly, each Highland battalion was ordered to hand in its kilts before embarking, although many officers retained theirs in their kit bags, as did the pipe bands. The 1st Battalion, The Gordon Highlanders, who were to join the Highland Division on 7 March in place of the 6th Gordons, had embarked with the 1st Division for France in September, just before the order to hand in the kilts was issued. It was not until December that instructions to switch to Battle Dress finally caught up with it, but few of its men were sad to see the back of the kilt.

During the latter months of 1939, the 1st Gordons had spent much time digging anti-tank defences near to the Belgian border. As they still had the kilt then, they were able to get some idea what it must have been like for their forebears in the trenches of the previous war when terrible sores from mud-caked kilts were an everyday occurrence. Furthermore, the Army had become largely mechanised since 1918, and wearing a kilt in a Bren carrier, a lorry or especially on a motorbike was hardly practical.

The Territorials of the 5th Gordons were much put out by the directive from the War Office and had marked the removal of their kilts in January prior to embarkation with a symbolic ritual. The Commanding Officer, Lieutenant Colonel Alick Buchanan-Smith, arranged a parade on the square at Bordon in which a single kilt was ceremoniously burnt as a symbol, so he said, that for 200 years the English had wanted to take away the kilt from the Highlanders and now they had succeeded. A little stone memorial to this effect was built on the spot, the inscription ending with the words: 'We hope not for long'.

Only one Highland battalion (not part of the 51st Division) managed to defy the War Office and go into battle wearing the kilt – the 1st Camerons. Some members of the battalion were still wearing kilts as they were herded off to prison camp.

* * *

At the end of March, the long awaited extension of the BEF front on the Belgian border got underway, and the 51st Division was moved into the front line around Bailleul. Meanwhile, the Finns had signed an armistice with Russia on 13 March, thereby releasing the divisions held back in Britain. In fact, the French government had just won Britain's agreement to open a second front in Finland, and so the Allies had been saved by a matter of days from a war with Russia as well as Germany.

2

The Saar

Thirteen April was to prove an inauspicious date. On that day word was received that the Highlanders would be the first division to do a tour of duty in the Saar area of Lorraine. Since early December, British infantry brigades had been sent to this sector in front of the Maginot Line to gain valuable combat experience against German troops, but by the end of March the French High Command had agreed to General Gort's request to extend the sector to divisional strength so as to accelerate the 'battle-hardening' of the BEF.

Initially, the Regular 5th Division was chosen, but with the German invasion of Denmark and Norway on 9 April it was earmarked to help the Norwegians. In its place would go the 'Fighting Fifty-First'. But this would be no ordinary division; it would have attached to it two pioneer battalions (the 7th Royal Norfolks and the 6th Royal Scots Fusiliers), two machine gun battalions (1st Kensingtons and 7th Royal North-umberland Fusiliers), and additional artillery and engineers bringing its total strength to a formidable 21,000.

The plan was for 154 Brigade and supporting troops to move into the original British sector on 21 April, with the remaining two brigades concentrating in the Metz area prior to taking over from the French on either side of 154 Brigade at the beginning of May. Fortunately, not all the Highlanders were strangers to the Maginot Line. Since the end of February, cadres of five officers and five senior NCOs from the infantry had been attached to the British brigade in the Saar sector for five day tours. Also, before its switch to the Highland Division, the 1st Black Watch had spent three weeks in December, including Christmas Day, in the Saar with 12 Brigade.

By 16 April, Advance Parties of 154 Brigade and its supporting arms had reached the Metz area. The following day the main body of troops arrived by rail and road. Coming from the flat and uninspiring landscape of the Pas de Calais, the rolling country of the Saar heartland was a more than welcome relief for the Scots. Peppered with huge beech woods and blossoming orchards, these much disputed fields of Lorraine – under German control until as recently as 1918 – could not have looked less like a battleground. Even the vaunted Maginot Line was not easily detected. Rather than a continuous line, it was a chain of concealed, underground fortresses with guns that rose hydraulically to their embrasures. Only the intervening blockhouses, the anti-tank ditch, the barbed wire, and the network of half-buried steel rails, acting as anti-tank obstacles, indicated a defensive system.

Acting in concert with the Maginot forts were a series of support lines, their number depending on the area: In the original British brigade sector there was a *ligne de contact* (front line), a *ligne de soutiens* (second line), a *ligne de receuil* (recoil line) and a *ligne d'arrêt* (final stop line); whereas the two new brigade sectors to be taken over by the British, either side of the old sector, had no *ligne de soutiens*. The idea behind the front two lines was that they would blunt an attack and prevent reconnaissance in strength of the Maginot Line itself. In the event of a serious attack, their defenders would withdraw to the *ligne de receuil*, but in no instances would the *ligne d'arrêt* – situated just behind the forts – be pierced. Nowhere, not even in the stop line, was there a continuous trench system, and to cover any possible withdrawal from the forward lines there were a series of *brisants*, or V-shaped works, just in front of the forts. But much work still had to be done before the half-finished stop line and *brisants* were effective. On his arrival in the stop line, the 4th Camerons' Pioneer Officer estimated that 80,000 sandbags, 2,000 'A' frames, 2,000 sheets of revetting material, 600 coils of barbed wire, and 1,200 wiring pickets were the minimum materials needed to make the defences secure.

Distances between five and nine miles separated the forts and the front line, with the second line usually only a mile or so from the first and the recoil line a few miles further back still. In this area east of the Maginot, farms and villages had been evacuated by the military, giving the landscape a ghostly feel. When the guns were quiet, only the singing of the ubiquitous nightingale gave evidence of life.

The Regulars of 154 Brigade, the 1st Black Watch, were the first to go into the front line, not least because they had gained valuable experience the previous December. On 20 April, the 7th Argylls took over the *ligne de soutiens* from the 5th Gloucesters, and a day later the 1st Black Watch relieved the 8th Worcesters in the *ligne de contact*. Both battalions had their headquarters in the village of Waldweisstroff. Defences in the front line were little more than a series of scattered outposts, usually holding a section, or ten men, and consisting of dug-outs and fox-holes surrounded by barbed-wire. Private Alan Brierley of A Company was in the first post to get a taste of action:

The first night we were in the trenches I was on barbed-wire patrol, which meant checking the wire around the perimeter for breaks with a lance corporal. We had to go back out again in the morning just before dawn and we had just returned when the Germans attacked us with mortars ... Eventually, one of our patrols cleared out the wood they were firing from.

The inside of my helmet was covered in blood, and the men at my back and side had been wounded with shrapnel. They started to carry one man back on a stretcher when the mortaring started again; the men carrying the stretcher just dropped it in the open and ran back to the trench. The wounded man was screaming his head off, so I ran out to see if there was anything I could do. But there was a big lump of shrapnel sticking out of his side and I knew he was a 'goner'. I got the signalmen to phone through to get someone up to take him away. They eventually did this, using a Bren gun carrier, but he died the next day.

After six days in the line, the Black Watch were relieved by men of the 7th Argylls, who were in turn relieved in the second line by the 8th Argylls. For most of the 7th Argylls, this was the first time in contact with an enemy. Second Lieutenant Diarmid Macalister Hall, a Supplementary Reserve officer aged just 20, was positioned with 8 Platoon of A Company in outposts in the middle of the left corner of the Hartbusch Wood. He and half the platoon were in the right post, a sergeant and the other half in the left. There had been a position right on the forward edge of the wood, but this had been attacked and eliminated during the winter and was never reoccupied. Macalister Hall recalls:

The waiting as dusk fell, wondering what was to come during the night, straining your eyes into the beech wood, was an unnerving experience. I already knew, and was to discover again, that if you stare at something in the dark long enough it moves. During our second night without sleep, a grenade was thrown into the trench, wounding three men. My Platoon Sergeant, Seatter, heard the grenade coming in and sent me flying round the corner of the trench. But for his quick action I would have been hit. We fired back, shooting blindly for a while and then stopped. Nothing more took place and because the wounded weren't serious, we waited until dawn to evacuate them. I remember having to explain and answer for expending a certain amount of ammunition with nothing to show for it.

The day before the 7th Argylls had moved into the front line, all nine infantry battalions of the 51st Division were issued with instructions on patrolling. As well as confirming the embodiment of brigade battle patrols, for 'enterprising' and 'active' work, battalions were also told to organise company patrols on a 'parochial' basis whose primary duty would be 'defensive'. The number suggested for the patrols was one officer and twelve men.[1]

Second Lieutenant John Parnell of the 7th Argylls, aged just 19, had gained a Regular commission from Sandhurst only the previous October. His first taste of the front line and local patrolling showed that no amount of Military Academy training could make up for combat experience.

> On patrol we wore the absolute minimum and just had our weapons and little else so that we could move quickly and get through fences. We didn't have sub-machine guns like the fighting patrols; the only weapons we had were the rifle and the Bren. I carried a revolver. It was only later, on the Somme, that I discovered how useless a revolver was and used a rifle instead. I don't think we blacked our faces or anything sophisticated like that, and we had no communications at all. We always went out at night and would move slowly and carefully on foot; if you started to crawl you would never get anywhere. We bumped a German patrol one night and I think both of us were equally frightened of the situation, fired like blazes and scarpered as quickly as possible. We weren't exactly experienced soldiers at that stage.

Among the first units of 152 Brigade to reach the forward area of the Maginot Line were its battle patrols. On 29 April, the patrols' commander, Major James Murray Grant of the 2nd Seaforths, moved his men into Waldweisstroff – the village that bisected the 152 and 154 Brigade Sub-sectors and was being used as headquarters by the two forward battalions of 154 Brigade. He was an unhappy man that day: the billets were very poor and he had just received word from GHQ in Arras that, other than the handful he had been issued, there were no more Tommy guns available for the fighting patrols, at least for the meantime.

The next day, Major Grant and his officers – Chandos Blair of the 2nd Seaforths, John Anderson and 'HAC' MacKenzie of the 4th Seaforths, and Donald Cochrane of the 4th Camerons – were taken by members of a French battle patrol on a reconnaissance of the forward area shortly to be taken over by 152 Brigade. But after a riotous lunch with drunken Frenchmen at their company post in the front line, involving much backslapping and innumerable toasts to the Allies, the 'recce' degenerated into a farce, with the French battle patrol commander using a grenade to blow up a garden fence. Grant later noted in his diary that 'had it occurred a few days later we'd have all been shot!!' Grant then visited the commandant of the French battalion in the front line. His record of this meeting indicates his dwindling confidence in the French will to fight:

> The Commandant was a nervy wreck. Obviously no proper patrolling had been done by them and the Germans had the upper hand and complete freedom of movement in that area. When I tried to get permission to take out my officers on patrol during the next few nights i.e. until 152 bde took over from the French, he nearly fainted. Shouted to me that there must be no movement at night and no contact with the enemy until they, the French, got out of the *ligne de contact.* Pointed out that the object of our coming up in advance of our units was to gain experience from his unit, to no avail.[2]

Despite repeated pleas, Grant was refused permission by the French to take his patrols out during the following nights and had to wait until his own battalion, the 2nd Seaforths, had moved up. His faith in French *élan* had been shattered, but consolation was near at hand with the rapport he struck up with the French battle patrols, and their generosity in leaving him five Skoda sub-machine guns and some offensive grenades. The night before they departed, the French patrol commander gave a party which began at 6.30 pm and ended some six hours later, with each side promising to meet again, two years to the day, in Paris at the Place de la Concorde. It was an engagement that few were in a position to fulfil.

Sergeant John Mackenzie of the 2nd Seaforths also sampled the unofficial French policy of 'live and let live' when, as part of an Advance Party from 152 Brigade, he spent the night of 1/2 April with members of the 102nd French Regiment, prior to his own battalion relieving them. Of greatest surprise to Mackenzie was the unspoken arrangement between the French and the Germans whereby parties of less than six were never fired on, and two ration trucks were allowed to move up unmolested twice a day as long as they stuck to the hours of ten in the morning and four in the afternoon. But this was nothing compared to the French lack of aggression at night:

> I decided to spend my first night in one of the outside posts to gain experience, and so at 20:30 hrs I crawled into my post with three French companions. I caused a good deal of consternation by trying to get in with bayonet fixed (as per regulations for night fighting), and my new friends, deciding that it was more unhealthy than anything Jerry was likely to provide for our night's entertainment, persuaded me to un-fix; and afterwards hid my rifle so that I was unable to find it for the rest of the night!
>
> Punctually at 21:00 hrs the fun began. The whole valley was filled with

an ear-splitting volume of sound. Things banged, boomped, screeched, whee-ed, whistled, and thumped. Lights flickered from gun-flash and shell-burst. Out in front sped line upon line of tracer, looking like red-hot bees, down and across the valley. I expected to be a very dead [sergeant] at any moment and was quite surprised to find the post and myself still intact at the end of the first half-hour. . .

The Foreign Legion on our right were busy searching the dead-ground in front of their position with rifle grenades, and my friends were annoyed about this as it tended to drive the enemy patrols too close to our position. They cheered-up when a couple of automatics started chattering in the wood behind us, and told me that Jerry was in our position and well on the way of his nightly prowl.

Later on, another party of Germans worked into position in the dead-ground . . . from where they peppered the Legion parapet with rifle fire. They were a dead easy target from our post, but our French inmates were certainly not going to go looking for trouble on their last night in Tiergarten! I was somewhat startled at this revelation of the 'offensive' spirit amongst our 'Invincible Allies' . . . I received lots of advice that night, mainly on how to keep out of trouble. I was advised to remove a vital part of each Bren, so that it could not be fired; never to fire at Jerry patrols unless they were cutting our wire; and never, under any circumstances to permit firing a mortar. They had, I was told, light-heartedly fired their mortar in January and within a few minutes Jerry had shelled the Tiergarten, destroying two posts and killing 15 men . . .![3]

By 2 May, all three brigades were in place in the enlarged British sector, and Advanced Divisional Headquarters had been opened in a château at Hombourg-Budange. On that day, 152 Brigade moved into the south sub-sector. A day earlier, 153 Brigade had taken over the north sub-sector. The centre sub-sector, the old British area, had been held by 154 Brigade since 21 April. Following the example of 154 Brigade, both newly-arrived brigades placed their Regular battalions in the *ligne de contact* first.

The day before the 2nd Seaforths moved up, the 1st Gordons arrived in 153 Brigade's sector of the new divisional front. In undoubtedly the most vulnerable position on the 1st Gordons' front was 10 Platoon of B Company commanded by Second Lieutenant Brian Hay. It occupied the deserted village of Betting in No-Man's Land, forming a dangerous salient in the already fragile defensive system of the *ligne de contact*. The Germans had the approaches to Betting covered during daylight and it was extremely hazardous for parties of more than three to attempt the trek to this isolated garrison. But this could have its advantages. Hay was left on his own for six days without interference from his company commander or his CO, a situation with which he, for one, was delighted.

Before his platoon arrived, Hay had spent the night with members of a Breton regiment holding the village. For once, the impression was favourable:

> They were well organised and had the area under control. There were a couple of graves of a German officer and an NCO they had knocked off which showed they weren't messing about. I spent the night with them there and the next morning, before it was light, my platoon came in and took over. We squared up the village a bit and put the manure heap in the right place. We were completely self-contained and had enough rations for a week.
>
> Almost every night we could hear the Germans round the wire. Being very logical, the French had left a way through the wire. They said the Germans always went through that way, and when I asked why they didn't wire it up they said the Germans would only go through another way and then they wouldn't know where they were. I thought that was entirely logical so we left it, but with two Mills grenades on a trip wire. There was no explosion and when we went to look the next morning, at dawn, we found a couple of German stick grenades there instead!
>
> We've always been told that the German troops down there were locals – I don't know if they were or not. But they certainly knew their way around. It was rather like playing boy scouts. During the day it was relatively safe as long as you didn't make yourself too obvious, but at night it was dangerous. It had all the fun of an exercise with a bit more danger, but no actual fighting. I thoroughly enjoyed it.

For Brian Hay and his men, part of the time spent in Betting was like an exciting holiday. Because of the informal truce the French had with the Germans, there was no firing at meal times and Hay's platoon was able to enjoy the fine Spring weather by eating outside. They found some wine, glasses and a quaint check tablecloth in an abandoned *estaminet* and, for the first few days, were able to enjoy typical French picnics. But when the 51st Divisional Artillery arrived in the sector on 6 May the atmosphere changed. Unused to cooperating with the enemy, the Royal Artillery fired whenever there was a target and the men in Betting suffered accordingly. In Hay's words, 'they kept firing on the German positions at feeding time and we got the shit back!'

Based in the village of Remeling, about a mile behind the front line, was the Advanced Headquarters of the 1st Gordons. Also in residence were the brigade battle patrols. One of the young officers was Second Lieutenant Johnny Rhodes, a huge man of six-feet four, educated at Eton, of English–American extraction, and with no celtic credentials other than a Mackenzie grandmother. He had been due to follow his father, uncle and grandfather, as a Regular in the 60th Rifles, but, on

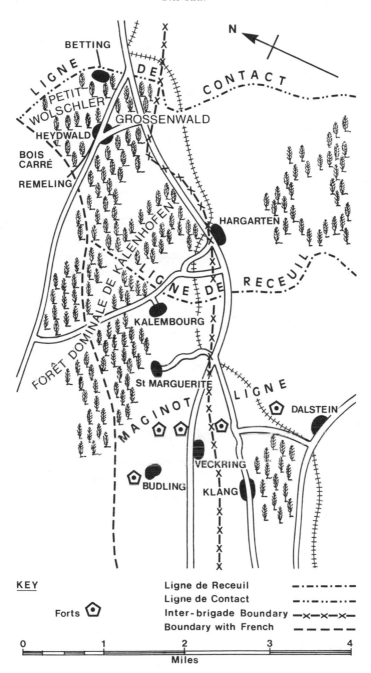

KEY

Forts ⬠

Ligne de Receuil   —·—·—·—·—

Ligne de Contact   —··—··—··—

Inter-brigade Boundary   —×—×—×—

Boundary with French   — — — —

0   1   2   3   4

Miles

Map 2. THE SAAR FRONT
(Based on a sketch by Second Lieutenant 'Ran' Ogilvie,
The Gordon Highlanders)

graduating from Sandhurst in the summer of 1939, when they decided to commission two terms together, his place was filled. Fortunately, there was a vacancy in the Gordon Highlanders which he snapped up. Perhaps because he was not a full-blooded Highlander, in some senses an 'outsider', he volunteered for the battle patrol.

Rhodes' clever personal training of his men undoubtedly contributed to the great success they enjoyed as a unit in the days ahead. Of particular use was his initiative to teach them to lisp; on a still night even the sound of a whisper can carry surprisingly long distances:

> You should have seen me sitting in a ditch with six of the hardest men in the battalion saying, 'Do you thee me thister thusy?' But we did it seriously and it worked. I used to go out on patrol with just 11 men, leaving my batman behind. We had about four sub-machine-guns between us, and I would always carry one. The normal method of moving was in a 'box' formation; it was the best because everyone covers everyone else. I would be in the centre of the front rank, but every commander did it his own way. We wore our Army boots, would make sure we didn't have anything that could shine, and wore Army jerkins which were super things. They go down to about your knees, are sleeveless, and made of leather on the outside and blanket-lined inside. We used to put a slash in the blanket lining, turn them inside out, and use the slash as a pocket for grenades.

* * *

Light reconnaissance tanks were probably the last weapon the infantry of the Highland Division expected to see used in the Maginot Line. There was the obvious problem of manoeuvring them in the hilly, wooded country where they would be vulnerable to anti-tank fire. Yet, initially, tanks were to play their part in the defence system. The original light tank cavalry regiment attached to the 51st Division was the 1st Fife & Forfar Yeomanry. But since its arrival in France in January, it had not shown up particularly well in training and when the decision was taken to send the Highlanders to the Maginot Line, Gort's staff decided to replace the Fife & Forfar with its sister regiment, the 1st Lothians & Border Yeomanry. Both regiments were Territorials from the Lowlands of Scotland, but the Lothians seemed to have gained the edge in efficiency following the arrival of a new commander – Lieutenant Colonel Mike Ansell – in March. This reshuffling was part of an unofficial policy to replace Territorial COs with Regulars, and in Ansell's case it made him, at 34, the youngest Commanding Officer in the British Army.

Formerly Second-in-Command of the 5th Inniskilling Dragoon

Guards, Ansell had a fine military pedigree: he was a descendant of that great soldier General Sir Thomas Picton, the commander of the 5th Division at Waterloo, while his father had been killed commanding the 5th Dragoon Guards at the cavalry Battle of Néry in 1914. Ansell, too, was a cavalry officer of the old guard: a first-rate horseman who competed in both show-jumping and point-to-points, and who would later become famous in the horse show world.

When Ansell was offered the command of the Lothians he was told by the general concerned that the former CO, Harry Younger of the Edinburgh brewing family, had decided to take a drop in rank and stay on as Second-in-Command rather than return home. He was also informed that if he did not feel this was working, he could insist that Younger was sent back to 'Blighty'. With this uncomfortable arrangement, and with the embarrassment of being younger than many of his junior officers, Ansell set about knocking the Lothians into shape:

> I don't think I've ever worked much harder than in the following few weeks. The Lothians were a splendid regiment, the officers all friends in civilian life, the men of high intelligence and even intellect – most of them from around Edinburgh. And they had to work. They knew virtually nothing: few could even throw a grenade or handle a rifle properly. I had a superb RSM in Mr Kerr, a tremendous disciplinarian; but discipline's not easy in the Territorial Army: it's better to lead than to order.[4]

Despite his unpopular early emphasis on smartness, it is generally accepted that Ansell succeeded. Troop Sergeant Major Jimmy Hogarth certainly thought so:

> When Younger was relieved by Colonel Ansell the feeling was very much against this Inniskilling wonder-boy coming in. He rubbed us up the wrong way to begin with; he brought a show troop over from the Inniskillings, painted and polished up to the nines. After this he issued us with paint and we camouflaged all the carriers. But he smartened us up. He was what was needed really.

And yet the men of the regiment could not help suspecting that Ansell was always trying to live up to his past. He quickly acquired the nickname 'Glory', and even the Padre, Eric Rankin, suspected he had had a hand in the transfer to the 51st Division:

> Mike was delighted with the move and I believe he had done much to secure it. He told us ... he was sure we should welcome an opportunity of seeing action at last. At the outset the majority of the Lothians were not so enthusiastic! It seemed to ask for trouble unnecessarily! However no

doubt it was in order to fight that we had come to the country, and a philosophic acceptance of the situation gradually supervened. It certainly was a bit of a distinction to be chosen to go. We were to be the first British tank troops on the ground, and the last.[5]

A cavalry reconnaissance regiment in 1940 did not consist solely of tanks. As well as 28 Mark VIb light tanks – with an armament of twin-mounted .5 and .303 machine-guns, a top speed of 40 mph, and a very thin skin of just 14mm of armour – it was equipped with 44 Bren gun carriers. These were similarly lightly armoured, but their tracks enabled them to carry a light machine-gun and a crew of three across country at speed.

The tactic intended for the tanks forward of the Maginot Line was one of counter-attack, and had been devised to combat the type of German assault that had recently overwhelmed a post of Duke of Cornwall's Light Infantry. A box barrage had accompanied the attack and prevented the arrival of reinforcements to aid the post. It was hoped to use tanks during such an occasion to outflank the attackers and cut off their withdrawal. But as Major Wattie McCulloch, commanding B Squadron of the 1st Lothians, noted in his diary: 'This was a plan which, in the possible event of the enemy being unaware of the presence of tanks, might be successful once but which, a second time, would be, to say the least, hazardous.'[6]

It was decided that one troop of three tanks would support each brigade, and be based in a village close to the front line. The remainder of the regiment was based in the village of La Croix near to the *ligne de receuil*, and the carrier crews of each squadron took it in turn to act as infantry in the *ligne de contact*.

3

Blitzkrieg

In the early hours of 10 May the long-awaited German offensive against the Low Countries – code-named *Fall Gelb* (Operation Yellow) – began with paratroops landing in Holland and armour pouring across the Luxembourg and Belgium frontiers. The first indication that the Maginot defenders received that an attack was underway was the sound of German planes droning across the frontier on their way to attack French airfields. Immediately the *Mise en Garde*, or full alert, was issued in the divisional sector and the reserve battalions occupied the *ligne de receuil* in preparation for a withdrawal from the front line. As it happened, the German thrust was concentrated to the north of the Maginot Line but local activity was expected to be stepped up, if only to distract attention from operations elsewhere.

General Maurice Gamelin, Commander-in-Chief of all Allied forces in France, responded with a 'Special Order of the Day':

> This morning the attack which we have foreseen since last October was launched.
>
> A struggle to the death has begun between ourselves and Germany. For all the Allies the watchword must be: Coolness, Vigour, and Faith. As Marshal Pétain said 24 years ago: '*Nous Les Aurons*' [we'll get them in the end].[1]

Manning the front line from right to left in the divisional sector were the 4th Camerons (relieved 2nd Seaforths on 8 May), 1st Black Watch (relieved 8th Argylls on 9 May), and 4th Black Watch (relieved 1st Gordons on 7 May). To encourage his men, General Fortune issued a Divisional Directive on 11 May. As well as stating that the enemy had achieved poor results against the Dutch and had been checked in Luxembourg (neither was true), and that Winston Churchill was the new Prime Minister, it also emphasised the 'importance of maintaining a firm front on the *ligne de contact*' and of 'obtaining an identity'. It went on:

> Patrolling must be active. Posts must be re-organised and well-wired – where scattered and un-wired localities have been taken over. Any attack

by the enemy must at once be exploited by the Tank Troop immediately information is received, or before if the enemy's artillery and mortar action is obvious.[2]

It was not long before the 1st Lothians had a chance to put this directive into effect. Holding the Betting salient and the posts behind it in 153 Brigade's front line was B Company of the 4th Black Watch. At 2 pm on 11 June, Captain 'Chick' Thomson, commanding B Company, and Second Lieutenant Garrett, commanding the Betting platoon, both of whom had been having lunch at company headquarters, tried to return to Betting but were prevented by fire from a machine-gun firing from the village of Waldwisse. They were forced to crawl back along the path to the nearest platoon position – No 9 Post – taking one and a half hours to do so.

A couple of hours later, after the two officers had returned to company headquarters, No 9 Post reported to Thomson that it was under fire. At almost the same time, the Betting platoon, now under the command of Sergeant Gibson, phoned in to say it was being surrounded. Immediately, Lieutenant Colonel Rory Macpherson, commanding 4th Black Watch, ordered the tank troop of Lothians at Remeling to proceed to Betting.

Under the command of Second Lieutenant Chambers, the three tanks moved off. Before they had even reached the right hand corner of Betting Wood, one tank had been lost (it had been knocked out by a shell, although the crew escaped unharmed). On returning to look for it, Chambers' own tank got bogged in some marshy ground. When the remaining tank tried to tow it out, it too got stuck. Although both tanks were eventually freed, by a clever use of tree branches, one – Chambers' – was soon irretrievably caught in a ditch. At this point two Bren carriers arrived to give assistance and Chambers decided to give up the ghost. He ordered the remaining tank back to Remeling, and his own crew to remove the firing blocks of the guns and to board the carriers. By this time, the crew of the knocked out tank had appeared. They too boarded the carriers. Unfortunately, the road back was barred by heavy shelling and the whole party was forced to spend a hair-raising night in a barn near Betting. After camouflaging the carriers, they returned to Remeling the following morning on foot.[3]

The counter-attack to rescue the Betting platoon had been a fiasco. If any evidence was needed of the unsuitability of light tanks for static warfare, this was it. One tank had been put out of action by boggy ground conditions, one was hit by shellfire. Yet it would take another equally costly action a couple of days later before this counter-attacking role for the Lothians was abandoned.

While the tanks were failing to reach Betting, the situation there was worsening. By 7 pm the platoon phoned to say they were being heavily attacked and shelled. Communication now ceased as the line was cut. Within an hour and a half, Sergeant Gibson decided to withdraw with two sections from the village and arrived at No 9 Post with five casualties at about 9 pm. The section he had left behind finally reported back to B Company Headquarters without any wounded at six-thirty the next morning.

Men were shot for leaving their posts without orders during the First World War. Gibson escaped without even a court-martial, and although his CO, Rory Macpherson, later condemned him in a letter (to Bernard Fergusson, the author of the Regimental History) for 'improperly' withdrawing his platoon, he excused him by attributing it to a 'misapprehension'. This apology may well have been prompted by the fact that Gibson was, in Macpherson's opinion, basically a 'sound man' who only weeks later was killed in action on the River Bresle. It may also have been prompted by Macpherson's recognition that many of the positions his battalion had been asked to hold in the *ligne de contact* were potential death traps, and none more so than Betting. In some places, the platoon posts were more than 500 yards apart, while their siting at the edge of woods meant they could not support each other with fire except over the killing ground in front. Once the enemy had infiltrated between them, they were on their own.[4]

On hearing of the tank *débâcle*, Colonel Ansell, true to his fearless nature and nickname of 'Glory', decided to leave his headquarters on the *ligne de receuil* and personally lead a daylight attempt to recover No 1 Tank. Unfortunately, the rescue was hampered by the fact that the tank's steel tow rope had got entangled in the track the previous evening, and as they were endeavouring to free it they were shelled with high explosive which wounded two men. The recovery had to be abandoned and only the radio was saved. Ansell's reckless disregard for his own safety did not go down well with his padre, Rankin, who expected a greater sense of responsibility from his commanding officer.

* * *

Any forebodings that the men of the 51st (Highland) Division might have felt as the last minutes of the pleasant summer night of 12 June ticked away towards a new day were entirely justified. Thirteen was not a number that was destined to be kind to the Highlanders, and 13 May was no exception. Up until this day, the efforts of the enemy had been largely localised to company, or at most battalion fronts. Now the Jocks were to be tested to the full as the Germans launched a large-scale assault across a two brigade front, and against the flanking French troops.

The first indication that something was 'on' came in 153 Brigade's sector when a battle patrol, led by Second Lieutenant Blair of the 2nd Seaforths, was caught in the open by an enemy force hidden in the edge of the Spitzwald wood. In the ensuing fire-fight Lance Corporal Robson was killed and two other ranks wounded. A couple of hours later, at 4 pm, heavy shelling began along the whole front, but was particularly severe in the 153 and 154 Brigade sectors. In the area held by the 1st Black Watch, SOS Very light signals – indicating an attack by infantry – were seen in Battalion Headquarters from the front line posts of both flank companies: A holding the Hartbusch wood and D holding the edge of the Grossenwald.

Captain Patrick Campbell-Preston, commanding D Company, had moved his forward headquarters up to the north-east of the Winkelmerter wood, about a mile to the rear of the Grossenwald, the day before, and was present when the SOS went up. Almost simultaneously, Lieutenant Howie, his second-in-command, telephoned through from a forward post asking for defensive artillery fire. Shortly after this request had been passed on to Battalion Headquarters in Waldweisstroff, and the desired effect achieved, the line was cut by shellfire, as were the lines forward to the platoon posts.

Howie, the former Regimental Sergeant Major, was normally to be found at company headquarters, but he had opted to spend this night with 17 Platoon, commanded by Platoon Sergeant Major McDonald, the right of the two platoons holding positions at the front of the Grossenwald. Howie recalls:

> I was in the right post of 17 Platoon known as F8 ... The barrage continued for about twenty minutes. As soon as it lifted, the platoon, according to a prearranged plan, set up a terrific all round fire. I could see no enemy, although grenades, rifle and automatic fire were directed at us from just outside our wire. The platoon commander then ordered the post to fire only when the enemy were seen or heard ... We remained in the post and managed to get in touch with the other two sections by shouting.[5]

Second Lieutenant John Moon was commanding the left platoon in the Grossenwald. Like 17 Platoon, it consisted of three posts each held by a section of ten men. At 4.20 am, both his forward sections were attacked and opened a heavy and continuous fire with Brens in response. By 5 am, the shooting had died down and Moon took the opportunity to crawl forward with his runner to the right post to check all was well. They told him that the enemy had been advancing from the left up the low ground in front of the wood and that they had shot a number of them, although others had penetrated the wire. Moon was impressed by the coolness of his men and later wrote in his report of the action that the 'attitude of this section was most aggressive: as soon as a German showed himself he was immediately shot at with accurate rifle fire'. Moon also mentioned that while he was with this section he heard a German officer shouting, 'trying to encourage his men to advance', and they were 'refusing'.

At 5.30 am, Moon could hear firing from his headquarters in the rear section, as well as sniping against the post he was in, so he decided to stay put. Half an hour later, a second short bombardment began, presumably to cover the withdrawal of the German wounded, but accurate rifle fire from Moon's post prevented this. At 6 am, Moon saw half a dozen Germans running from the Grossenwald across to the Lohwald, and at least two were hit by Bren gun fire. But by now ammunition, especially for the Bren gun, was running perilously low.[6]

All the while, Campbell-Preston was out of contact with his forward platoons and feared they were being overrun. At 5.15 am, the telephone line back to Battalion Headquarters had been repaired and Campbell-Preston was able to speak to his CO, Lieutenant Colonel Eric Honeyman. After asking for more ammunition, he mentioned that he was considering making an immediate counter-attack with his reserve platoon to relieve the posts in the Grossenwald. Honeyman stalled this initiative by saying that he was sending up a section of light tanks to help, and that when they arrived, Campbell-Preston should keep them behind the forward edge of the wood, to prevent them being hit by their own artillery, and to use them down the safer road running through the Grossenwald.

At 6.45 am, the clank of caterpillar tracks signalled to D Company Headquarters the arrival of No 1 Troop of three tanks under Lieutenant Johnston of the 1st Lothians. Amazingly, accompanying the ammunition on the back of one of the tanks was Captain Bill Bradford, the Adjutant of the 1st Black Watch, who had managed to persuade the CO that he might be of some use at the forward posts. It was quickly agreed that both Campbell-Preston and Bradford would ride on the tanks to deliver the ammunition. But Campbell-Preston failed to heed his CO's advice to keep the tanks under some form of cover through the middle of the wood and instead decided to use them round the southern edge where they could, in his opinion, bring effective fire into the Lohwald, the enemy-occupied wood facing the Grossenwald, and possibly cut off any attacking troops. This was the classic counter-stroke role for which the tanks in the Maginot had been intended, but it ignored the unsuitability of the terrain.

With the two Black Watch officers clinging to their hulls, Lieutenant Johnston's tanks rumbled off, but as they were skirting a roadblock on the edge of the Winkelmerter one tank got ditched. There was no time to offer assistance and the remaining two continued on up the road to the back edge of the Grossenwald and then moved along its western edge until they were 150 yards from the corner of the wood, hidden from the enemy-held Hermeswald wood by a crest. Campbell-Preston and Bradford dismounted, and set off in the direction of Post F8 carrying a box and some bandoliers of small arms ammunition between them. In his report of the action, Campbell-Preston admits it was unfortunate that he 'gave no definite orders' to Johnston, 'except that an effective attack might be made round the southern corner of the wood'. He added in his own defence that, despite this advice, he thought 'they would remain behind the wood' until either he or Bradford returned.[7] Bradford is certain that his own instructions to Lieutenant Johnston could not have been misconstrued: 'I told them to stay there until I came back to tell them where to go'.

Confused by unclear and apparently conflicting orders, and spurred by a fresh outbreak of shell and machine-gun fire against the post towards which the two Black Watch officers were heading, Johnston decided to follow Campbell-Preston's advice and attack with his two remaining tanks round the southern corner of the Grossenwald. On arriving at the corner, Johnston's tank was unable to obtain an adequate field of fire and he decided to circle back through a gap in the wire and go round the wood to a position where he hoped he could enfilade the Lohwald. Unfortunately, as soon as the tank came into view of the enemy it was hit by anti-tank fire, blowing off one track and wounding the gunner, Corporal Akers, in the leg. The tank was now disabled and, despite a gallant attempt by the wounded Corporal Akers to turn the turret to get the gun into action, two more high explosive shells hit it from close range. Akers was killed instantaneously. Johnston then ordered his remaining crew member, the driver Lance Corporal Burkhart, to bale out and try and reach a Black Watch post in the Grossenwald, which he duly managed. For a few precious seconds, Johnston struggled to remove the gun locks, but they were jammed and he soon gave up. He too reached the safety of a Black Watch post.

The second of the two tanks had fared no better. After rounding the corner of the wood, it too had been knocked out by anti-tank fire, which killed its commander, Sergeant Grant. The rest of the crew – Lance

Corporal Fraser and Trooper Crooks – leapt out and made for the woods, firing their revolvers at an enemy patrol which was hoping to capture them. Unable to locate the Black Watch posts, they wandered lost in the wood for some hours until they were both wounded by shrapnel. They were eventually picked up by stretcher-bearers and evacuated.[8]

Unaware of the tanks' fate, Bradford and Campbell-Preston had managed to get the ammunition up to the posts, but not without problems of their own. Bradford takes up the story:

> Patrick [Campbell-Preston] and I set off, revolvers in hand, carrying several bandoliers and a box between us. There was a lot of firing in front, and we rather wished we had got an escort. After some 600 yards, we got within sight of the most forward section posts, having passed the other to the right. Someone shouted to us to look out and then they opened rapid fire away from us. We doubled through the wire entanglement, and into the trench, to find the Germans were only 30 yards in front, in some thick bushes.
>
> One could see movements in the bushes, but it was difficult to get a shot. The Jocks just couldn't reach them with a grenade so Patrick and I got some, and landed them right among the bushes, causing shouts and forcing them to move to where we could get shots at them.
>
> Soon we had cleared up that lot and, rather miserably, I decided I had better go back to tell the tanks about the mortar and machine-gun to our right flank. Patrick wanted to come too, or go instead of me.
>
> They arranged to fire like hell, while I got out. Of course I couldn't find the exit through the wire, but did at last. I felt very silly looking for it while some people were shooting at me. When I got back near to where I had left the tanks, I saw some men there, but as I got near them they fired at me, and I saw that they were Germans – a small patrol I suppose. I dropped down, fired back and crawled away. I got round and found that the tanks had gone out in the open and had been knocked out.
>
> I set off for [company HQ] when an automatic opened up on me from my left rear, so I had to crawl again. Then they began shelling the road, exactly where I was. An Observation Post must have been able to see me, and was amusing itself, as each salvo was exactly on my line. I covered about 100 yards between each salvo, but the last lot landed all round me – the nearest was in my ditch and six feet from my head. Just as I was getting into cover, someone shot at me with a pistol – and I found the driver of one of the tanks – very shaken poor chap. They were shelling [company HQ] fairly well, and just as I was going to leave, there was a terrific explosion, which shifted tree tops, sandbag emplacements and men. (The 6ft thick sandbag walls moved sideways complete!) I was 20 yards or so away ... and thought everyone must be dead, but went over and found them all right. The anti-tank minefield in front had been hit

and an acre had gone up at once. After a decent interval I set off for Battalion Headquarters.[9]

After Bradford had left to get in touch with the tanks, Campbell-Preston moved across from 17 Platoon's position to the rear section post of 16 Platoon. There he found Second Lieutenant Moon, recently returned from his forward posts, who told him that his men were desperately short of ammunition. Moon also gave him an account of the battle so far, pieced together from the information he had got from his sections up front. The Germans had attacked from the Lohwald around his post (F9) and towards Post F8. The attack had consequently crossed in front of both his forward sections and the enemy had suffered accordingly. A few Germans had managed to get behind them but they were accounted for by his rear section. Later this section had been shelled and one of its occupants, Private Barty, killed by a sniper. Campbell-Preston congratulated Moon on his good work, promised to send up ammunition as soon as possible, and then left for his headquarters.[10]

After another huge barrage had descended on the front of the Grossenwald, Campbell-Preston proved as good as his word and arrived back at Post F9 at 9.30 am with ammunition and stretcher-bearers. Second Lieutenant Moon quickly set out to deliver some to his forward posts, and was surprised to find another assault in progress. The enemy were on three sides but had not got through the wire. When the attack was beaten off, and he was able to get into the post unscathed, Moon realised what a close call they had had. One of the Bren gunners had been killed by a sniper, the section commander and the stretcher-bearer had been wounded, and only the resolute firing of the crew of the remaining Bren had saved the post.[11]

By now the attack was effectively over, and two further barrages and intermittent machine-gun fire during the day could not alter the fact of a German defeat. The failure to take the posts in the Grossenwald had cost the enemy heavy casualties. Second Lieutenant Moon's platoon claimed it had killed at least 40, with 14 bodies found in front of one post alone. Yet British casualties on D Company's front were just five dead (two tankmen) and eight wounded (again two tankmen). And all this despite the fact that the Germans had attacked with vastly superior numbers, and were supported by eight artillery batteries, compared with the 1st Black Watch's support of just two troops of the 17th Field Regiment and a troop of French 75s. Booty, picked up by the forward platoons and the brigade fighting patrols (who also helped evacuate the wounded), included rifles, a light machine-gun with 500 rounds and two prisoners. Not surprisingly, Lieutenant Colonel Ansell was in on the act of recovery again, leading a party to rescue the radios, maps and gun locks from his knocked out tanks. They also managed to bring back the body of Corporal Akers, though Sergeant Grant had to be left. In this act, Ansell was assisted by a fighting patrol under Second Lieutenant David Campbell of the 1st Black Watch. For the untiring work of his patrol this day, and for driving off an enemy patrol the previous day, Campbell became one of two officers to win a Military Cross for gallantry on 13 May – the first in the division.

If the men of the 1st Black Watch thought they had been hit badly on the morning of 13 May, it was nothing compared to the hammer blow that fell on their neighbours. As Lieutenant Colonel Rory Macpherson of the 4th Black Watch was quick to realise, the defences available to the battalions in the original British sector were infinitely superior to those in the two flank sectors that had been taken over from the French. Consequently, the 4th Black Watch were to suffer more heavily from the bombardment and subsequent assault – and they were not alone. On the evening of 12 May, 11 officers and 123 men of the 5th Gordons had arrived to spend the night with their respective companies in the 4th Black Watch, prior to relieving them the next day.

As in the neighbouring sector, it had been a particularly quiet night until a violent barrage, lasting 50 minutes, opened up at around 4 am. Within 20 minutes, SOSs were seen from both C and D Company areas, and by 4.30 am the artillery had begun to fire its defensive fire plan. But it was A Company, holding positions to the left of the 1st Black Watch in the Grossenwald, that was subjected to the heaviest early pressure. No sooner had the barrage lifted than an infantry attack was put in against all three forward platoon positions and company headquarters. The posts on the extreme right of the battalion, occupied by 7 Platoon, had been virtually flattened by the shelling and despite tenacious resistance had later to be evacuated with heavy casualties including the commander, Second Lieutenant Larg, who was severely injured.

In charge of one of the sections was Sergeant Sidney Newman. In his report of the action he noted that the Germans used a myriad of armaments against his post. 'The barrage was immediately followed by an attack in which the enemy used grenades, sub-machine-guns, and flame throwers against us,' he wrote. 'A mortar was also in action against the post, while on the road we could see two vehicles, and about 400 yards away . . . an anti-tank gun.' In response, Newman's post put down Bren and rifle fire, as well as hurling grenades. It was not until 8 am, after a battle lasting more than three hours, that the Germans withdrew.

But they were not finished. Intermittent shelling continued until midday when a fresh barrage was unleashed and machine-gun bullets began to rip into the flimsy wooden outpost from all directions. Finally, at 1.20 pm, a runner arrived with orders to evacuate the post and the gallant defenders successfully fought their way back to company headquarters.[12]

For his work that day Newman was awarded the Distinguished Conduct Medal – the highest award for gallantry available to an Other Rank bar the Victoria Cross. Typically, in his report, Newman left out the details of his own deeds, but the citation for his award reads as follows: 'Sergeant Newman gave a fine example of bravery under heavy fire during repeated enemy attacks, by encouraging everyone and himself carried a [Bren gun] to various positions, firing on the enemy, and so repelling the main force of the attack on his post.'[13]

While 7 Platoon was taking a hammering, the other two platoons, less battered by artillery shells, were holding out. Platoon Sergeant Major McLaughlan, commanding one of them, was first aware of enemy infantry in the vicinity when he heard a voice the other side of the barbed-wire shouting, 'A Company, 4th Black Watch, surrender your arms!' In response he ordered his men to open up with everything they had – grenades, Brens and rifles. The fighting continued throughout the morning and at 10 am Second Lieutenant How arrived with some rum for the men. On hearing that McLaughlan's men were down to just 40 rounds per man, How mentioned that there was a box out in the open in the wood behind and two volunteers were needed to collect it. Private Bennet of the Gordons' advance party and Private Murphy of the Black Watch stepped forward, and successfully retrieved the ammunition despite continuous enemy fire.[14]

A Company's success in repulsing the Germans was due in no small part to the bravery shown by men like Sergeant William Clark. His post was having difficulty locating a group of Germans lying in some dead ground 60 yards to its front, so Clark, disregarding the danger, climbed onto the top of the parapet and proceeded to shoot several magazines from his Bren gun, drawing onto himself a hail of bullets and stick grenades. He was finally killed by a burst from a machine-gun. His CO, Macpherson, put him forward for a DCM, but, due to the War Office policy that the only medal that could be awarded posthumously was the VC, his gallantry was never officially recognised. By the time A Company was relieved that evening, by the same company of the 5th Gordons, it had lost two dead and 14 wounded. The advance elements of the 5th Gordons who had been with them during the attack had suffered two dead and one wounded.

*

B Company, under Captain 'Chick' Thompson, was holding the left edge of the Grossenwald and the Betting salient. It had been in action on and off since 11 May. The day after its evacuation, Betting had been reoccupied by Second Lieutenant Garrett's platoon, with the assistance of Johnny Rhodes' Fighting Patrol. Now it, No 9 Post behind it, and the rest of the company were facing an even sterner test.

When the barrage lifted, intensive firing broke out along the front edge of the Grossenwald. With the lines cut to the forward posts, Captain Thomson could only guess on the course of the fight until Sergeant Cowie, by now in command of No 9 Post, arrived and reported that the Germans had been repulsed and could his men have some breakfast. This was arranged, but only minutes after its arrival a new attack was put in.[15]

The battle continued to rage in B Company's area through the day, and it was not until 7 pm that company headquarters got its first news about Betting. No 9 Post rang through saying Betting was being heavily shelled and the path from the village machine-gunned. Soon after another message came through saying that Betting was on fire; in response, Captain Thomson instructed No 9 Post to cover the Betting platoon if it came out. By 9 pm there was still no sign of a withdrawal, so Captain Thomson took the last resort of sending Johnny Rhodes and his fighting patrol – who had arrived to cover the company's relief by the 5th Gordons – to get the platoon out. After managing the feat without suffering any casualties, Rhodes returned with his patrol to Remeling. But when he reported to Colonel Macpherson he was given a 'roasting' for having evacuated Betting before the 5th Gordons' relief could take place. Despite this chastisement, Macpherson was sufficiently impressed with Rhodes' work over the previous few days to recommend him for a Military Cross, which he was duly awarded. Six men, including one officer, had been wounded in B Company's area.

C Company was unlucky enough to be holding the Grand and Petit Wolschler woods – the second, along with the Grossenwald, of the two German objectives in the battalion area. Holding 'Goat' Post in the front edge of the Grand Wolschler was a platoon under the command of Second Lieutenant David Elder. After the preliminary bombardment of high explosive and shrapnel, a German force of at least 150 men attacked this position, but by keeping up a continuous volley of rifle and Bren gun fire, the defenders managed to hold on and inflict severe casualties. Elder was particularly prominent in organising the defence and encouraging his men, despite the fact that they were outnumbered by five to one. By 5.30 am, the enemy began to retire, taking as many of their dead and wounded as they could. But at least one fit German remained and he soon became a considerable irritation, sniping at the posts with, in Elder's words, 'considerable skill'. At 7.30 am, Elder set off on a tour of his section posts, accompanied by Private Small. As they were nearing the last post, Small was shot by the sniper. At great danger to himself, Elder went back for Small and dragged him to the safety of the post. The skill of this German marksman was underlined when he hit two of the defenders of the post shortly after Elder had staggered in.[16]

Elder was not the only one in difficulties. At company headquarters, sited towards the back of the Grand Wolschler, a fierce two hour infantry assault was being put in. In the opinion of Second Lieutenant C Millar, second-in-command of C Company and the commander of No 2 Post at company headquarters, it was only a second German barrage, which fell short and caused many casualties among its own side, that saved company headquarters from being overrun.

By 11.30 am, during a period of relative calm at company head-quarters, Millar was ordered by his company commander to form a fighting patrol and attempt to establish contact with 'Goat' Post. As the patrol was moving out of company headquarters it discovered four dead Germans, one with a flamethrower, actually in the wire. Luckily there was no opposition in the wood on the way to 'Goat', but on arrival Millar discovered Elder immobilised in one of his posts by a sniper. Two men of the patrol – Company Quartermaster Sergeant Samuel Taylor and Private Grogan – volunteered to go out and deal with him, and within minutes the sniper was dead. Millar then handed over the 2,000 rounds he had brought up with him, took details of the numbers of wounded, promising to send up stretcher-bearers, and returned with the patrol the way he had come.[17]

Once back at company headquarters, Millar found that the phone line to Advanced Battalion Headquarters in Remeling was still cut, and he was forced to continue his march there in a quest for stretcher-bearers. On his return to the Grand Wolschler in the afternoon, there was still no news from Second Lieutenant Robbie's platoon, holding the isolated positions of 'Hare' Post in the Petit Wolschler. The last communication between 'Hare' and company headquarters had been in the early hours of the morning, before the bombardment, when Robbie remarked on the eerie quietness of the night.

Millar's solution was to send a patrol of four men to try and discover what had happened, but on entering the Little Wolschler wood they were fired on and forced to retrace their steps. As a last resort, Second

Lieutenant Scott Raeburn of the 5th Gordons' Brigade Fighting Patrol, who had arrived in C Company Headquarters to supervise the planned relief of the 4th Black Watch by his battalion that night, offered to take just two of his patrol to try and get through. By using all the skill of their specialist training, they managed to get within calling distance of 'Hare' unmolested, where they fired off some shots and called out to indicate their presence. They were answered by a combination of German expletives and bullets, in response to which they retired. They arrived back at company headquarters at 6 pm with the bad news.

Second Lieutenant Robbie and his entire platoon of 30 men had been lost: some killed, most taken prisoner. Also captured were eight members of an advance party of 5th Gordons who were spending the night with Robbie's platoon; among them was Second Lieutenant Innes, who later died of his wounds. The end had come not long after 8.30 in the morning when men in 'Goat' Post had seen large numbers of Germans entering the Petit Wolschler, loaded down with ammunition.

A second tragedy had yet to be played out at No 8 Post, the second of the two platoon positions still holding out in the Grand Wolschler. As it was starting to get dark, the men of the 5th Gordons' C Company arrived in the wood to take over from their respective company of the Black Watch. Second Lieutenant Millar, accompanied by Scott Raeburn, was given the job of organising the switch.

> I led Mr Raeburn and the No 8 Post personnel to [platoon headquarters] and was changing over personnel while Mr Raeburn was changing over the other posts, guided by a corporal of the new unit who knew the post. When I went forward I found Mr Raeburn dead on the wire and the corporal dying.[18]

Second Lieutenant Raeburn had been shot by the jittery defenders of the post he was trying to relieve. He was aged just 23. One of three pairs of brothers who were officers in the battalion – his brother, George, was the Mortar Officer – he was immensely popular with the men, and was considered a natural soldier with a great future. His fellow patrol officer, Johnny Rhodes, is convinced Raeburn was not to blame for his own death:

> He knew his business absolutely perfectly. He got to where the post was and he knew that the nearest foxhole was just behind the nearest tree. So he got all his men to lie down – he couldn't have done better if he had been a Regular soldier with years of service – and he called out, 'C Company, 4th Black Watch, it's Mr Raeburn!' He repeated this call twice

and there literally wasn't a sound. So he came out from behind his tree and they blasted him in half with two Bren guns and the rest of the rifles. I presume they were probably napping, because if they hadn't been, why didn't they answer.

It was not until the morning of 14 May that Second Lieutenant David Elder and his platoon in 'Goat' Post received word that the company had been relieved, and that they could hand over and march out. For his excellent work during the attack, Elder was decorated with the Military Cross. Company Quartermaster Sergeant Samuel Taylor emulated Sergeant Newman of A Company by being awarded the DCM. As well as knocking out the sniper harassing 'Goat', he had been prominent in the initial attack on company headquarters. Part of his citation reads: 'At one stage he was firing a Bren Gun when it was hit by a stream of bullets ... he was knocked backwards several yards, received a cut and severe bruises, but undeterred he quickly changed the barrel and continued firing with complete calm and accuracy.'[19] Strangely enough, Second Lieutenant Millar, who performed so many gallant acts on 13 May, was not decorated, despite being recommended for an MC by Colonel Macpherson.

Casualties for the 4th Black Watch on 13 May were six killed, 25 wounded and around 30 taken prisoner. Advance elements of the 5th Gordons lost three killed (two officers, Raeburn and Innes, and Platoon Sergeant Major Massie), one seriously wounded and seven taken prisoner. As the 4th Black Watch moved back to Budling for a well-earned rest, plaudits for its performance were rolling in. General Fortune wrote to Brigadier George Burney, commanding 153 Brigade:

> Please convey to the 4th Black Watch my appreciation of how they have defended the *ligne de contacte* against repeated enemy attacks.
> The normal holding of this line is an exhausting operation [and] is contrary to our principles, teaching and training.[20]

But not everyone came out of the day smelling of roses. As well as the 'friendly fire' shooting of Scott Raeburn, there had been a serious altercation between the CO of the 5th Gordons, Lieutenant Colonel Alick Buchanan-Smith, and Brigadier Burney over the question of a counter-attack to assist the 4th Black Watch. Originally, the Gordons had been due to relieve the Black Watch at dawn on 13 June but, because of the attack, Colonel Macpherson told Brigadier Burney that he could not disengage until after dark that evening. Instead, at 5.30 am, with the battle at its height, Colonel Buchanan-Smith was ordered by Brigade to send up a section of carriers to Remeling. An hour later, he was told to send a company to join the carriers and make a strongpoint around Remeling. Soon after that, a second company was requested, for use in a possible counter-attack. This was too much for Buchanan-Smith. Aged 42, a quiet, sensitive man with an academic pedigree – his father had been Principal of Aberdeen University for 26 years, while he had been a lecturer in Animal Genetics at Edinburgh University since 1925 – he regarded his battalion like a family, its men his sons. Lance Corporal George Maclennan, the medic, was present at the showdown:

> We were lying in reserve in a big wood when Brigadier Burney arrived and ordered our CO, Buchanan-Smith, to send up all his carriers and two companies into Remeling to help the Black Watch withdraw. Buchanan-Smith replied, and I was there with the doctor when he said this, 'Remeling is one of the most stupid positions any men could be in. This battalion is like my family. When I go up, I'm going up with the whole battalion. I'm not sending part of it up to be sacrificed.' It was at this point that Burney threatened him with a court-martial and in the end he was forced to send up some carriers and one company.
>
> But he was right all along, it was a stupid position. Soon after, he was relieved. This was because he was suffering terribly from shingles. I used to have to dress him twice a day. It was the doctor who insisted he went to the Clearing Station and they sent him home from there.

That evening Buchanan-Smith watched his men march up the line to begin the relief of the 4th Black Watch. His thoughts at the time illustrate the predicament of a sensitive man caught up in war: 'I remember being very much struck by a seriousness in their faces and how they put their confidence in the officers. I wondered how many would ever again possess those boyish faces.'[21]

The next day, 15 May, Buchanan-Smith was replaced by his second-in-command, Major Rupert Christie – a Regular soldier. This episode illustrates both the strength and weakness of the Territorial battalion. On the one hand its close-knit nature meant its men worked and fought well together; on the other, casualties were felt all the more personally and such considerations could undermine military efficiency. Buchanan-Smith's departure meant there was just one non-Regular commanding officer of an infantry battalion left in the 51st Division – the 4th Cameron's Earl of Cawdor, and he would not last to the end of the campaign.

The day after the Battle for Remeling, as the action fought on 13 May is known, the 5th Gordons enjoyed a period of relative calm. But it only presaged a new storm, as the German pressure against 153 Brigade resumed. The main focus of the attack this time was the Heydwald wood, held by D Company under the command of Captain Lawrie.

Just before dawn on 15 May, the shelling intensified in D Company's area and communications between company headquarters and the two forward platoons on the front edge of the wood were broken. At 6 am, when the barrage lifted, German infantry attacked but were initially repulsed. Another bombardment came down, lasting three hours. Completely in the dark, Captain Lawrie sent forward a patrol to try and make contact with his platoons, but it was driven back by machine-gun fire that appeared to be coming from the direction of the Gordons' own posts. In despair, Lawrie sent back a runner to Advance Battalion Headquarters in Remeling with a message that he was holding his headquarters with just 28 men and had no news of his other units. Battalion had no option other than to send in Second Lieutenant 'Ginger' Gall and his fighting patrol to see if they could make contact. Private Tom Anderson, a member of Gall's patrol, remembers the occasion:

> We had been out all the previous night on patrol and were sitting on the steps of this farmhouse when Gall came back and said, 'Right lads, I've just had a message that we're to go back out because we've lost contact with D Company. We're to find out what's happened. I'm looking for volunteers.' We all had our heads over our porridge and kept them there. I always remember what he said then, 'Oh, if that's the way you feel about it, we'll all go back out.' All 13 of us, with the officer, went out. We didn't normally go out in daylight so we had to crawl a good way up a ditch until we got into the cover of the wood. When we arrived at company headquarters, a lot of Germans were around but they soon cleared off.

At 3 pm the patrol arrived safely at D Company Headquarters, whereupon Second Lieutenant Gall was briefed by Captain Lawrie and asked to patrol up to the forward posts of the right platoon and find out what had happened. Curiously, the commander of this unit, a platoon sergeant major, was present. The evening before, while his posts were being shelled, the platoon sergeant major had arrived unbidden at company headquarters and had been told by Lawrie to stay there. Second Lieutenant Norman Duncan was sent forward to take his place. Gall was less than ecstatic when this sergeant major was detailed to guide him up:

> I said to Bill Lawrie, 'I know where it is roughly', and he replied, 'Oh well, the platoon sergeant major is here and he knows exactly where it is.' So we set off with the PSM theoretically 'leading', but he was in a jittery state

and stayed at the back of the patrol passing on the directions to me at the front.

It was eerie going through that wood. They had blasted it and the company had really been given a hot strafing by shells. When we got near the post I sent a message back to the PSM to ask how close we were. All of sudden here's this German, about six foot tall, machine-gun in his hand, running the other way. So up with the tommy-gun. It was the first time I had fired it in anger and the bullets went behind him. Nowhere near him. But I said to myself in consolation, 'I couldn't have shot the guy in the back anyway'. By now I was within calling distance of the forward post so I shouted who we were. There was no reply and I realised that they had been swamped.

Gall immediately gave the order to move back, and without incident the patrol reached the relative safety of company headquarters.

Lance Corporal George MacLennan was at Advanced Battalion Headquarters in Remeling when the remains of D Company marched in at 6 pm, with Gall's fighting patrol covering them.

Bill Lawrie got permission to withdraw from his position and when the remnants, just 28 men, returned they had no equipment. Lawrie had told them to dump everything they had, and just take their rifles, grenades and as much ammunition as they could carry. I was told he was going to be charged for loss of equipment, but it was quashed. When the platoon sergeant major arrived he said to me, 'My platoon's lost, Mac!' He was shaking life a leaf.

At 4.30 pm Brigadier Burney had given orders that the battalion and its attached troops were to withdraw to a position south of Remeling, while still holding the village itself. By 6 pm this was changed to a full withdrawal behind the *ligne de receuil.* This second order had been issued by General Condé, commanding the French Third Army, and was to apply to the whole of the 51st Division. The two French divisions on either side of the 51st had also been under heavy attack and had given up some ground, and the withdrawal was intended to iron out any salients.

Second Lieutenant George Raeburn, the Mortar Officer and brother of the unfortunate Scott Raeburn, was at Advanced Battalion Headquarters when the order to move back was received:

We were to withdraw at dusk. I was hanging about at Battalion HQ in Remeling after my men had come in when a runner arrived and reported to Major Tony Bruce, who was in command of HQ Company at that time: 'They're through Sir, they're through!' he said. Tony assumed he meant the Germans and said to me, 'George, take 20 men and go and stop them!' Immediately I shouted, '20 men follow me!', but not a man moved. I was forced to fish my own platoon out of a billet where they were playing poker, and without much enthusiasm we took up positions at the north entrance to Remeling. I hadn't been there very long when another runner came through and said, 'It's all right sir, C Company are through.' I was then able to report back to Tony Bruce that all was well and it was no longer necessary to have my 20 men sacrificed. Even after this I was foolish enough to stay hanging around and was grabbed again by Tony Bruce who said, 'Take seven men and go and patrol out there!' I knew that 'out there' was absolutely swarming with our machine-guns and all sorts and that it would be fatal to try. So I took seven men, went round a corner and said to them, 'Get the hell out of here! Hide!' I don't think Tony Bruce – who was a great friend of mine – was scared for himself but he was jittery and panicked a bit.

'Ginger' Gall, whose fighting patrol was once again covering the withdrawal, remembers a similar state of confusion:

There was an all round panic when we withdrew from Remeling. The Brigade Major, Captain Macpherson, had come up because of all the hoo-ha that was going on and started to give orders. I didn't know who the hell the guy was. He says to me, 'You'll take your fighting patrol and you'll go up there,' pointing towards the German lines. 'I'll do nothing of the kind,' I replied. He then asked me if I was contradicting him and I told him there was nothing out there except barbed-wire. I thought we'd done pretty well already. We'd got D Company out, but the boys were all shaking, and I said, 'There's no way I'm going out again into that position. I'll cover the roads, where they'll be coming down, if they're coming.' They were worried that the Germans were advancing but there wasn't any advance. We were the last to leave Remeling.

The battle for Heydwald wood had decimated D Company. Two officers and 60 men were missing, and six wounded. Second Lieutenant Mike Langham, another of the three sets of brothers, had been taken prisoner along with his platoon in the morning and was being interrogated at a rear German headquarters by 10 am the same day. Second Lieutenant Norman Duncan had been shot in the head by a sniper, and many people never forgave the man he had relieved for his death. At the conclusion of the campaign, that same man managed to evade the fate of most of his comrades by escaping from the Germans and returned to Britain. On the recommendation of Lieutenant Colonel Alick Buchanan-Smith, his former CO, he was awarded the Military Medal and was later commissioned. The one consolation from this dismal episode was the Military Cross awarded to Second Lieutenant 'Ginger' Gall for his patrol's gallant relief of D Company, and for his own good work later in the campaign on the Somme – he was the third fighting patrol officer to be decorated.

4

'We Have Lost the Battle!'

As the Highlanders withdrew closer to the forts of the Maginot, the Allied armies in the north were facing a far more serious predicament. Just five days after the offensive had opened, Holland had surrendered and no less than seven panzer divisions had breached the French defensive line of the River Meuse between Dinant in Belgium and Sedan in France, threatening to cut the communications of the divisions to the north. The French Ninth Army, holding these positions, had been routed. Outstripping all other German forces was General Erwin Rommel's 7th Panzer Division, which by the evening of 15 May had reached Cerfontaine, over 20 miles behind the original French lines. The 'Ghost' Division, so called because of its ability, over the next few weeks, to appear where it was least expected, as if spirited there, was destined to meet the 51st Division at a small seaside town in Normandy, and there seal its fate.

That morning, Winston Churchill, who had taken over as Prime Minister from Neville Chamberlain on the day the offensive began, received the first indication that French morale at the highest level was cracking in an extraordinary conversation with Paul Reynaud, the French Premier:

> ... I was woken up with the news that M. Reynaud was on the telephone at my bedside. He spoke in English, and evidently under stress. 'We have been defeated.' As I did not immediately respond he said again, 'We are beaten; we have lost the battle.' I said: 'Surely it can't have happened so soon?' But he replied: 'The front is broken near Sedan; they are pouring through in great numbers with tanks and armoured cars' – or words to that effect. I then said: 'All experience shows that the offensive will come to an end after a while ...' Certainly this was what we had always seen in the past and what we ought to have seen now. However, the French Premier came back to the sentence with which he had begun ...: 'We are defeated; we have lost the battle.'[1]

From here on, as the military situation worsened, Churchill was forced into an intricate game of political chess, with the 51st Division as a pawn, as he tried desperately to persuade the French to continue the fight.

* * *

For the first week of the campaign, General Fortune was largely unaware of the seriousness of the breakthrough further north, and the possibility that his division might be severed from contact with the rest of the BEF. But on 17 May, there was an ominous development when the French division occupying the sector to the south of the Highlanders was withdrawn and sent north to try to help stem the German advance, and 154 Brigade was ordered by General Condé to take over part of its former area. The 7th Argylls remained behind to man 154 Brigade's share of the *ligne de receuil*, the new front line in the British sector. Also holding this line were the 2nd Seaforths and the 1st Gordons. From now until its withdrawal from the Maginot Line on 22 May, there were no serious attacks on the 51st Division and most of the confrontations were between patrols.

At the southern end of the divisional sector, the 2nd Seaforths was based around Gueling Pouderie. C Company was holding the Villerwald wood and the Bibiche-Neudorf road. On the night of 18 May, one of its officers – Second Lieutenant Colin Mackenzie of 13 Platoon – went out with six men on a local patrol:

> After going no further than 300 yards from our lines we met a heavier German patrol of about 15 men who opened up on us and caused some casualties. I ordered the men to stay where they were and went off with one other chap, Macloughlin, with the intention of drawing the Germans off the wounded. So we fiddled about for some time without really achieving anything, but as we were still within earshot of our forward posts I shouted back for them to give covering fire while at the same time shouting to my patrol to move back. Under cover of this fire all members of the patrol managed to get back; I personally helped one of the wounded in.

True to form, Mackenzie underplays his role in this action for which he was to receive a Military Cross. Part of the official citation reads: 'When almost surrounded by a strong patrol of ... Germans he fearlessly drew one half of them off by ... showing himself and thereby allowing the remainder of his patrol of five men to slip through the gap. He subsequently rejoined them and assisted to get in three men who were wounded ...'[2]

Mackenzie was not the only officer to win a medal for gallantry in this latter phase of the division's sojourn on the Saar. The following day, in the neighbouring sector held by the 7th Argylls, some Germans were spotted at noon entering the deserted village of La Croix, out in front of the battalion's positions. Captain Jack Ritchie, Second Lieutenant Alan Orr-Ewing and the latter's battle patrol were sent down to investigate. Their progress towards the village was watched with interest by Second Lieutenant Diarmid Macalister Hall:

> My platoon was in a trench on the forward slope of a hill looking right down on La Croix, about 1,000 yards away. It was a reasonably sunny day and we knew the battle patrol was going out because some Germans had been seen going into a house in the village. The patrol got down on either side of the village and we could see them advancing from two sides on this house. Then we heard some shots, they threw some grenades and eventually came out with three German prisoners. I was tremendously impressed with the whole performance. By now the battle patrol had cut their teeth and they were a capable and competent formation.

In fact, that capture of the Germans had not gone as smoothly as it looked from a distance. After searching two buildings without result, Orr-Ewing went up into the attic of a third alone and came face to face with a German officer. The German opened fire first with his Biretta pistol and missed, enabling Orr-Ewing to beat a hasty retreat. Once outside, he ordered the house surrounded. After a brief fight, three Germans surrendered.[3] For this, and for good work earlier on the *ligne de contact*, Orr-Ewing was awarded the Military Cross – the fourth fighting patrol officer to win one in front of the Maginot Line.

Considering the danger of their work, it was enough if the members of these élite units left the Saar with their lives, let alone a medal. One officer who did not was Second Lieutenant Donald Cochrane of the 4th Camerons. On 19 May, Cochrane was ordered to take his patrol up to Beckerholtz – the former home of his battle patrol, now in No-Man's Land – to see if it was occupied. After passing through the 2nd Seaforths manning the *ligne de receuil*, the patrol reached their objective and discovered it to be empty. On his own initiative, Cochrane then led his patrol up to the top of the ridge overlooking the next village – St Oswalds Château. Unfortunately, Germans were in residence there and they opened up on the unsuspecting Scotsmen with machine-guns and mortars. Private 'Sandy' Russell remembers the first chaotic moments:

> The patrol was uneventful until we came to a hedge near some houses. All hell broke loose and in the first burst of German fire our officer fell shot several times through the head and body. Lance Corporal Laing was

killed by a mortar and our second scout [Private Grant] was killed by a burst from a sub-machine-gun. We were completely in the open and how any of us escaped I don't know. After an exchange of fire lasting ten minutes, our PSM Maclean, from the Western Isles, ordered us back. We fell back in reasonable order with one lot covering the other and eventually got away. Two more men were wounded but not seriously . . .

At General Fortune's request, the guns of the Maginot fired 800 rounds in retaliation and flattened both Beckerholtz and St Oswalds. The following day, all the division's battle patrols were disbanded and returned to their units. It was one day too late for Cochrane, Laing and Grant.

* * *

On 20 May, the Highland Division was removed from the command of General Condé's Third Army and put into reserve, under the direct control of the French High Command, with orders to move on the 22nd to the concentration area of Étain, about 20 miles west of Metz. This was to be the first stage of a plan to return the division to the main body of the BEF – in action further north – the policy that had been agreed with the French in the event of a German offensive when the division moved down to the Saar.

On hearing of their departure, General Condé sent the men of the division a letter of congratulation:

> For five months the Third French Army has had the honour of counting British soldiers in her ranks; five months of fights side by side, crowned by the arrival of the 51st Division.
>
> After contacting the enemy in a remarkable way, thanks to the ardent fighting qualities of its men, the Division of Highlanders had soon mastered him. From 11 to 15 May, in spite of a very violent shelling, the defenders of the Grossenwald, whose strength is hardly that of one battalion, dislocate a regiment armed with flame-throwers, inflict heavy losses, and capture prisoners . . .
>
> From this very moment, the Highlanders of 1940 have renewed the tradition of Beaumont-Hamel.[4]

By the morning of 23 May, the concentration of the division in the Étain area was complete. The next stage in the move was scheduled for Pacy, near the River Seine to the north-west of Paris. But before the troops could continue their journey by road and rail, General Fortune received orders to hasten instead to the Varennes area, some 30 miles from Verdun. The Highlanders had been lent by the French High Command to its Second Army who wanted to employ them as a reserve behind the French troops holding the southern shoulder of the German breakthrough near Sedan.

There were more last minute changes of plan. By the early hours of 25 May, most of the division had reached Varennes, but there was no news from six battalions that had left the Étain area by train the previous evening. It was only later that day that Fortune's infuriated staff were informed by the French that these battalions had been re-routed to Rouen, while the move to Pacy for the remainder of the division was once again on.

To reach Pacy, the division was instructed to take a route south of Paris via Fontainebleu. But as movement tables were being issued, and staging and advanced parties despatched, still more amended instructions arrived changing both the route and the destination. The road parties, consisting of the wheeled divisional transport, would now travel round the top of Paris to Gisors, 40 miles out to the north-west. The rail parties, made up of the marching troops and the tracked vehicles, would follow the route of the six missing battalions by moving in a huge loop to the south of Paris with the Neufchâtel area as the terminus.[5]

Because of the speed of the German advance – the supply lines to the Allied armies in Belgium had been cut by panzers on 21 May – it was now no longer possible, if it had ever been, to reunite the Highland Division with the BEF. The new plan, outlined to General Fortune by General Georges, the French Deputy Commander-in-Chief, on 26 May, was to hold the line of the Rivers Somme and Aisne with the remaining Allied troops. Without the men trapped in Belgium and north-east France, the Allies could muster just 65 divisions, of which the 51st and the recently arrived 1st Armoured Division were the only trained British formations.

The role of the Highland Division was to hold the extreme left of the Somme position, with its flank on the Channel, under the command of General Besson's 3rd Group of Armies. The one condition Fortune insisted on, when he saw Besson in the afternoon of 26 May, was that the division had to be allowed to concentrate properly before being committed to an operational role – his memory of the recent removal of six of his battalions without notification was still fresh.

Fortune got his way and on 27 May, at the headquarters of General Robert Altmayer – commanding *Groupement A*, an improvised formation (later to become the French Tenth Army) under whose immediate orders the Highland Division had been placed – he discussed his final troop dispositions. It was agreed that both the rail and road parties of the division would concentrate between the Béthune and Bresle rivers, and then move forward to the line of the Somme from the sea to Pont-

Remy in order to take over from two French light cavalry divisions on 2 June.

* * *

As the 51st Division was making its disjointed progress towards the Somme, the scene of such terrible carnage in 1916, the overall strategic situation was worsening. Reynaud, the French premier, had replaced his septuagenarian Commander-in-Chief, General Maurice Gamelin, with another, General Maxime Weygand, on 19 May, but within a few days it was clear that Weygand's plan to counter-attack north to regain touch with the Allied armies in Belgium and northern France was doomed to failure.

On 23 May, General Gort, convinced that a counter-attack from the south was not going to materialise, ordered the withdrawal of his two divisions around Arras back to the Haute Deule Canal. This effectively ended hopes that the two portions of the Allied armies could be reunited and was the first step along the road back to Dunkirk and evacuation. Gort had in fact disobeyed the express orders of General Weygand that he remain in position ready to attack south to meet the promised counter-attack. He later justified his decision by arguing that he had fulfilled his side of the bargain by counter-attacking south of Arras on 21 May. That operation, undertaken by just two battalions of infantry and 74 tanks, because the rest of the BEF was engaged on other fronts, had met with initial success because the thick armour of the British tanks was proof against the German 37mm anti-tank gun. The advance of these tanks caused the crack *Totenkopf* (Death's head) SS Motorised Infantry Division to retire in some disorder, panicking some elements of Rommel's 7th Panzer Division. But the tanks were stopped, and eventually forced to withdraw, after Rommel had personally supervised the use of his heavy 88mm anti-aircraft guns to penetrate their armour.

General Gort had been given the moral authority for his decision to abandon Arras, and subsequently to retire to Dunkirk, by the clause in his operational instructions that allowed him to appeal to the British Government if he felt an order from the French High Command was endangering the BEF. He had been given an inch and he took a mile. He did not bother to request permission from his own political masters for his actions on 23 May because he was well aware that their response would have been a flat 'No'. At that time, Churchill and his ministers were still pinning their faith on Weygand and his ability to effect a breakthrough; three more days would go by before the British Government could bring itself to accept Gort's *fait accompli* by authorising an evacuation. When a dilemma similar to Gort's arose for General Fortune, he, as a lowly divisional commander, did not feel he had a similar mandate to throw off the shackles of French control.

Just one day after Gort's brave decision, Reynaud learnt for the first time that two of his key military figures were already considering peace. One of them was General Weygand, his new Commander-in-Chief; the other, Marshal Philippe Pétain. On 17 May, the 85-year-old hero of Verdun had been recalled by Reynaud from his post as Ambassador to Madrid to take over as deputy Premier, in the hope that his presence in the government would put some backbone into the war effort. Reynaud could not have been more wrong. He later wrote:

> I knew on the 24th [May] that Weygand, and with him Pétain, were to form a coalition in order to demand an armistice, if, as unfortunately there was some reason to believe, the battle which was to be waged on the Somme were lost. It was a cruel betrayal for a man who had just, a few days previously, placed his confidence in them.[6]

In the evening of the following day, the French War Committee, a combination of politicians and generals, met in the Élysée Palace in Paris. Weygand's pessimism was evident as he painted a gloomy strategic picture in which, not counting the troops trapped in Belgium and north-east France, the Allies were outnumbered by as much as three to one. He concluded by saying that the only option left to the French Army was a fight to the death:

> We shall not have the reserves needed to carry out a retreat in good order, under pressure from the enemy, from the Somme–Aisne line to the lower Seine–Marne line. No methodical retreat is possible with such an inferiority in numbers.
>
> We must hold the present Somme–Aisne position, and defend ourselves there to the last extremity. It has many weak points ... We may therefore be penetrated. In that case the fragments will form points of resistance. Each of the parts of the army must fight to exhaustion to save the honour of the country.

It was during the subsequent discussion that the possibility of an armistice was first mooted by the President, Albert Lebrun. The problem, as he saw it, was how to get round the agreement with the British that neither could seek peace without the permission of the other. 'Certainly, we have signed engagements which forbid us a separate peace,' Lebrun began. 'If, however, Germany should offer us relatively advantageous conditions, we ought to examine them very closely.' After a lively discussion it was agreed that the British Government should be warned of the possibility of the total destruction of French forces if the Army fought to the finish, and the danger this would pose for the maintenance of order. In other words, the necessity to negotiate an armistice.[7]

Earlier that day, Major General Edward Spears had arrived in Paris as Churchill's personal liaison officer with Paul Reynaud. He was ideally suited for the job. As a young subaltern on attachment to the French War Office in 1914, Spears had reached France just as the First World War began; within days he was acting as liaison officer to the French Fifth Army, and by the end of the war he had progressed to Head of the British Military Mission to the French government, with the rank of Brigadier General. Such was the surprise of his appointment in 1940 that Spears had to ask friends to sew new buttons on to his old army tunics, and to borrow a forage cap from a military outfitters because there was no time to find a proper hat to replace his gold-braid versions from the last war.

The scale of his task had been made evident when a messenger arrived at his home in the early hours of 25 May with a copy of a 'Most Secret' telegram from Reynaud to Churchill that had just been received. Spears recalled the episode in his memoirs:

> Its sense was as follows: 'You telegraphed me this morning that you had instructed General Gort to persevere in carrying out the Weygand plan.
> General Weygand now informs me that, according to a telegram from General Blanchard, contrary to the formal orders confirmed this morning by General Weygand, the British Army has decided upon and carried out a retreat of 40 kilometres in the direction of the harbours, while our troops, starting from the south, were gaining ground to the north to meet the Allied Armies of the north.
> This withdrawal has naturally compelled General Weygand to modify all his dispositions. He finds himself compelled to give up his attempt to close the breach and re-establish a continuous front. There is no point in insisting on the gravity of the consequences which may follow'.[8]

It was already plain that the French High Command was anticipating defeat by looking for a scapegoat. Gort was ideal because his withdrawal towards the coast, in contradiction of Weygand's orders, provided the ideal excuse for the failure of a counter-attack from the south that could never have succeeded given the disorganisation and paucity of forces available. It was up to Spears to convince the French that Gort's move towards the coast did not signify Britain's desire to leave the French to their fate; far from it.

After an uneventful flight, strapped into the machine-gunner's chair of a Blenheim bomber, Spears arrived in Paris before midday and went straight to the Ministry of Defence in the Rue St Dominique to meet Reynaud. He had hardly finished shaking hands before Reynaud referred to Gort's precipitous withdrawal by commenting on 'how British generals always made for harbours'. Spears retorted by imploring him to 'set his face against recriminations'. The Allies' only hope, he continued, was to 'act together as brothers'. These words seemed to have the desired effect as Reynaud 'nodded in approval'.[9] Spears was then invited to sit in on a meeting of the French War Committee – the first of two that day – which was about to take place in Reynaud's office. Present were Pétain, Weygand, Admiral Darlan, the Naval Minister, and Paul Baudouin, the Secretary to the War Committee. Weygand had brought with him Commandant Fauvelle, a liaison officer from the headquarters of General Blanchard – the commander of the Allied armies encircled in Belgium and northern France – and requested that he be heard. Spears noted:

> The idea of defeat, or even the shadow of such an idea, never crossed my mind, but, as Commandant Fauvelle told his story in fragments, revealing an appalling state of affairs, and as I realised that his catastrophic defeatism seemed to some extent at least to be accepted as the reflection of the real position, I felt cold fingers turning my heart to stone.[10]

Despite censuring Fauvelle for intruding into politics by ending his report with the words 'I believe in a very early capitulation', Weygand made his own feelings clear when he said acidly to Reynaud: 'This war is sheer madness, we have gone to war with a 1918 army against a German Army of 1939. It is sheer madness.'

In the afternoon, Spears went to see Georges Mandel, the anglophile Minister of the Interior. Mandel gave him his opinion of why the French Army had performed so badly. France's morale had been 'sapped by the feeling of the last 20 years that there would be no war like that of 1914', he told Spears. In other words France would never again take the vast majority of the burden of fighting, she would not fight without 'strong allies'. But, Mandel continued, the British 'certainly could not answer that description, and the United States do not exist as far as Europe is concerned'. He concluded: 'As no one wanted to fight, why should France?' Mandel went on to tell Spears that the other factor undermining morale was the belief that even if there was a war, the Maginot Line would prevent an invasion. The implication was that now the Line had been circumvented, all confidence had drained out of the French people because they did not feel 'strong enough to face the Germans in the open field ...'.

As their conversation switched to the present, Mandel began to outline to Spears the complete breakdown of the civil authorities and the apathy of the population in the face of the German advance. He concluded the conversation by advising Spears that the 'best way of strengthening French opinion' was to make it understand the 'unflinching resolution of the British people'.

The following day, Spears had an interview with Marshal Pétain, who 'stated in so many words that he could see no way out'. Spears was now convinced that Mandel's suggestion was the only course left, and that evening he cabled Churchill to this effect. 'My conclusion was,' Spears later wrote, 'that to drive home to all, including Pétain, the truth that the British were completely, absolutely, fanatically resolved to fight on offered the best, perhaps the only, chance of shaking France out of her trance'.[11]

On 26 May, as a consequence of the War Committee meeting the evening before, Reynaud flew to London. At a lunchtime discussion he told Churchill that given the disparity in numbers of three to one 'the war could not be won on land'. When Churchill argued that the Germans might not attack the new French defensive line but instead direct their efforts against Britain, Reynaud countered with his belief that 'the dream of all Germans was to conquer Paris'. Finally, in response to the British Prime Minister's plea that 'if only we could stick things out for another three months, the position would be entirely different', Reynaud simply repeated that although Weygand was willing to fight on, he 'could hold out no hope that France had sufficient power of resistance'.[12]

Following this *tête-à-tête* with Churchill, Reynaud was taken to the Admiralty for a meeting with the Cabinet.

> I revealed to them how dangerous Britain's position would be if the Battle of France was lost because of this new aggression, for the Germans would hold the French coast from Brest to Dunkirk. I added that I thought it my duty to warn them that I would have difficulties with my Government if the Battle of France were lost, for Pétain would speak in favour of an armistice ... I thought Lord Halifax was struck by my arguments. He expressed his willingness to suggest to Mussolini that, if Italy would agree to collaborate with France and Britain in establishing a peace which would safeguard the independence of these two countries, and was based on a just and durable settlement of all European problems, the Allies would be prepared to discuss with him the claims of Italy and the

Mediterranean and, in particular, those which concerned the outlets of this sea. It was agreed that the British Cabinet would discuss the matter and that I should be kept informed.[13]

Winston Churchill was severely shaken by the events of 26 May. First, Reynaud had told him that the French Army was as good as finished, and that when this happened there would be pressure from within his government from no less a figure than Marshal Pétain for an armistice – implicitly ruling out the possibility of guerrilla warfare or fighting on from abroad. Then he had discovered that members of his own War Cabinet, led by the Foreign Secretary, Lord Halifax, were all for offering concessions to Italy in exchange for her interceding with Hitler for a negotiated peace. He was being squeezed into a corner with only one obvious way out – armistice. But was there another? That evening he asked his three Chiefs of Staff to examine Britain's prospects of 'continuing the war alone against Germany and probably Italy'.

The following morning they reported back: As long as the Royal Air Force was 'in being', they wrote, it and the Royal Navy together 'should be able to prevent Germany carrying out a serious sea-borne invasion of this country'. If Germany obtained air superiority, the Royal Navy could hold up an invasion 'for a time' but not 'an indefinite period'. The 'crux of the matter' was air superiority. At last, here was the substantive support he needed to defeat the doves in the Cabinet and enable Britain to continue the fight.[14]

That same day, news arrived from Washington to give Churchill added hope. Lord Lothian, the British Ambassador to the US, sent a telegram describing a conversation he had had with Roosevelt in which the American President had suggested that if the Allies really were *in extremis* then the US would come in. He had gone on to say that provided their Navies remained intact, the resources of the Allied empires would allow the war to be carried on from abroad, possibly Canada. Here was American support for an option Churchill had already considered: the continuation of the war even if Europe was conquered.[15]

By the evening of 27 May, the pieces of Churchill's jigsaw were beginning to fall into place. His Chiefs of Staff had advised him that a German invasion would not necessarily succeed, and there were signs from Washington that the US might join the war in the not too distant future. Even so, the uncertainty about France's long-term participation in the war was worrying. If she sued for peace, Germany would almost certainly gain control of her powerful Navy, and this might tip the balance and make an invasion of Britain possible. Churchill was convinced that for this reason alone, Britain should do everything it could to keep France in the war. The other advantages were obvious. If the French Government decided to fight on from its colonies or the New World, this would provide invaluable assistance in the struggle against Hitler. If it chose to fight to the end on the soil of Metropolitan France, any prolonging of the death throes would allow Britain much-needed time to build up its defences, especially in the air, before Germany turned on her. From here on, all Churchill's efforts were geared towards convincing France that there was still hope. To this end, he would heed Spears' advice and use the tactic of insisting to the French that even if they capitulated, Britain would fight on. This method gained added impetus by virtue of the fact that it was not a bluff.

On 31 May, Churchill flew to Paris for a meeting of the Allies' Supreme War Council, determined to do all he could to bolster French morale. Spears, who was at the airport to meet him, was surprised at his vitality:

> He was as fresh as a daisy, obviously in grand form. He might not have had a care in the world. This was, perhaps, due to the fact that he had had a rest in the plane, but was more likely generated by the sense of danger in such a journey. Danger, the evocation of battle, invariably acted as a tonic and a stimulant to Winston Churchill.[16]

After lunch at the British Embassy, Churchill was driven to the Ministry of War, where the Supreme War Council was being held. It opened with Reynaud expressing his dissatisfaction that only 10 per cent of the 150,000 Allied troops rescued from Dunkirk so far were French. Appreciating the possible political repercussions, Churchill insisted that this was because the French commanders had not yet issued the necessary orders. For the remaining 24 hours of the operation, he promised, the troops would be taken off in equal numbers and the British, not the French as previously agreed, would provide the rearguard. The conversation then turned to the war effort. Reynaud wanted the British troops already evacuated from Dunkirk to be sent straight back to France to rejoin the battle. He also asked that more guns, planes and tanks be sent. Churchill's response was hardly encouraging. Any initial aid 'would of necessity be small'. He pointed out the fact that two British divisions were already on the new Somme line, that Britain needed to defend herself, and, in any case, the re-equipping of the BEF would take time. There were no fighters to spare after the losses over the Dunkirk beachhead. Yet, he continued, if the Germans could be held until Autumn, then the United States might come to the Allies' assistance. And even if Roosevelt could not declare war he 'would soon be prepared to give us powerful aid', Churchill predicted.[17]

Nicely warmed up, he then launched into a stirring speech about British resolution to continue the fight. Spears' record is as follows:

> 'I am absolutely convinced,' the words were rolling on like waves, symmetrical and formidable, crashing on our consciousness, 'that we have only to fight on to conquer. If Germany defeated either ally, or both, she would give no mercy. We should be reduced to the status of slaves for ever. Even if one of us is struck down, the other must not abandon the struggle. Should one of the comrades fall in the battle, the other must not put down his arms until his wounded friend is on his feet again.
>
> 'We shall,' he said, 'carry on with the war if every building in France and Britain is destroyed. The British Government is prepared to wage war from the New World if through disaster England herself is laid waste. The British people will fight on until the New World re-conquers the Old. Better far that the last of the English should go on fighting and *finis* be written to our history than to linger on as vassals and slaves.'
>
> Everyone in that room was deeply moved, carried away by the emotion that surged from Winston Churchill in great torrents. It was not necessary to understand his words to seize his meaning . . . It was a pity that it fell on such barren soil . . . It would have been greeted at home with the mighty roar of approval only the British can give. But it was heard by a tiny audience of men who, with one or two exceptions, were already half enemies . . .
>
> Then Reynaud spoke and I began to write again.
>
> . . . The morale of the French nation was very high. He did not think the morale of the German people was as high as their victories would justify. The French would hold the Somme. If France could hold the Somme until Britain and America could make up for the disparity in arms, then victory was certain . . .[18]

This was just what Churchill wanted to hear; for Reynaud to speak in this manner was evidence that his morale, at least, was improving. But reading between the lines Spears knew it was all up for the French, and he suspected Churchill knew as well:

> . . . I knew, more from his tone than from a few words Winston had said when he walked over to me as I stood alone for a moment before taking leave, that he realised in his heart that the French were beaten, that they knew it, and were resigned to defeat. He had not said so, it was as if he would not permit the thought to dwell consciously in his mind. But he knew. This affected me perhaps less because I had felt it to be true for some time, though I would not admit it either.[19]

If Spears was right – that deep down Churchill accepted that France would not fight for much longer – then his decision to leave the 51st (Highland) Division and other troops in France can only be seen as a political gamble with very long odds. It was a risk he was prepared to take because, according to the report by his Chiefs of Staff, planes – and not troops – were the key to Britain's survival. If the loss of one or two divisions did not keep France fighting, then it would at least signify to the world that Britain had not deserted its ally in her moment of need. This might be an important factor in bringing the United States into the war.

5

The Somme

While the fate of the Highland Division was being determined by the calculations of politicians and generals in London and Paris, its soldiers were sorting themselves out after their 400 mile trip across France. On 28 May, Advanced Divisional Headquarters opened at St Léger-aux-Bois, in the Basse Forêt d'Eu south of the River Bresle, and later that day Victor Fortune was visited by Major General Evans, commanding the British 1st Armoured Division, which was to come under Fortune's control.

This formation, the only British one of its type – the Germans had ten and the French three – had been rushed out to France on 14 May, underequipped and understrength. Unable to join the main body of the BEF, and before it was properly concentrated, it was used on 27 May by *Groupement A* in an abortive attack without artillery and infantry support against the German bridgeheads over the River Somme at Abbeville and St Valéry-sur-Somme. The Armoured Division had suffered heavily in these attacks for which it was neither trained nor equipped, and General Evans had come to St Léger-au-Bois to tell Fortune that, without a period for drastic overhaul, his division would soon be defunct. Fortune decided on a compromise. From 2 June, when the relief of the French on the Somme was due to be completed, all vehicles needing overhaul could be withdrawn to workshops in the rear, but any serviceable tanks and troops should remain. In the event, the 51st Division was left with a composite regiment of tanks and the largely intact Support Group comprising an infantry battalion, a Royal Engineer company and a light anti-tank and anti-aircraft regiment. Lieutenant Colonel Harry Swinburn MC, Fortune's senior staff officer, later wrote of his disappointment:

> Coming at this juncture when obviously the next week or two would be critical, this news was most disturbing. As events proved the Armoured Division, if it had been able to operate, might have made the difference during the next eventful fortnight.[1]

There was more bad news. Another visitor that day was Brigadier AB Beauman, Commander of the Northern District of the BEF's Lines of Communication. A glittering military career had seemed assured for

Beauman when he won a DSO during the First World War and was promoted to brigadier at the age of 27, the youngest in the British Army. But after the war he had not fulfilled that promise, and was one of the many Army officers 'bowler-hatted' by Hore-Belisha, the Secretary of State for War, in 1938. On the outbreak of the Second World War he had been recalled from early retirement.

Beauman was responsible for the logistic support of the forward combat troops, but since the links to the BEF had been cut, he had hastily formed some of his half-trained and poorly-equipped soldiers into three improvised infantry brigades known as 'Beauforce' (later called Beauman Division). He told Fortune that Le Havre was nearly evacuated and that Rouen would now have to serve as the supply centre for the Highlanders. He also told him that the only troops protecting the rear of the 51st Division were his mish-mash brigades, holding a huge line along the River Béthune from Dieppe down to Rouen. Appreciating the reality of the situation – the Highland Division was expected to hold an unprepared front of 18 miles without a reserve, while the conventional deployment was one division per four miles of properly entrenched positions – the two commanders then got down to business. Lieutenant Colonel Swinburn was present at the discussion:

During [Beauman's] visit, the question of any arrangements existing in the case of a withdrawal was brought forward. The position then being taken up bore a very close resemblance to that in which the BEF had found itself in Belgium, for any penetration at Amiens, where the enemy then had a bridgehead, would automatically isolate all forces to the North whose only way of re-effecting junctions with the main Allied Army in case of withdrawal would be either through Rouen or embarkation in the North and thence to Cherbourg. It was learnt that Dieppe was impracticable for any embarkations, being heavily mined with magnetic mines, whilst the port and harbour had, in addition, been seriously damaged by air attacks. Further, no lines of defence west of the River Béthune to Le Havre had been prepared, although this latter was the only real port left in the area if embarkation were decided on. The grave dangers of joining up through Rouen were that not only would the few crossings of the River Seine constitute serious bottle-necks but also the enemy might well anticipate the force at Rouen, since the Allied forces would have to execute a pivotal manoeuvre whilst the enemy would be moving on a direct and shorter route. At this meeting Brigadier Beauman and [Fortune] made an outline plan to fall back on Le Havre whereby 51 Div and Beauforce ... working together, would leapfrog backwards. The dispositions of the Support Group when made were framed with this in mind, as they covered the right flank of the 51 Div and linked back to the positions held at that time by Beauforce.[2]

Fortune and Beauman had anticipated the likely pattern of events and had made a sound plan accordingly, but the British Government's insistence that they act only under the orders of the French meant they were inhibited by the cumbersome and increasingly despondent French chain of command. There was no overall British commander who, like. Gort, had a right of appeal back home. Instead, each formation was answerable to a different master: The Highland Division came under the orders of General Altmayer's Army, the 1st Armoured Division had to answer directly to the French High Command, while Beauman's troops were the responsibility of Lieutenant General Sir Henry Karslake, sent out as Commander of all Lines of Communication troops on 23 May. The obvious solution would have been to appoint Karslake, the senior British officer in France, as a Corps Commander in control of all BEF troops south of the Somme. Indeed, this appointment was made verbally to Karslake by General Sir Edmund Ironside, the Chief of Imperial General Staff, on 25 May. It was never confirmed in writing because General Sir John Dill replaced Ironside as CIGS on 27 May, and Karslake was seen as Ironside's crony.

Irked that his appointment had not been confirmed, and conscious of the need for someone, anyone, to be made overall commander, Karslake sent a memo on 31 May to the Chief of Military Operations in London, Major General Dewing, arguing that if it 'should ever be decided to withdraw to positions south of the Seine the operation would be less difficult if it was co-ordinated by a central Commander'. Dewing, in turn, passed on his own thoughts a day later in a memo to the new CIGS, General Dill:

> An important decision on policy is required in relation to our forces remaining in France. It seems to me that we must appoint a C-in-C, to the BEF in France. The role that he is to be given must be either:
>
> (a)   to be placed at the complete disposal of the French,
> (b)   to be an independent commander acting in co-operation with the French, but responsible for the security of his force and its L of C,
> or (c) some compromise between (a) and (b).
>
> In deciding which of these roles should be adopted, we have to balance our desire to give sufficient support to the French to keep them in the war against the importance of preserving the security of our troops and of their L of C. The military contribution which we can make during the next few months to the security of France against German land attack is negligible. Even if it were to amount to five divisions (which is far in excess of what is immediately possible), it could hardly make the

difference between the success and failure of the French defence. The value of our force in France is therefore chiefly moral. I suggest that we should give this moral support to the French if we can convince them that we honestly intend to reconstitute a field force for co-operation with the army. Our difficulty will be to convince them that this field force cannot be reconstituted for several months.

To leave our two divisions at the complete disposal of the French would mean that in the event of a successful German attack southwards – particularly if this attack should penetrate south of the Seine – our L of C might be entirely uncovered.

If we withdraw our two divisions entirely from French command, it will be difficult to make the French believe that we really mean to reconstitute a field force for co-operation with them. The policy I suggest is therefore a compromise. I suggest that we should tell the French that our two divisions now in France are the nucleus upon which we intend to re-form a fresh field force. That they will remain under French command, subject to the restriction that they should be employed on the left flank. That should the Allies be forced to carry out a further withdrawal from the Somme, these conditions would stand, unless a withdrawal south of the Seine became necessary. Immediately this became necessary, the British division would cease to be under French command, and their commander would be ordered to manoeuvre to cover his communications back to Nantes.[3]

In this memo, Dewing accurately articulates the dilemma that faced Churchill and the British High Command. If military considerations had been uppermost, then the British forces in France would have either been withdrawn or, at the very least, removed from French command. But, of course, a political factor held sway – namely the need to keep France in the war – and against this the well-being of a handful of divisions was small beer. In the event, General Dill largely agreed with Dewing, but insisted that no mention was made of a withdrawal south of the Seine, lest it sounded defeatist, and that the commander should be given the usual right of appeal. But time was now the key. If there was any hope of salvaging the British troops in France, and those the government was planning to send, in the battle to come, then the immediate arrival of the new commander was paramount.

On 2 June, Lieutenant General Alan Brooke, a corps commander with the original BEF and just returned from Dunkirk, was summoned for an interview with General Dill. Brooke later recorded his memory of their conversation:

I sat in the chair next to the CIGS's table . . . and asked him what he now wished me to do. His reply was: 'Return to France to form a new BEF.' As

I look back at the war, this was certainly one of my blackest moments. I knew only too well the state of affairs that would prevail in France from now onwards. I had seen my hopes in the French Army gradually shattered throughout those long winter months; I had witnessed the realisation of my worst fears concerning its fighting value and morale and now I had no false conceptions as to what its destiny must inevitably be. To be sent back again into that cauldron with a new force to participate in the final stages of French disintegration was indeed a dark prospect.

I asked Dill whether I could refit the 3rd and 4th Divisions so as to bring out some seasoned troops. He said that there was no time for this, that I should be given the 51st Division, the 52nd Division, the remnants of the Armoured Division, Beauman's force, and the 1st Canadian Division ...

... He was very charming ... and finished by asking me whether I was satisfied with what was being done for me. I think I astonished him by replying that I was far from satisfied. That the mission I was being sent on from a military point of view had no value and no possibility of accomplishing anything. Furthermore, that we had only just escaped a major disaster at Dunkirk and were now risking a second.

I continued by stating that possibly this move had some political value ... There might be some reason connected with the morale of the French Government and efforts to maintain them in the war. All that was not for me to judge, but I wanted him to be quite clear that the expedition I was starting on promised no chances of military success and every probability of disaster ... I left his room with the clear conviction that what I was starting on was based purely on political requirements, and from what I had seen of the French up to date I had very great doubts as to any political advantages to be gained.[4]

Not only had Brooke, a seasoned soldier and destined to replace Dill the following year as Chief of the Imperial General Staff, enunciated his conviction that the French had no chance of holding the Germans, but he was also suspicious, rightly as it turned out, of the immediate political gains. His own feelings were based on his experience of fighting alongside the French in Belgium. He was convinced that the French did not have the stomach to continue the fight come what may; it followed from this that any troops left to fight in France would be sacrificed for nothing.

Probably because it was difficult to assemble a staff from the chaos of troops returning from Dunkirk, possibly because of his belief that the task he had been given was hopeless, and perhaps because the War Office was worried he might quickly come into conflict with the French, Brooke was not to arrive in France until the evening of 12 June – a full ten days after his appointment and too late to save the 51st Division

* * *

The plan agreed with the French for the 51st Division's defence of the Somme sector was to have 152 and 154 Brigades up (right and left respectively), 153 Brigade in reserve, holding the River Bresle, with the 6th Royal Scots Fusiliers (one of the pioneer battalions), and the 1st Armoured Division's Support Group and composite tank regiment dug in on a line linking the Bresle with 'Beauforce' on the Béthune.

Before the relief of the French was carried out, General Charles de Gaulle was instructed to reduce the all-important Abbeville bridgehead. Having begun the war as a colonel, de Gaulle had been speedily promoted as one of the few French commanders who had met with any success during the disastrous campaign. On 28 May, his 4th Armoured Division had attacked the high ground above Abbeville with 140 heavy and medium tanks. Because his tanks were more heavily armoured than the lighter models prevalent in the British 1st Armoured Division, and could withstand hits from the German 37mm anti-tank gun, they had more success than the assault a day earlier and by nightfall were in possession of the crest of the Bailleul valley – a sizeable inroad into the bridgehead. The following day the attack was renewed on an angle north towards Beinfay and Moyenneville, with inroads again being made to the line Cambron–Yonval–Caubert. Flushed with even this limited success, de Gaulle was determined to eradicate the bridgehead with one final tank attack on 30 May, supported by the remaining armour of the French 2nd Light Cavalry Division (*2me Division Légère Cavalerie*), and he requested that some of the foremost troops of the 51st Division be placed in reserve to the French to release more soldiers for the attack.

Accordingly, Fortune agreed to allow the 1st Black Watch to hold a position from Toeuffles to Miannay, while the 4th Seaforths with one platoon of 1st Kensingtons and supported by one battery of the 1st Royal Horse Artillery were moved into reserve in the Béhen area. But, Colonel Swinburn recorded, the troops were only released on condition that:

> As they had no adequate supporting weapons it was agreed by the French that these troops would on no account be used in the attack but only as a reserve to hold rearward positions. Here again the differences between the French and our own conceptions of matters was demonstrated, for at 1400 hours the Battalion Commander of the 1st Black Watch received orders from the French to attack at 1600 hours.[5]

Once again the French had gone behind the back of the divisional staff and had issued orders directly to the units involved. The 1st Black Watch CO, Lieutenant Colonel Honeyman, was told that his objective was a wood called the Grand Bois on the right flank of the Abbeville bridgehead. When Honeyman complained that two hours was not nearly long enough to carry out the reconnaissance necessary for such an attack, the start time was put back a paltry quarter of an hour. There was no opportunity to appeal to his brigade or division, and the advance by just one company began on time with no previous reconnaissance.

Although there were no enemy in the wood, its size and the incoming fire made the going tough before B Company wearily reached the far side. Unfortunately, the French attack had been largely a failure and B Company were ordered out in the afternoon so as not to be left hanging in the air. Just as the withdrawal was about to begin, the wood was heavily bombarded causing some casualties. The report of these casualties to Divisional Headquarters was the first indication Fortune received that his troops had been used without him being consulted, and, as Colonel Swinburn recorded, 'in direct contravention of the agreement made with him when he made the troops available'. According to Swinburn, this 'incident', following on from the removal of the six battalions on 24 May, 'seriously shook the faith of the Division not only in the French staff but in the reliance which could be placed on their agreements'.[6]

Despite the failure of de Gaulle's final attack, and the strained relations it placed on the Allies, the relief of the French went smoothly and was completed on 2 June, although the earlier plan to have 153 Brigade holding part of the River Bresle had been amended. By the afternoon of 2 June, 154 Brigade was holding from the sea to Saigneville; 153 Brigade (with the 1st Black Watch attached) was next in line from Gouy to Moyenneville; then came 152 Brigade holding the villages of Bienfay, Villers and Huchenneville; and finally the tanks and carriers of the 1st Lothians were on the right flank from Bray to the bank of the Somme opposite Pont-Remy. The German front line ran from Le Hourdel at the mouth of the Somme estuary, round the St-Valéry-sur-Somme bridgehead which included the strongly guarded woods between Pendé and Boismont. There it retreated behind the Somme Canal, forcing the Highlanders to occupy a dangerous salient. At Abbeville the second German bridgehead began. Its western face was from the same Grand Bois the 1st Black Watch had taken and then relinquished, running along the Cambron valley, whilst the eastern face traced the ridge from Abbeville to Mareuil. Linking the edges were a series of posts on the Miannay–Moyenneville plateau, in the long wood in front of Moyenneville and on the end of the Mareuil spur – the Mont de Caubert. There were no permanent German positions from the bridgehead to Pont-Remy, but frequent heavy patrols were mounted in the southern heights of the Somme valley.

Although the coming battle was commemorated on the colours of some of the regiments involved as 'The Somme, 1940', to distinguish it from the carnage of the previous war, its geography should not be confused. Unlike the 1916 battle, that took place on the flat land to the north-east of Amiens, this time the action for the British was centred on the lower Somme, including its canalised form from Abbeville to the sea. Here the water flowed through a narrow valley, dominated by a series of prominent bluffs on each bank. In places, small valleys cut between the bluffs allowing tributaries a passage to the river. But away from the river the land was generally flat, apart from the Mareuil spur capped by the Mont de Caubert and held by the Germans. Covering the countryside were a series of sprawling agricultural villages, typically French, with small interconnecting farms, orchards and outhouses. Because of the excessive size of the British sector, it was impossible to hold the whole line and companies were usually holding these villages as unconnected strongpoints. Harvest time was near and standing crops covered many of the fields between the villages.

* * *

On 1 June General Fortune had received a memo from General Altmayer, now commanding the Tenth Army, which had grown out of *Groupement A*, ordering an attack to be carried out on the Abbeville bridgehead at or as soon after noon on 3 June as possible. Only two days earlier, following the failure of de Gaulle's last attack, Altmayer had ruled out a further assault by insisting simply that the present line should be held. But since then he had come under pressure from his High Command to eliminate the bridgehead and stabilise the defensive line on the Somme.

Fortune was given command of the attack because he was the senior general in the sector, despite the fact that it would be carried out largely by French troops. These were: the *Groupement Cuirasse* (the remnants of the 2nd Armoured Division), consisting of 86 medium and heavy tanks, a regiment of armoured cars, and around 50 artillery pieces; and the 31st Mountain Division, of six battalions of Pyrenean *Chasseurs* and a further 80 guns. The commanders of these two formations, Colonel Perré and General Vautier respectively, arrived at Advanced Divisional Headquarters – by then at Hélicourt in front of the Bresle – in the afternoon with the news that they could not possibly be in position to attack before the morning of 4 June at the earliest. Fortune agreed to this small concession, but was not prepared to allow them longer because Altmayer had impressed upon him that the longer they delayed, the less their chance of success.

The obvious person to consult for this ominous task, already attempted four times with strong armoured forces and only limited success, was General de Gaulle. He told Fortune that, in his opinion, the key to the attack was the ridge running north-west from Villers-sur-Mareuil and that only by taking the Mont de Caubert could the Abbeville bridgehead be snuffed out. After digesting this information, and examining the ground as exhaustively as possible, General Fortune came to the conclusion that he would have to use some of his own troops to cover the flanks of the French attacks, which could then be made at full strength.

The final plan decided on was for an assault by the armoured *Groupement* along the western slopes of the Mareuil ridge with one battalion of 153 Brigade in support, whilst the 31st Division on its left was to move from the line Moyenneville–Bienfay through the long wood in front of the former to Yonval and Rouvroy. Both flanks were to be secured by Highland troops: the left by 153 Brigade sending a battalion through the Grand Bois to the Bois de Cambron; the right by 152 Brigade taking the villages of Mareuil and Caubert on the east of the Mareuil ridge. But the key to the attack, according to Colonel Swinburn, was the armoured assault against the Mareuil ridge:

> The whole success of the operation depended on the tanks, since capture of the ridge would automatically cover the 31st Div forward, whilst their advance avoided the exposed Miannay–Moyenneville plateau which would be cut off from Abbeville once the two main attacks reached their objectives. From the outset, any success along the ridge very seriously threatened the whole of the communications of the bridgehead with Abbeville.[7]

Zero hour was set at 3.30 am, just before dawn and the time best suited for a tank attack. Ten minutes of concentrated artillery fire against the German front lines would begin at 3.20, covering the approach of the armour to its Start Line, then it would lift and move forward in a 'rolling' barrage just in front of the tanks.

But for all the theory, there were many practical problems. As Swinburn wrote later, the biggest of these was the lack of reconnaissance:

> The dispositions of the enemy defences were only vaguely known, no photographs of the area were available nor any received until the 3rd when some rather inferior ones were delivered, too late for them to be studied by units ... participating in the attack. An RAF officer did come up from Rouen in connection with 'air photos' but as the air cooperation

squadrons were to work from England, that intimate touch so necessary for an organised attack was not possible. The artillery were perhaps the most handicapped by this lack of information and close air cooperation. No flash-spotting or sound-ranging existed in the Division and to try and deal with counter-battery work a counter-battery officer and staff had to be improvised from the HQ 51st Medium Regiment. A Lysander was arranged for spotting but it had no W/T [radio] and its communication had to be done by message dropping, a very slow process indeed.

The cumulative effect of all these factors made the production of even a mediocre counter-battery programme one of extreme difficulty, which in turn meant that the neutralisation of the enemy artillery would be as no means as effective as one could have desired.[8]

A second major problem encountered on 3 June was the uncertainty surrounding the arrival of shells for the French artillery. The 31st Division was a mountain formation and its 75mm field gun used ammunition different to the standard French version. General Vautier had told Fortune that he doubted whether there were any such shells available north of Paris, and repeated representations to the Tenth Army Headquarters produced promises but no results. The ammunition eventually turned up late on 3 June, only because a French artillery officer had spotted its train standing in a station without orders and had used his own initiative to unload it and send it up.

It was not just the shells that were arriving late. The French reconnaissance parties only showed up in the afternoon of the 3rd, and then proceeded to examine the enemy positions like a herd of wildebeest searching out a waterhole. According to Colonel Swinburn's diary, the clouds of dust raised by these groups as they raced in their cars from point to point 'must have clearly indicated abnormal activity to any enemy observer on the front of the proposed attack'.

* * *

The layout of the Highlanders' front line on the evening of the 3 June was as follows: 154 Brigade, which was to play no active role, was holding from the sea to Saigneville, with the 8th Argylls on the left and the 7th Argylls on the right. The 1st Black Watch had been moved over the 153 Brigade, and were near the village of Miannay preparing to support the 1st Gordons in a very limited attacking role.

153 Brigade was in control of the Gouy–Miannay valley feature, with the 1st Gordons based at Cahon and the 5th Gordons holding the villages of Béhen and Moyenneville, from where the main French infantry attack was due to begin. The 4th Black Watch had been put into Divisional Reserve at Le Plouy.

Immediately to the right of the 5th Gordons were the 4th Seaforths of 152 Brigade in the villages of Bainast and Zailleux. A little ahead of them were the 2nd Seaforths at Bienfay. Next, across the Blangy–Abbeville *Route Nationale* were the 4th Camerons, based around the villages of Huchenneville and Villers-sur-Mareuil. The 1st Lothians were still holding the bluffs of the Somme from Bray to Pont-Remy.

Spread between all three brigade sectors were elements of the five divisional artillery regiments, the two machine-gun battalions, and the pioneers of the 7th Royal Norfolks. The other pioneer battalion in the division, the 6th Royals Scots Fusiliers, was holding the Bresle with the Divisional Royal Engineers.

* * *

As the last minutes of midsummer daylight ticked away on the evening of 3 June, the mood among the troops due to go forward the next morning was mixed. Some, like the men of Sergeant John Mackenzie's platoon, were relieved:

> The men cheered-up somewhat, at the news. Anything, we thought, was better than this static warfare, having to take it in the neck under a continuous barrage day and night.[9]

But most were tense and nervous, even reflective and fatalistic, as men tend to become before a battle. Major Iain Shaw-Mackenzie MBE, Second-in-Command of the 4th Seaforths, a battalion with one of the most onerous tasks the following day, was in a contemplative mood:

> I wrote a letter to B. [his wife] and managed to get it off with our Padre who had come up for a brief daily visit ... I made no mention to her of our coming action for I felt it was no use worrying her and, in any case, by the time she received it much would have happened and the fates would have decided one way or another as to our future. Nevertheless home, family and all that was worthwhile in one's life was very close at that moment...
>
> Harry [Houldsworth, his CO] had arranged supper for all the officers at 11 pm ... We sat down at full strength and drank a toast to the success of the operation. It was a fairly cheerful gathering but I could not help but think that never again would we all be together for whether or not the attack on the morrow was successful the days and weeks ahead must see hard fighting now that the issue had been joined with the German Army.[10]

In the same diary entry, Shaw-Mackenzie – a 41-year-old former adjutant of the 2nd Seaforths from the Black Isle who was destined to become the 21st Chief of the Clan Shaw – wrote of his 'grave doubts' as to the success of the operation the following day:

> [It] seemed to me that much would depend . . . on the capture of the high ground on the right and the destruction of the enemy there by barrage for failure would permit the enemy to enfilade our attack . . . In addition, the *Groupement de Gaulle* had already made an attack with tanks in this area on 30 May and had failed, so presumably the enemy had taken all precautions against further attacks. Also, I was astonished at the lack of knowledge as to known enemy defences, the whereabouts of [machine-guns], [anti-tank guns] etc which if not knocked out by the preliminary bombardment might somehow escape the barrage. And lastly, I was appalled at the hasty attacks to be undertaken in conjunction with tanks of another nation whose language we did not speak ... We had never practised any such attack ourselves and had only seen a singularly unimpressive demonstration at Aldershot. I could not but help remembering the Aldershot Tank Corps Commander's lecture when he emphasised the absolute importance of long rehearsals and precautions ... he had said that in 1918 all such attacks not so prepared had failed! I kept my fears to myself but I prayed that the Goddess of Luck would be on our side.[11]

6

The Highlanders Attack

As the morning of 4 June dawned, the omens for the attackers were good. A low summer mist embraced the Somme valley which, it was hoped, would mask the advance of armour and men until they were nearly upon the enemy. Most of the troops involved had had little sleep the night before, partly because of nerves and excitement, but mainly because they had been roused at 12.30 am by their NCOs to form up and move down to the Start Line in readiness for the attack. Men swore in whispers as they bumped into each other in the darkness while collecting their kit, checking their weapons, and priming their grenades.

At 3.20 am the combined thunder of 268 Allied artillery pieces of all calibres opened up. British 25-pounders and 6-inch howitzers joined in a terrible cacophony with French 75mm, 105mm and 150mm field guns for a ten minute barrage of high explosive that pounded the enemy lines. Some German infantry, alerted to the likelihood of an attack by the reckless activity of the French the day before, had withdrawn slightly behind their original positions and were able to escape the worst of the murderous bombardment. The less resourceful had to sit tight and hope for the best. Major James Murray Grant of the 2nd Seaforths described the barrage in his diary as a 'magnificent sight, a sheet of flame right across the horizon'. Sergeant John Mackenzie of the same battalion remembered the brief blitz in a less aesthetic light: 'The din was infernal,' he wrote. 'The air above was a mass of screeching, whistling metal and I was grateful that it was our guns and not Jerry's which were responsible for the racket.'[1]

The barrage was one of the few elements of the attack to go to plan. The key to the assault was the *Groupement Cuirasse*'s tank attack on the Mareuil ridge, which 24 *Chars B* heavy tanks were to spearhead with an escort of light tanks, followed by the 4th Seaforths also accompanied by light tanks at the scale of one per ten men in the leading wave. As the heavy tanks reached their successive objectives – the line of a road crossing the ridge, the line east and west through the bend of the ridge, and finally the end of the spur – they were to be assisted by French motorised infantry (*Chausseurs Portées*) in troop carriers who would hold the objectives until relieved by the slower moving Seaforths.

But the *Chars B* and their escort were late to their Start Line, lost the cover of the rolling barrage that had moved forward, and then stumbled into a minefield between Villers-sur-Mareuil and the Bois de Villers, where a number were blown up. A report that this area was suspected of being mined had come in the night before, but as the Bois de Villers was held by the Germans it was impossible to check it. The tanks that survived the minefield pressed on but, as they came into view of the ridge, they were fired on by artillery and anti-tank guns and many more were knocked out.

The heavy tanks were not the only ones late. At Zero hour the men of B and C Companies of the 4th Seaforths, with bayonets fixed, were anxiously awaiting their armoured escort on the Start Line, 600 yards in front of a track from the *Route Nationale* to Boëncourt where the follow up companies – D and A – were forming up. A few finally appeared, but it was not until 35 minutes after Zero – again too late to gain protection from the barrage – that B Company moved off with three tanks to the left of the Bois de Villers, which the 2nd Seaforths were in the process of taking bloodlessly. Ten minutes later, C Company advanced to the right of the wood, also accompanied by just three tanks.

Attacking with B Company that day was the Intelligence Officer, Lieutenant Hugh Macrae. He had joined the Territorial Army a year earlier, when the battalions were duplicated. Now, aged 38, he was older than many majors in the British Army. Describing his experiences in the attack, he wrote later:

> We were advancing up a gentle slope, over bare fields which were topped by a line of well-spaced trees which had raised earth field boundaries running along between them. Immediately we reached this spot, German machine and anti-tank guns opened up on us. The enemy had this line very well covered by their fire.
>
> At once the infantrymen threw themselves flat on the ground, as they were trained to do, but the firing continued for some considerable time. At least it seemed like an age to me. Personally, I could hear, and in some strange way could almost feel, the bullets passing extremely close to my head . . .
>
> . . . Although a few men and one or two tanks were hit, the advance continued. The tanks went forward and we followed. The Germans kept up their fire. About half-a-mile further on the heavy tanks ran into a minefield. Several were blown up almost at once and caught fire . . . Both light and heavy tanks were being put out of action, the force of the explosions lifting them into the air, toppling many right over on their sides. Amid the smoke, there were tongues of flame and the shouts of the

men still trapped inside their vehicles.

The Germans were now using additional anti-tank guns and at least three machine-guns were concentrating their fire on us, sweeping the bare slopes, one to our right front, one to our left and another to our right rear. Our men were being hit at an alarming rate and such was the concentration of fire against us, together with the devastation being caused by mines to our tanks, that the advance appeared to have come to a complete standstill.

I saw a heavy tank standing stationary some distance away. It was not on fire, but there was no sign of the crew. It occurred to me that I could make good use of this tank as cover from the machine-gun bullets, but on running across I found that no matter to which side I went, bullets were either striking the ground very close to me or hitting the tank and ricochetting off the metal sides.

I had just come round the rear when something hit me in one of my legs, knocking me down. Surprisingly, I felt little pain. As I sat on the ground I saw bullet strikes sending up dust to my left front and also swinging right towards me at about 12 to 15 inch spacing. It was obvious that if I stayed where I was, within a couple of seconds I would be hit low down in my abdomen. I raised myself on my hands and feet, praying that the gunner would not get me in the wrists. Bullets were thudding into the ground all around me, in front of my face and on either side and just as I thought I had escaped that particular burst I felt one bullet graze my ankle. In that instant I noticed a shell hole only a few yards away.[2]

Crawling, it seemed an age before he covered the short distance to safety. Once in the hole, he used his field dressing to bind his wounds as best he could, noting with relief that the blood congealed and that the ankle bone did not seem to be broken.

Macrae had reached the foremost point of the battalion's attack. He lay out in his shell-hole all day, in the burning summer heat. When night fell, he managed, despite his wounds, to gather together about half a dozen other casualties and painfully led them the two miles back to the overworked Regimental Aid Post. For his gallant action he was awarded the Military Cross.

But Macrae was lucky. Out of 100 men of B Company who moved off that morning, only 17 escaped becoming casualties. All the company officers were killed except Captain Gascoigne, the Second-in-Command, who had been left behind. Major Simon Fraser, the Company Commander and winner of an MC in the previous war, had sensed his time was up even before the attack. His last words the previous evening to his old friend and fellow company commander, Major The Viscount Tarbat, had been: 'Wonder when our next meeting will be – I suppose the Somme, possibly Hades'. In the morning, Fraser was led up to the point from which his company was to advance by Lieutenant 'Bim' Young, Second-in-Command of D Company. With his task over, Young turned to Fraser and, half apologetically, told him that he would not be going forward in the attack. Fraser quietly thanked him for his help, and as he turned to walk away said matter-of-factly: 'By the way, I'm not going to come back'.

The men of C Company, who had started a little later, were not faring any better. In textbook fashion, the company was moving with two platoons forward and its headquarters and remaining platoon slightly to the rear. As the forward troops passed the left of the Bois de Villers they moved past a number of German positions, their defenders sprawled in grotesque figures of death, victims of the terrible bombardment. Once clear of the wood, the platoons continued to advance down the valley with minimal opposition until suddenly they, and the tanks accompanying them, came under a hail of machine-gun, anti-tank and shell fire. The Germans had cleverly held their fire until the company had moved parallel to a small wood they held called Les Trois Mesnils, marking the left flank of the 4th Seaforths attack. Then they opened up with everything they had, managing to catch the Scots soldiers in a deadly crossfire. Private Donald Maclennan, a company runner, recalls the horror of the attack:

> We advanced with three tanks in support. A French officer was directing them from behind. They were a help but soon got knocked out because they were so slow – they were sitting ducks.
>
> Being a company runner, I had a bicycle. Imagine going through fields with a bicycle and having to fight at the same time! It didn't last long. A shell burst in the middle of us and the bicycle went sky high – I don't know where it went. One or two boys disappeared then – I think they must have got a shell to themselves.
>
> We were fighting from shell-hole to shell-hole and all the time were being bombed by Stukas. I saw one chap, Willie Mackenzie, with two bullets through his helmet that knocked the rubber out of the inside but never scratched his head. Another man, a piper called Malcolm Robertson, had the point of his thumb knocked off by a bullet and he was only worried that it would be spoiled for piping! Out of the whole company, only 21 of us survived that lot.

Like B Company, C Company was held up just short of their first objective and most of the handful of survivors retired to the front edge of the Bois de Villers which the 2nd Seaforths were holding, though some, possibly including Private Maclennan, continued to try to advance under Second Lieutenant Shearer. Two of the other three officers, Second Lieutenants Smith and Grieve, had been killed.

A little after C Company set off, it was followed up by A Company under the command of Major The Viscount Tarbat, an ex-Regular officer and son of the Earl of Cromarty. By 4.50 am the front ranks had cleared the left side of the Bois de Villers where, as the surprise was being sprung on C Company up ahead, the Germans opened up on them with machine-guns from the high ground to the front and the Les Trois Mesnils wood, about 1000 yards to their left front, causing some casualties. Now all contact was lost with C Company, who had been allowed by the Germans to veer off to the right down the valley. Tarbat decided that to try and advance past the flank of Les Trois Mesnils was inviting annihilation. His company's only hope was to take the wood first:

> My reception became warmer as I worked forward towards Trois Mesnils using, as far as possible, folds in the ground on the left of the valley. By 0600 hrs we had cleared up some German infantry in positions forward of Trois Mesnils and were about 600 yds from the wood itself. We were now being shelled as well as [machine-gunned] but casualties were incredibly light considering that the whole atmosphere seemed to consist of bullets and shells. A German [machine-gun] not yet cleared up started on my right rear from Bois de Villers direction. I decided that the best way to get forward was all together in a rush, to some cover – a re-entrant 30 yds from Trois Mesnils. So I accordingly led A Coy forward in a good old fashioned charge and though the air sang we did not have one casualty – some Germans decided not to await our arrival and retired back to Trois Mesnils. Meanwhile two light tanks (French) made a very ineffective attack on this annoying wood and failed to silence any of the [machine-guns]. When engaged by anti-tank guns in the wood they cleared off. About 50 German prisoners were marched back down the valley – they had been caught by the heavy tanks. The French on my left were mostly dead – though some further over had got forward. Several tanks were smouldering ruins – those inside being a horrible sight, though one seemed to regard so many horrors from a completely detached viewpoint . . . There were at least two anti-tank guns in the wood and more in the right of the valley. I tried to get some returning tanks to help me get up to the wood but they were not for it . . . I had under my command a section of our Carriers and they did admirable work . . . By one of them, I sent back a message giving the situation and asking for some sort of fire – mortar or [artillery] to help me up to Trois Mesnil . . . I got no support. Any further move forward was met by a hail of fire.[3]

By now it was clear to Tarbat that an attack up the right flank of Les Trois Mesnils wood would be suicidal and the only hope was up the left. But before risking his company, he decided to make a personal recce through the dead French in a Bren gun carrier. This was aborted when a hail of bullets smashed the observation slit and an anti-tank gun opened up narrowly missing them. Tarbat now realised that only tank or artillery support could enable the wood to be taken, and he sent back a message to this effect. It never arrived. As A Company tried desperately to dig in at its advanced position, Tarbat reflected wryly on the idiocy of the War Office decision to remove entrenching tools from the kit of the infantryman.

At 10 am, some French motorised infantry arrived, over six hours late, and took up positions to the left of A Company. But when they were dive-bombed an hour later, they leapt into their armoured vehicles and headed to the rear, setting off a chain reaction with other French troops to their left. As this was happening, Tarbat was holding a conference with his officers to discuss the next move and they were unable to prevent some men of A Company also getting carried back. The company's flank was now up in the air, and Tarbat decided to withdraw 200 yards to where there was a more suitable defensive position.

> I waited till all were clear and started back, but didn't get very far when a shell arrived ... and knocked me down into a shell-hole. I was unhurt but a bit concussed and knocked out for a moment. When I came to I was the only one on the left as the [company] had gone back too far towards Bienfay. As soon as I started back I became a target for several [machine-guns] and a field gun, so retired to a shell-hole. Soon got tired of this and very hot ... A bit of shell had crushed my flask (1790–1830 great-great-grandfather) so desired stimulant was missing. So I risked it and went back, luckily the shooting was bad and my guardian angel still present. I collected the [company] and we took over a gap in the line 2/Seaforth area in front of Bienfay.[4]

And here A Company remained until 11 pm when it, the remnants of B Company, and the 2nd Seaforths were relieved by a rather shaken French unit. Compared to the other companies, Tarbat's men had got off lightly: just two killed, ten wounded and one missing. For his work on the Saar, his leadership this day and in the days to come, Tarbat was awarded the Military Cross.

As the attack by the 4th Seaforths was in progress, its Second-in-Command, Major Iain Shaw-Mackenzie, was fretfully awaiting news back at Rear Battalion Headquarters in the château at Bainast. His CO, Lieutenant Colonel Harry Houldsworth MC, a 44-year-old Regular from Moray, had followed up the forward companies with his Battle HQ. Shaw-Mackenzie wrote:

> I wondered what was happening and started to become anxious, as no

message had come back from Harry and I was expecting orders to send
up the 3" Mortar [Platoon]. Hours seemed to pass when, at about 9 am,
a runner appeared with a message from Harry. Briefly it said that the
French tanks had arrived late and, in consequence of this, had not
benefited from the barrage and that the [battalion] was held up short of
the 1st Objective, having suffered heavy casualties in the leading
companies. Further that the tanks had also suffered considerably and
were taking no further part in the operation, also that the *Chasseurs
Alpines* [motorised troops] had not played at all.[5]

There was no further news until 11.30 am when a despatch rider
arrived from 152 Brigade Headquarters at St Maxent with a message
that Lieutenant Colonel Houldsworth was a casualty and that Shaw-
Mackenzie was to proceed there immediately. On arrival, he was
relieved to discover that Houldsworth's wound, in the shoulder, was not
serious, but that he was being evacuated. He had been hit by shrapnel,
along with Captain Macbeth, the Carriers Officer, and Lieutenant
Lindsay, the Signals Officer, from a direct hit on the trench they were
occupying. Of greater concern to Shaw-Mackenzie was the lack of
information provided by his brigade commander, Brigadier Herbert
Stewart DSO, a 53-year-old Lowlander who had served with the Royal
Scots Fusiliers in the previous war. Shaw-Mackenzie wrote:

> I asked for information about the progress of the attack elsewhere but he
> had no news. I then asked if he could say what the future plan was to be
> and whether we should be relieved but he could tell me nothing. He
> asked me to see Lt Col Barclay [2nd Seaforths CO] and to fix up with him
> details for holding a combined front.[6]

Frustrated, Shaw-Mackenzie quickly set off for the 2nd Seaforths' HQ
at Boëncourt, taking the opportunity to stop at the château in Bainast
on the way to see if there was any news from the front. He was surprised
to find in residence Captain Pat Munro of Foulis, the commander of C
Company. As Shaw-Mackenzie later wrote, Munro was 'very shaken and
could give no clear account of the attack on the left other than that his
company had been practically wiped out'. Telling Munro to rest in the
château until further orders, Shaw-Mackenzie left for the 2nd Seaforths'
headquarters in the school at Boëncourt, arriving about 1.30 pm.

Shaw-Mackenzie paused briefly at the door of the combined Regimental Aid Posts of both battalions, at the back of the school. Inside,
Lieutenant Duncan Macrae, the Medical Officer of the 4th Battalion
and a Scottish Rugby International, was hard at work on a man whose
stomach had been torn open by shrapnel. All around men lay in rows
waiting to be operated on, moaning softly. To one side, those who had

not made it lay covered by sheets. The smell of blood and death was too much for Shaw-Mackenzie, and he did not linger.

Once inside the main building, he quickly sought out Colonel Barclay, who told him that C Company men had joined his forward company at the front end of the Bois de Villers and that A Company had also come in. Barclay then asked Shaw-Mackenzie to take command of the right and put it into a state of defence – effectively the remnants of B, D and HQ Companies of the 4th Seaforths – while he would form a strong point around the Bois de Villers and Bienfay with the rest. Just before Shaw-Mackenzie arrived, the 2nd Seaforths had sent a message to 152 Brigade Headquarters asking for reinforcements and for permission to evacuate the Bois de Villers, which was suffering heavily from counter-battery fire. The reply was uncompromising: 'Take 4th Seaforths under your command and hold on at all costs'.

Shaw-Mackenzie went forward in a carrier, with the intention of searching out the 4th Battalion's Battle Headquarters. After passing up the right side of the Bois de Villers, he found it and the remaining carriers in orchards on the western outskirts of Villers-sur-Mareuil. Captain 'RAAS' Macrae, the Adjutant and temporary commander, was sitting forlornly in a small trench with just two runners for company. Both were relieved to see the other, especially Shaw-Mackenzie, as he had heard a rumour while at Boëncourt that 'RAAS' had been killed. In reply to Shaw-Mackenzie's query as to company positions, Macrae pointed up ahead, to the front edge of orchards just to the north of the first houses of the village, where HQ Company had dug some shallow weapon pits behind a hedge and a low mud bank.

The two set off to find D Company, and finally located it in orchards to the north of HQ Company, manning a similar ditch and hedge and overlooking a grassy valley with the Bois de Villers about 200 yards to its left, the battalion's first objective 200 yards ahead in a hollow, and beyond it the Mont de Caubert ridge, the final objective, running round to the left. From the commander of D Company, Captain Ronnie Pelham-Burn, Shaw-Mackenzie discovered that a platoon of 7th Norfolks and seventeen survivors of B Company were also manning the defences. All three officers then anxiously surveyed the ground ahead, half expecting a counter-attack. As Shaw-Mackenzie recorded, a particularly grisly sight greeted them:

> Together we looked across the open fields and the hollow to our front on the lower slopes of which were lying the bodies of most of B company, mown down by [machine-guns] from camouflaged and well-dug positions towards the top of the ridge and from the wood and hedges half right.

[Pelham-Burn] told me how Simon Fraser had come back to say he had been held up and had requested him to try and deal with the nearest [machine-gun] in the hedge on the right and how [Second Lieutenant John] Anderson's platoon had been nearly wiped out in trying to do so, 2/Lt Anderson together with L/Cpl McBean and Pte Finlayson managing to get within a few yards of it when, after throwing hand grenades, they were all wounded.[7]

Soon after this disaster, Pelham-Burn had sent a patrol down to try and locate Anderson; but without success. He suspected, as he told Shaw-Mackenzie, that Anderson was one of two men who had been picked up by the Germans shortly before this. Shaw-Mackenzie later wrote of the painful decision he and Pelham-Burn now had to take:

We came to the conclusion that none of the men of B Coy could be alive for they had lain without moving for upwards of ten hours under a blazing sun. As they lay in the open and close to [machine-guns] which opened fire on any movement and as a counter-attack might be expected it was considered hopeless to try any rescue operations.[8]

They were wrong, as the gallant Lieutenant Hugh Macrae and his six walking wounded were to prove. Furthermore, Anderson, although severely wounded, had not been captured. Like Macrae, he waited until nightfall and then crawled painfully back to the British lines, ending up with a platoon of 4th Camerons to the left of D Company in Villers.

At 2 am the following morning, the remnants of B, D, and HQ Companies of the 4th Seaforths were withdrawn and joined A and C Companies in brigade reserve at Limercourt, about two miles to the rear of Villers down the *Route Nationale*, ostensibly for a well-earned rest. The battalion had been decimated. Five officers had been killed, six wounded and a further 223 Other Ranks were casualties. This represented about half the battalion's true 'fighting' strength, as opposed to its administrative, or back-up, strength.

The day, necessarily, was full of heroic actions. As well as the decorations already mentioned, a DSO went to Colonel Houldsworth, for his leadership and in recognition of the battalion's courageous sacrifices. Private James Morgan was awarded the DCM for carrying in a severely wounded comrade nearly two miles under cover of darkness, even though he himself had been hit by several bullets in the arms and shoulders and had been lying all day in the open. The same award went to Sergeant Donald MacLeod, who had continued to lead his platoon forward, after his platoon officer was killed, until alone and badly wounded he reached his objective. Over the next two nights he evaded capture and finally managed to work his way back through enemy positions to the British lines, which were some way distant, due to a subsequent German attack.

* * *

While the forward companies of the 4th Seaforths were being cut to pieces in the main assault on the Mont de Caubert, the men of the 4th Camerons to their right were faring little better. Supported by the guns of the 1st Royal Horse Artillery, the 23rd Field Regiment and the 215th Medium Battery, the battalion's mission was to take the village of Mareuil-sur-Somme, and from there to prevent any enemy attempts to cross the river to reinforce the bridgehead, and later to assist the infantry following the tanks in clearing up the ridge. This position would also enable direct observation of an enemy artillery concentration located south-east of Abbeville.

Prior to the attack, the 4th Camerons were deployed with: Battalion Headquarters in the Château de Huchenneville; A Company was some way forward to the right, on the high ground immediately behind the hamlet of Tourbieres; B Company was between these two positions in a wood in front of Huchenneville; C and D Companies, and a platoon of 152 Brigade Anti-tank Company, were holding the village of Villers, about a mile to the north of Huchenneville and strategically positioned on the *Route Nationale.*

It was decided that the assault would be pressed on a two company front: B Company would move forward and take the strongly-held Hedgehog Wood, to the left of A Company's posts which would provide covering fire. D Company would follow a quarter of an hour later, parallel to the *Route Nationale,* and capture the crossroads at Mareuil. C Company's role would be to thin out its defences and take over D Company's vacated positions. Yet, because of the loss of one of D Company's platoons to shell and mortar fire the day before, 14 Platoon of C Company under Second Lieutenant Johnston would accompany D Company leaving only two platoons to defend Villers.

At Zero hour, B Company, made up of men largely from the islands of Harris and Skye, moved off towards Hedgehog Wood, aptly named as its defences were bristling with machine-guns and rifles. Leading was Second Lieutenant Clark's platoon on the right, Second Lieutenant Robertson's on the left, with Captain The Viscount Fincastle, B Company Commander, following up with his headquarters and the last platoon under Second Lieutenant Spiers. The company moved in extended order, 126 men strong, across a broad expanse of flat ground with little cover. There were no ditches and only a few shallow

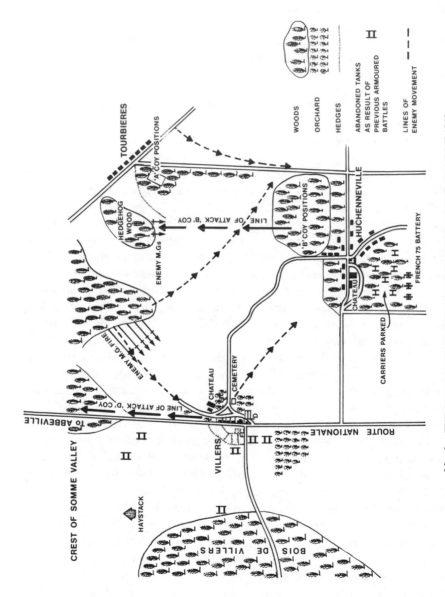

Map 3.   THE 4th CAMERONS ON THE SOMME - HUCHENNEVILLE 4 JUNE 1940

depressions in which to hide from the bullets and shrapnel that were about to consume them. Confidence had already been dealt a blow by the inaccuracy of three French planes which, a few minutes earlier, had bombed the company positions by mistake. This misfortune was compounded when the barrage that was aimed at the front edge of the Hedgehog fell short, leaving its defenders unscathed and ready to reap destruction. The left hand man of the left hand unit, 12 Platoon, was Private Sandy Russell, the former battle patrol member:

> The whistles sounded and we were on our way. When we left the trenches and looked towards Hedgehog Ridge all was smoke and fumes, and aerial and ground explosions. The enemy was supposed to be no nearer than that ridge and it came as an unpleasant surprise when we came under intense machine-gun and mortar fire after having gone only about 100 yards. On my left was a large field of waist to shoulder high wheat, and I was tempted to go into it for some kind of cover. However, when I saw large swathes being cut in it by opposing fire I decided to carry on where I was.
>
> The racket was hellish with Jerry mortars falling in all directions and men spinning and falling or being blown up. I saw my old friend from schoolboy days hit by a burst from a machine-gun, followed by Neil Mackenzie and several others being hit in succession. I came to a small hole and from it chucked two or three grenades in the general direction of the Jerry machine-gun. I think I might have stayed there all day, but Lieutenant Robertson came along shouting, 'Come on, come on we can't stay here!' I followed him quite closely until we came to a hedge about half a mile from our objective. He called on us to dig in but already there was a line of slit trenches and a small orchard. I, along with Robertson, was furthest on . . .
>
> I fired two shots out of my rifle when, suddenly, there was an almighty red flash and a bang and I found myself sitting in the bottom of the trench on top of some guy who was semi-conscious. Another mortar landed on top of the trench area about one and a half yards away and blew a heap of earth on top of me. The Jerries seemed to have this hedge well ranged because, for the next 20 minutes, it became a living hell. When the barrage eased off, we got the order to join A Company at the far end of the orchard about 200 yards further back.

The order had come from the company commander, Lord Fincastle, who with the remnants of the company had arrived in that area. Amazingly, at this point only one man of Russell's section was a casualty and that was by friendly fire in the heat of battle; every man in the remaining two sections – around 20 men – of 12 Platoon had been killed or wounded, other than Second Lieutenant Robertson. Despite the failure of the barrage, that fell short a second time, Robertson and

Russell had reached the foremost point of B Company's advance and had forced at least one machine-gun post to withdraw.

Moving up in the centre with B Company Headquarters was Company Quartermaster Sergeant Gregor Macdonald:

> By the time we were half-way to the objective we had seen a number of our men go down – if the casualties were close at hand one tried to help, but our objective was first priority and we were forced to leave many where they fell. Then, quite suddenly, there appeared before us what must have been at least two enemy companies who had been lying unseen in the rye crop and only appeared when we were within 100 yards. They greeted us with a hail of fire from their Spandau machine-guns and huge gaps appeared in our formations. By this time we were getting near our objective and, with a final desperate effort, we reached the edge of the escarpment bordering the River Somme. In the confusion of battle, we had veered slightly to our right and found ourselves very close to our A Company position ... The last 100 yards had cost B Company dearly and at roll call only 41 men stood up. Of the officers, only Captain Fincastle and Second Lieutenant Robertson survived the advance ..., while two sergeants were killed and three wounded, leaving the Sergeant Major and I as the only surviving senior ranks.[9]

There were now two pressing problems for the survivors to face: defence against counter-attack and evacuation of the many wounded. The first was 'solved' by pushing forward 12 men to defend the front of the orchard, while Company Quartermaster Sergeant Gregor Macdonald and the Company Sergeant Major – also named Macdonald and known to his men as 'The Muc', or pig, in Gaelic because of his reputation as a hard disciplinarian – began to gather the wounded together. During his rounds the 'Muc' noticed that Captain Fincastle had been hit in both legs by machine-gun bullets, and he hurried over to dress them. Seeing Company Quartermaster Sergeant Macdonald nearby, he shouted for help.

> I made my way to where the Company Commander lay, and was cutting the stitching on my battle dress pocket where the first field dressing was carried when the mortar battery again concentrated on our position. Unlike artillery fire, the mortars give no warning and my first recollection was being thrown to the ground by the blast and trying to regain my feet. The Sergeant Major, his face covered by blood, shouted 'QMS give me a hand – I think the Company Commander has had it'. I moved across to where Captain Fincastle lay to find that the last mortar had landed on him and he was already dead. I hurriedly put a plaster on the Sergeant Major's own wound but he assured me it was not serious. At that moment, another mortar landed between us and I felt a burning sensation in my head.

When I retrieved my helmet, I found that a piece of shrapnel had gone in below the rim and out through the crown, leaving me with an uncomfortable head wound ... By this time, a number of the men wounded in the final assault had crawled into the orchard, while others were being carried in by their comrades. We used the ammunition truck to take these men to the Regimental Aid Post, packing in 20 wounded.[10]

Before leaving Fincastle, the 'Muc' retrieved his personal effects. He could not help looking at his pocket book in which there was a family 'snap' of Fincastle, Lady Fincastle and their little boy, who was just two years old. Faced with this, tears started rolling down the cheeks of the Sergeant Major who, it was said, would have put his own grandmother on a charge.

In the afternoon, after a hazardous trek, the company cooks managed to reach the survivors of B Company with enough food for 130 men. They found less than 40. But Sandy Russell was famished and, because there was so much extra food, he remembers the meal of bacon and bread as the best feed he had had in the Army, even though it was rudely interrupted by another mortar barrage, causing three more casualties. Following this happy diversion, Russell was brought back down to earth by the unenviable task of gathering the corpses.

> We started to assemble the dead and it was a harassing duty to see all our good friends lying there in such a grotesque look of death. Our company commander was amongst the slain and he was well-loved and respected. Lieutenant Robertson departed for Battalion Headquarters to make his report and the rest of us came under the leadership of CSM Macdonald. He was here, there and everywhere encouraging us, showing us where he wanted slit trenches dug and generally keeping us busy to ensure discipline would not slacken.

It was lucky that the attack was not resumed from A Company's positions because the Germans had anticipated this, and had vacated the front edge of the Hedgehog to allow it to be bombed by their Stukas. Eventually orders came for the 'Muc' to leave a party of 13 to assist A Company – Sandy Russell was amongst them – and to withdraw after dark with the remaining 26 men to their original positions in the wood in front of Huchenneville. There they were met by D Company of the 5th Gordons who had been rushed across in the evening to stiffen the 4th Camerons, now so seriously depleted after their heavy casualties.

* * *

The second part of the two-pronged attack by the 4th Camerons, undertaken by D Company, was planned to start at Zero plus 15 minutes to allow B Company time to neutralise the Hedgehog Wood. This never happened and, during the advance, D Company was machine-gunned from both the front and the flank.

While forming up, D Company had suffered another misfortune to add to the loss of one of its platoons the previous day: The commander of the leading platoon, Platoon Sergeant Major Noble, was killed by shellfire. His place was taken by the Company Second-in-Command, Captain Burton. Second Lieutenant Macdonald was to follow with his platoon on the left, and Major Threlfall, the company commander, would bring up the rear with his headquarters and Second Lieutenant Johnston's platoon from C Company. As the forward platoon moved off, Second Lieutenant Macleod, commanding the 152 Brigade Anti-tank Platoon in Villers, arrived on the Start Line – between the *Route Nationale* and the Château de Villers – with some more, unwilling, participants. These 18 sheepish-looking soldiers were the reinforcements who had arrived the day before and who had been overlooked in the preparations for the attack; Macleod had found them fast asleep in their farmhouse billets. It would not be long before they wished they were back there.

Watching the troops move off was Private Alexander Grant of the 3-inch Mortar Platoon, positioned in a sunken road near to the Start Line. He and his comrades were waiting for the forward troops to take a clump of trees directly ahead at the top of a wheat field, which would be the signal for them to rush up in support:

> We heard a whistle blow, then the bagpipes and soon after we saw Piper Mackay coming out leading the advancing troops of D Company; the Germans waited until they were 50 yards up and then opened up with their spandaus from this group of trees to the front. The piper went down and soon after Major Threlfall was hit. He was a big man, very tough, but a lot of people say he had a bottle of gin inside him that morning. We couldn't believe our eyes, it was suicide. Men were going down like flies, falling all over the place. What sheer madness, they went forward without a tank, without anything.

Major Threlfall was seen to rise after he was hit, and then fall once more close to the *Route Nationale*, up the right of which the company was advancing. He was dead. Second Lieutenant Ian Macdonald was hit in the bullet-swept orchard beyond the hedge marking the Start Line but was later evacuated to safety. He later spoke of being fired on by a number of tanks and it is almost certain that these were the French tanks in the 4th Seaforths sector who mistook the Camerons for Germans. Second Lieutenant Johnston was also hit soon after starting and lay out in the open all day until, like Lieutenant Macrae of the 4th Seaforths, under cover of darkness he crawled back to safety. The most progress was made by Captain Burton and the remains of his platoon on the right, but soon they too were pinned down. Burton, like Threlfall, was seen to fall as if hit and he was later reported as presumed killed. But he was a hardy fellow and later made it back to the British lines. Out of the whole company, only a handful had made it past the scanty cover of the orchard in front of the Start Line, and into the wheat field beyond.

The enemy machine-gun, mortar and shell fire had grown in intensity as the attack progressed, and there was little hope of hitting back because of the inadequacy of the artillery observation. In any case, the artillery had largely missed its front line targets and was now following a prearranged timetable of bombardment against targets beyond.

All the while the wounded were making their way back to Villers and at 9 am Company Sergeant Major Simmons arrived at the old company headquarters, which had since been taken over by C Company. He had with him the remnants of the company, about 50 men, including a number of the 4th Seaforths who had strayed across from the other side of the *Route Nationale*.

At 9.45 am Company Sergeant Major Simmons returned from C Company Headquarters at the bottom of the village and placed himself under Second Lieutenant David Ross of C Company who, with his platoon, was holding a position to the right of the *Route Nationale* near the Start Line. After receiving an instruction from his company commander, Captain Ross (no relation), to act at his own discretion, Ross decided to form the returned D Company and 4th Seaforths men into two groups – one under Company Sergeant Major Simmons and one under Sergeant Macleod – to resume the attack. The results were tragic and inevitable: after advancing just 200 yards to the front of the orchard the attack was halted by murderous machine-gun fire from the wood off to the right, and the survivors finally crawled back in under the cover of a shallow ditch.

After this, Second Lieutenant Ross liaised with Captain Pelham-Burn, the commander of D Company of the 4th Seaforths dug in across the main road, and together they organised parties to collect the wounded and carry them back to the château.

Later in the day, after a visit by the battalion Second-in-Command, Major Stanley Hill, a platoon of 7th Norfolks pioneers was sent up to strengthen the position. They were joined by 12 other Camerons under Second Lieutenant Slater, a reinforcement officer, and used to strengthen the position to the right of the château which was already being held by Lance Corporal Walsh and 17 men who had survived the two attacks. The Norfolks protested strongly that as pioneers they were not equipped to be used as front line troops, but every man was needed and their protests were ignored.

The remaining hours of daylight on 4 June were used by C and D Companies to continue to evacuate the wounded. The RAMC had prohibited the use of ambulances in front of Huchenneville, and so this was carried out by the anti-tank lorry and the ration truck when it came up. There was no news of a relief.[11]

152 Brigade's casualties on 4 June were a crippling 20 officers and 543 other ranks, the major proportion being borne by the 4th Seaforths and 4th Camerons. In effect, these two battalions were now down to 50 per cent of their fighting strengths.

* * *

To the left of the main tank attack, aided by the 4th Seaforths, was the push made by the French 31st Infantry Division and one battalion of light tanks under General Vautier, with its objectives as the long wood in front of Moyenneville and, finally, the Somme Canal to the west of Abbeville. In support were 80 *Soixante-quinze* field guns and 16 of the heavier 105mm calibre. The right flank of this attack was Les Trois Mesnils wood, the village of Yonval and finally the Vaux Farm on the Mareuil ridge. The left flank was a track leading from Moyenneville to Rouvroy.

To get to their Start Line the French troops had to pass through positions in Moyenneville and Bienfay held by the 5th Gordons and 2nd Seaforths respectively. Second Lieutenant Donald Ritchie was in Moyenneville and remembers the slapdash way the French infantry went to war:

> I was absolutely amazed at the casual way the French *poilus* went into battle. They were still wearing their long coats, with great long rifles slung over their shoulders, and smoking the inevitable *gauloises*. They just sort of shambled out to the battle area. They weren't at all convincing. You felt, 'My god, that's no way to go into battle.' One or two officers passed through us and they weren't much better.

Ritchie's fears were soon realised. Although the start of the attack went to plan, going in at 3.30 am after a heavy ten minute bombardment and, thanks to the ground mist, making some good early progress, the troops soon began to falter. Despite initial reports that the eastern edge of the long wood had been taken, and that the tanks were being moved around the flank to enable the whole wood to be cleared, the sight of large numbers of the attackers returning to the Start Line seemed to contradict this. Captain Geddes, Adjutant of the 5th Gordons, estimated that within an hour the majority of the French, less the killed and wounded, had returned to the Gordons' lines.

Once back on their Start Line, the French made little effort to take cover or dig in and, as the mist lifted, the Germans in the wood and on the Mareuil ridge were able to engage them to good effect, causing many casualties. An excuse given for the speedy retreat by many of the returned French soldiers was that they were counter-attacked. This was not true, and the only explanation is that they mistook French tank crews and walking wounded of *Groupement Cuirasse*, returning from the direction of Les Trois Mesnils, as Germans attacking.

The 5th Gordons had not been idle during this abortive assault. As well as providing covering fire with all weapons, a platoon under Second Lieutenant Thom went forward to help in the attack on the long wood, albeit without success.

Despite a subsequent attempt by some French tanks to take the long wood, by 8 am the attack had irretrievably failed even though, at this stage, less than one regiment had been used. The concentration of disorganised French troops inevitably attracted an artillery bombardment on Moyenneville which lasted until 11.30 am. When the French moved back to Béhen, the enemy fire followed them and was supplemented by dive-bombing attacks in the afternoon. Undoubtedly the German command of the air, and the freedom this gave to its stukas and artillery spotter planes, markedly increased the discomfiture of the Allied troops.

Certainly the French had not fought with their customary *élan*, taken for granted in earlier wars and so sadly lacking from most of the engagements of the 1940 campaign. There were some mitigating circumstances: most of the commanders of the forward troops had only arrived in the area two hours before the attack and many of the troops themselves were not even in position at Zero. But they do not disguise the apathetic and half-hearted attempts by the French troops to advance, and their willingness to retire at the first sign of trouble, real or otherwise. This feebleness only serves to highlight the heroic efforts made by the Highland soldiers that day, and the terrible casualties they suffered accordingly.

At 4 pm the CO of the 5th Gordons, acting Lieutenant Colonel 'Sailor' Clark – a Regular Gordons' officer who had taken over from Major Rupert Christie on 20 May, the latter reverting back to Second-in-Command – received orders from Brigadier Stewart, commanding 152 Brigade, to send one company immediately to the assistance of the

4th Camerons, with the rest of the battalion to follow that night. He sent D Company and one section of carriers, and it was they who were in position in the wood in front of Huchenneville when the remnants of B Company, 4th Camerons, returned. The plan was that the 5th Gordons' former positions would be taken over by French troops, but when the commander of these troops arrived in the evening he refused to assume responsibility. 152 Brigade Headquarters then ordered the 5th Gordons to leave in any case, and by 9 pm the movement was underway.

The final, and only successful, attack of 4 June was put in by the 1st Gordons, supported by the 1st Black Watch and machine-gunners from both the Northumberland Fusiliers and the 1st Kensingtons. There were two tasks: first to clear the Grand Bois from the north west, then to move on to the Bois de Cambron. This latter wood dominated the valley running south from Cambron to Moyenneville and when held would, in Colonel Swinburn's estimation, 'both cover the left flank of the final stages of the 31st Division attack and also cut off the garrison of the enemy posts on the Miannay–Moyenneville plateau'.

Two companies of the 1st Gordons, B and C, were due to storm the Grand Bois from their positions along the Cahon valley while elements of the 1st Black Watch attacked the Petit Bois, a much smaller wood to the south from where they could cover the Gordons' advance. A Company of the 1st Gordons was to remain in position at Gouy, on the banks of the Somme Canal, while D Company would be waiting in reserve behind the forward companies.

At Zero hour, again after a ten minute bombardment, the 1st Black Watch moved off and, unopposed, quickly took the Petit Bois. The Gordons came up against somewhat stiffer opposition. Spearheading the right-hand company (C Company) was 13 Platoon. Its men were to advance with bayonets fixed up a narrow sunken lane, across some fields and into the right-hand edge of the wood, about half way up, to take the defenders by surprise. Once in, it was to swing right and continue to the end. Leading 13 Platoon that day was Second Lieutenant Charles Barker:

> On the way forward a young soldier lost his nerve and shaking said he had left his rifle behind! I threw him mine, which I had decided to use, and told him I'd shoot him if he continued to shake! He reacted immediately and carried on. We gained complete surprise until a vast Bosche sentry yelled 'Achtung!' and then lunged at me with his bayonet. It scraped my face drawing blood and for his audacity he received a number of bullets from my .38 pistol and reeled to the ground. The Jocks were pouring in behind me with bayonets fixed. I told Sergeant Geerie to go further into

the wood and to swing right while I took the near side. Unfortunately he was killed by Spandau fire while doing that. Germans were firing from all directions; some were in trees, some in dug-outs. It was chaos really, one didn't know friend from foe. When we had captured our objective I rushed off to organise the position and to see what had happened to Sergeant Geerie. Bullets were still streaming in from beyond the wood because the Germans knew we were there. While I was away the Germans who were still in the position were coming out, pretending to surrender, and then playing tricks on the Jocks. One incident that was reported to me when I returned was of some Germans throwing what looked like a water bottle among the Jocks; it exploded killing one and wounding five. I doubt if those who fought on survived. We probably took about 20 prisoners.[12]

After the initial incursion by his forward platoons, Captain Donald Alexander, commanding C Company, quickly followed up with his headquarters. Attached to Alexander's headquarters for the assault was Private Tom Copland, a member of the Intelligence Section. He remembers that as they approached the Grand Bois, most enemy fire was directed towards the 1st Black Watch entering the Petit Bois.

When we reached this wood, a steep bank of gorse faced us, with narrow footpaths through the gorse leading into the wood. An enemy soldier was standing at the top of this footpath with his hands raised as if he was surrendering. Captain Alexander went up the path to capture him, but the German had a dagger hidden in his hand and attacked Alexander with it, cutting the point of his chin and one of his thumbs. They both landed at my feet with the enemy soldier on top and we quickly finished him off. C Company reached its objective but only after heavy loss of killed and wounded on both sides.

Carrying out the left wing of the attack on the Grand Bois was B Company, commanded by Major Douglas Gordon. Recently a member of General Gort's staff at General Headquarters in Arras, Major Gordon had wanted to do his bit by serving with a front line unit and had asked to be transferred to the 1st Gordons. One other explanation, popular in the battalion at the time, is that he had fallen out with General Gort. Whatever the reason, he would not live to regret it.

Like Captain Alexander, Major Gordon was following up his lead platoons with his headquarters. By sheer bad luck he and his men ran into a well-concealed machine-gun post that had been passed unnoticed by his vanguard troops, with the result that Gordon was killed and his Company Sergeant Major, Jack Kean, and two company runners were seriously wounded. Despite this setback, Lieutenant Colin Denniston-

Sword, the company Second-in-Command, took over and the advance continued.

Moving up behind the two attacking companies, into a position where it could quickly go forward if necessary, was D Company. Commanding its 16 Platoon was Johnny Rhodes, looking to add to the MC he had won in the Saar:

> We got down to the bottom and I came across a man called Friel, a B Company Bren gunner who had refused to advance. I said, 'Right, I'm going to shoot you!' At that moment a runner came tearing back and saved his life. He said that B Company's Headquarters had been hit and Major Gordon was dead. They sent me up to find out why.
>
> So I took my platoon and we wandered along until we came to a fairly big ride through the wood. It appeared dreadfully silent. There were no birds singing and no rabbits moving. I suppose after all the artillery it wasn't surprising. They had said that the forward elements of B Company had been killed by machine-gun fire and I realised that there might be a machine-gun platoon or half a company right across the ride from me. I tried tossing a bomb to make something move, but nothing did. So I got three men and we doubled across and suddenly found ourselves among what had been half a company of machine-gunners – they'd all gone and left their weapons! There were little fox holes and machine-guns all over the place.
>
> Then I debouched towards the forward edge of the wood and on the way found Douglas Gordon lying dead with Private Will, one of the oldest men in the battalion, and a couple of others.

By midday, B and C Companies, with some elements of D Company in support, had reached their first objective, the high ground at the far end of the Grand Bois, and were eager to carry on to the Bois de Cambron beyond. Indeed, Lance Corporal Denholm and some of his platoon had initially continued on regardless, until recalled. But no orders to this effect ever arrived, and the rest of the day was spent digging in and keeping out of the way of the incoming fire. Casualties for the battalion were just 40 killed and wounded, while around 50 Germans were killed and many more wounded and taken prisoner. Considering that an attacking formation should expect to lose men in a ratio of at least two to one compared to the defence, this was a remarkable achievement in an otherwise depressing day.

But it was now clear to General Fortune that the attack on the Abbeville bridgehead had failed, and that to continue the advance of the 1st Gordons was pointless. As it was, the abandonment of the assault by the French 31st Division to the right had left the Gordons' flank dangerously exposed. General Fortune's initial plan, as communicated to General Altmayer of the French Tenth Army that afternoon, was for the 1st Gordons to consolidate, all attacks in other areas to be suspended, and to try to exploit the gains made by the Gordons on the morrow. Altmayer agreed to this, but by late afternoon the incapacity of the men under Fortune's command to continue the attack the next day was recognised and that night the 1st Gordons had to relinquish their hard-won ground.

As well as the bravery, determination and sound tactics demonstrated by its well-trained officers and men, the success of the 1st Gordons on 4 June was due in no small part to the close support given by the British gunners behind. A clever system of notifying the artillery of the progress of the forward troops by Very lights, so allowing the barrage to creep just in front of the advance, was highly successful. Although not given the toughest tasks – these fell to the 4th Seaforths and 4th Camerons – it is probably not a coincidence that the only Allied troops to achieve their objectives during the attack were the three Regular battalions of the Highland Division. Also indicative was that not one member of the 1st Gordons was awarded a gallantry medal for the attack on 4 June. Even to be recommended as a member of a Regular battalion required an act well beyond the call of duty.

After accepting that the attack had stalled, General Fortune was given an opportunity to reduce the frontage to more manageable proportions by using the remainder of the 31st French Division to take over the line from the *Route Nationale* at Villers to Moyenneville. This was the move that enabled the 4th Seaforths to withdraw that night to Limeux, and the 5th Gordons to sideslip to the right to Huchenneville. By the morning of the 5th, the front was held as follows: 1st Lothians were still holding from opposite Pont-Remy to Bray; 152 Brigade was next in line with the 5th Gordons and the 4th Camerons up between Bray and Huchenneville, and the 2nd and 4th Seaforths in reserve at Limeux and Limercourt respectively. To the left of the brigade, was the French 31st Division, flanked by 153 Brigade holding up to Gouy on the Somme Canal. The 1st Black Watch were holding the villages of Bouillancourt and Miannay, and the 1st Gordons extended the line up the Cahon valley to the canal. 154 Brigade had not moved from its positions from Saigneville to the sea. The 4th Black Watch was still in Divisional Reserve at Le Plouy.

But the omens were not good. All day, information about enemy reinforcements arriving in the area had been coming in to the Fortune's Battle Headquarters at Martainneville. Prisoners talked of reaching Abbeville shortly before the attack, after long marches, while motor transport columns had been reported nightly along the Somme valley. Colonel Swinburn recorded:

> Everything pointed to an early enemy action against the river Somme position and from prisoners' statements the impression was gained that the enemy had himself contemplated local attacks on the 4th June to widen his bridgeheads. Fears that a German attack was brewing further south at Amiens, the other major bridgehead over the Somme, were heightened when Perré's *Groupement Cuirasse* was withdrawn from General Fortune's command and sent there on the night of the 4th.[13]

The intelligence assessment proved correct, for on the same day that the 51st Division launched its first major attack of the campaign, Dunkirk fell and the German Army was preparing to strike at the remaining Allied forces holding the Somme–Aisne line. Although over 224,000 British and 110,000 French had been evacuated from Dunkirk, there were still 160,000 British troops left in France. The vast majority of these were lines of communication troops, and the 51st (Highland) Division was now the only British formation still in the front line.

* * *

Even as the last full-scale Allied attack of the 1940 campaign was being planned, the British Government was being pressured to send ever more military aid to France.

While holding out little hope that the Germans could be held for long, General Weygand was determined that France would not go down without a fight. He was equally determined that Britain would pull its weight in this final struggle by supplying its most valuable commodity – aircraft. As he knew that the RAF was Britain's only hope to stave off invasion, it is tempting to conclude that he did not wish to see Britain escape France's fate. On 1 June, he sent Churchill a personal telegram demanding that 'the maximum of British aviation, both Fighters and Bombers, should continue to make maximum effort in forthcoming land battle'. General Vuillemin, the commander of the French Air Force, was more specific in a letter to Weygand which the latter passed on to Churchill with his own telegram. In the coming battle, he argued, French fighters of which there were just 350 left 'would soon be overwhelmed' if they were not '*heavily* reinforced' by British fighters. Vuillemin ended his letter by insisting that 'if possible' all fighters based in England should intervene in the battle on the lower Somme, and to cover the rest of the expected battlefield 'it would be necessary that 20 Squadrons (320 aircraft)' should be based in France.

These demands from the military were backed up by the politicians when Reynaud sent an even further-reaching telegram on 2 June. Not only did Reynaud request the immediate despatch of three infantry divisions, followed up by units from Dunkirk as they were re-equipped, he also asked for bomber assistance and for fighters 'whose role will be decisive'. The number was not specified; he simply asked for a 'still greater extent than during the battle in the North', adding that they could not operate effectively from England. Given that every available fighter was used at Dunkirk to create an aerial umbrella virtually 24 hours a day, the implication was obvious.[14]

But as well as being the head of the government, Reynaud – along with Mandel – was one of the few members of the French Cabinet keen to fight on at all costs. For both reasons, his requests carried more weight than the military, whom Churchill suspected were already anticipating defeat. It is in this perspective that the British Prime Minister's response should be viewed.

At an evening meeting of the War Cabinet in London on 2 June, Churchill pointed out that if they were 'to decline to respond to M. Reynaud's appeal there was a considerable danger that a point might be reached at which French resistance might collapse', and if Paris fell the French might be 'tempted to conclude a separate peace'. This, he continued, would pose the awful possibility of a French Government 'not merely out of the war, but actually hostile to us'. In reply, Clement Attlee, the leader of the Labour party and the Lord Privy Seal in Churchill's coalition cabinet, pointed out that it was vitally important not to 'impair the essential fighter defences of this country', not least because, in his view, it was 'doubtful whether the French had evolved any new methods' of countering the German panzers. Instead it was necessary to 'do something to hearten the French' such as the offer of one or two divisions, as a 'token' of the British Government's 'sincerity'.[15]

This argument struck a chord with Churchill. He knew that Britain almost certainly had to look to its own security, especially in the air, in anticipation of the defeat of the French armies, but he also realised that to ignore French pleas might give the defeatist elements within her cabinet and military command the opportunity to ignore the joint agreement and seek peace unilaterally with all the consequences that would entail. That evening, John Colville, Churchill's personal private secretary, was to argue just such a point in his diary:

> Reynaud has telegraphed for more fighters, more bombers and more troops in order to withstand the great attack expected shortly on the Somme and on the Aisne. This annoys Winston who considers the French

grasping and whose main energies are now turned to consolidating our
home defences, conserving our air strength, and building up a new army
from the remnants of the old and from the troops now left in India and
Palestine. However, it is vital to sustain French morale and give no excuse
for a collapse.[16]

The result of the War Cabinet's deliberations, after consultation with
the Chiefs of Staff, was close to Attlee's suggestion. In a telegram sent
to General Spears in Paris for communication to Reynaud on 4 June,
Churchill offered the following: To reconstitute the BEF by sending a
headquarters and three infantry divisions, one within seven days and
the remaining two as soon as possible after that; and to bring up to
strength the three fighter and six bomber squadrons already in France.
In other words, contrary to the requests, no extra squadrons would be
sent. Instead, the French would have to make do with what they had,
plus three divisions whose arrival was uncertain to say the least. As an
excuse for the paltry aircraft offering, Churchill cited the 'very serious
losses of the last three weeks' and the time it would take to overhaul the
squadrons and replace the losses.[17]

Churchill was playing a dangerous game. He and his Cabinet were
prepared to sacrifice soldiers, in Colville's words, to 'sustain French
morale', but they were far less willing to do so with the RAF – and this
could not escape the notice of the French. Indeed, Churchill might
have been doubly nervous had he been present at the meeting of the
French War Committee in Paris on 3 June in which Weygand accused
Churchill of having abandoned France to her own resources by playing
a 'double game' since 16 May. As evidence, he gave two examples: Gort
had only disobeyed his orders and marched to the coast because he had
received orders to do so from London, and, contrary to what had been
agreed on 31 May, the rearguard at Dunkirk was French.[18]

Churchill would also have been alarmed if he had seen the telegram
that the anglophobe US Ambassador to France, William Bullitt, sent to
his Secretary of State in Washington, Cordell Hull, on 4 June. Bullitt
reported a conversation with Marshal Philippe Pétain, Reynaud's
deputy, in which the hero of Verdun ran through a catalogue of 'Albion
Perfidy' since the beginning of the campaign, concluding that 'unless
the British Government should send to France, to engage in the battle
which was imminent, both its air force and reserve divisions the French
Government would do its utmost to come to terms immediately with
Germany'.[19]

Both Weygand and Pétain, the men who since 25 May had talked of
the possibility of an armistice, were blaming Britain for the disastrous

campaign and were preparing the ground for a renunciation of the agreement with the British that denied either country the right to seek peace unilaterally.

But while Churchill was preoccupied with the political considerations of the BEF fighting in France, his generals in the field were gradually making him aware of the military realities. On 4 June, Lieutenant General James Marshall-Cornwall, the British officer who on 2 June had been attached to the Headquarters of General Altmayer's Tenth Army, sent a report to General Dill, which was quickly passed on to Churchill. In it Marshall-Cornwall made clear his lack of faith in the French ability to resist on their present line by suggesting that a 'policy should be laid down covering the routes of withdrawal of the British Troops in the event of a German break-through further east'. He went on to specifically warn that there was a danger of the 51st Division being 'driven into' the Le Havre peninsula and 'trapped there' as the bridges at Rouen were bound to be destroyed. His solution was for alternative crossings to be prepared on the Seine below Rouen, but this would need to be squared with the French High Command.[20]

But given the delicate nature of Anglo-French relations at this juncture, there was no way that Churchill was going to suggest to General Weygand, or his deputy, General Georges, that they should make plans for a withdrawal from the Somme Aisne Line; especially as an order had already been issued by Weygand that this was a final line, that there would be no retreat, and that its defenders would die where they stood.

7

'Operation Red'

In the early hours of 5 June, the German offensive against the Somme–Aisne line – codenamed *Fall Rot* (Operation Red) – began. The forces ranged against France that morning were divided into three army groups, comprising a total of 139 divisions. Of these, 104 were to take part in the attack, including all ten panzer formations; the rest would hold the German frontier opposite the Maginot Line.[1]

To repel the assault the Allies were holding from Luxembourg to the sea with just 51 divisions: the 51st (Highland) Division, the 1st Armoured Division (with a third of its tanks), the hotch-potch Beauman Division, and 48 French divisions, some still being formed and most understrength. The remaining 17 French divisions, producing a grand total of 68, were manning the now largely-redundant Maginot Line and the Swiss and Italian frontiers. The Germans, therefore, had a numerical superiority of two to one, and an even greater imbalance of tanks and planes.

German confidence in the offensive, understandably, was sky-high. On 31 May, the Commander-in-Chief of the Army, Field Marshal von Brauchitsch, had issued an order that read:

> Operational enemy reserves in considerable numbers need no longer be expected. It will therefore be possible first to break down under heavy assault the hastily constructed enemy front south of the Somme and the Aisne and then, by rapid, deep penetration, to prevent the enemy from carrying out an ordered retreat or from forming a defence line in rear.[2]

The plan was for von Bock's Army Group B, on the right, to attack first on 5 June, followed four days later by von Runstedt's Army Group A. Forming the right flank of Army Group B, in opposition to the French Tenth Army, was von Kluge's Fourth Army. Its ten and a half divisions were ordered to advance towards Le Havre, with the bridgeheads over the lower Seine at Rouen, Les Andelys and Vernon as the preliminary objectives.

The main hammer blow against the Highland Division, wielded by the 11th Motorised Brigade and the 12th Infantry Division, was to fall, aptly enough, on the two forward battalions of 154 Brigade who had not been involved in the attack the previous day: the 7th and 8th Battalions, the Argyll & Sutherland Highlanders, facing the German bridgehead at St Valéry-sur-Somme from Saigneville to the sea.

Prior to the attack, the layout of the battalions was as follows: the 7th Argylls were up on the right with Battalion Headquarters and HQ Company in Franleu, A Company nearby in reserve at Quesnoy, and B, C and D Companies holding from right to left the villages of Saigneville, Mons-Boubert and Catigny respectively; the 8th Argylls were on the left, nearest the sea, with Battalion Headquarters, HQ Company, and D Company in reserve in St Blimont, and A, B and C Companies in position around the villages of Sallenelle, Lanchères and Pendé respectively.

The Argylls held a broken line of strongpoints, with companies up to a mile apart. The only means of immediate communication within battalions was by telephone lines, but they usually went no further than company headquarters and could easily be cut by hand or shellfire. Contact with platoons was kept by runner or despatch rider.

Just after dawn, Second Lieutenant Moore, commanding 13 Platoon of C Company, in position on the forward edge of the Bois de Nevers, a large wood to the left front of the main company positions in the twin villages of Mons-Boubert, heard shouts from his sections posts. Moore's platoon headquarters was set 150 yards back from the fringe of the wood, and he had not even covered half that distance when he was met by a runner from his centre section who reported that large numbers of enemy infantry were advancing on the wood. To save time, Moore ordered the runner to return to his section commander with instructions not to open fire until the enemy were within range, while he himself ran back to his headquarters to fetch a Very pistol in case an SOS for artillery assistance was necessary.

Once again, Moore set off for the front of the wood and no sooner had he reached it than he was greeted with the chilling sight of a long, extended line of Germans approaching through the high corn that fringed the wood. At about the same time the enemy opened up with mortars. Wasting no time, Moore found a clearing to fire the SOS before returning to his headquarters to send a despatch rider, Private Malone, direct to Battalion Headquarters to warn them of the situation. No defensive artillery fire ever arrived because the gunners of the 17th Field Regiment had problems of their own: soon after the firing of the SOS, the observation post that would have directed the fire was abandoned under enemy pressure, and within half an hour the troop of guns further back had been captured.[3]

At about 4.10 am, Private Malone arrived on his motorbike at Franleu, about two and a half miles to the rear, and lost no time in locating the CO, 'Copper' Buchanan, in the schoolhouse that was serving as Battalion Headquarters. In response to Malone's message that 13 Platoon was being heavily attacked on all sides, Buchanan ordered a section of four carriers under Second Lieutenant Robert Powell to move up to Mons-Boubert and report to the C Company Commander, Captain Hewitt. Within 20 minutes of Malone reaching Franleu, Powell's carriers had arrived at the roadblock to the south entrance of Mons-Boubert. It was dismantled to let them through, but the man in charge, Company Sergeant Major Milne, told Powell that they could not drive up the road leading out of the village to the west because there was another block there that could not be moved. The only solution was to dismount the Brens, and to get the carriers under cover. As this was being done in a farm yard, Captain Hewitt arrived and agreed to accompany Powell to find a suitable spot to site his guns. Powell's account reads:

> Some 400 yards out of the village I made a recce for suitable gun positions to cover the open fields and soon found a good position looking towards the slight slope between Boubert and Bois de Nevers. Immediately after this position had been taken up, two parties of the enemy each some 20-30 strong appeared crossing the open to our left front. Each party was wheeling four or five bicycles ...
>
> The enemy were some 200–300 yards away when we first saw them. I ordered two guns on the right to open fire from their concealed positions. Our fire was effective and the enemy were almost all hit, the survivors turning and running from the direction they had come. We then saw further larger parties of enemy on our extreme left and right flanks and engaged them at longer ranges. As the enemy appeared to be more numerous on the right, Capt Hewitt was very concerned about the possibility of them surrounding the village. He ordered me to cease fire, to return to the Carriers, and carry out Carrier action against the enemy, as the road block had by then been removed.[4]

Meanwhile, Second Lieutenant Moore, under siege with his platoon in the Bois de Nevers, was unaware of the attempts by the carriers to clear a passage between him and the village. After sending off the despatch rider, Moore had returned to his centre section who were firing furiously from the front of the wood. But such was the strength of the German attack, and the intensity of the fire needed to repel it, that by 4.30 am the ammunition of the centre section had all but run out, while that of the right and left sections was also perilously low. In view of this, the heavy mortaring, and the attempts by the enemy to work

round the left of the wood, Moore gave the order for the centre section
to withdraw first to the rear edge of the wood, and then into the
standing corn to the left of the track running up the side of the wood.
No similar order ever reached the other sections. Moore, along with his
platoon sergeant and runner made for the junction between the track
and the Arrest–Mons-Boubert road to the south of the wood.

> My intention here was to rally my sections, who were rather disorganised
> by this time, owing to heavy enemy mortaring. Shortly after my arrival at
> this junction, one single enemy appeared a short distance to my right,
> [and] doubled across the road. I fired at him. He returned my fire. A
> second German now appeared from the place where the last one had
> come from and fired at me. He missed, and I returned his fire. He fell.
> I was then hit in the left arm. I swung round to fire again at the first
> German. He was aiming at me with his rifle. I took a deliberate aim with
> my revolver. We appeared to fire at the same time. I fell wounded in the
> thigh. He appeared to let out a groan and fall backwards.[5]

Moore was captured at about 5.30 am, and the remaining opposition
in the Bois de Nevers was also mopped up around this time. Unfortunately, because of the parlous state of communications, this fact was
unknown at company headquarters. If it had been, Second Lieutenant
Powell might never have taken his carriers on a raid up towards the Bois
de Nevers to make contact with 13 Platoon. On the first attempt, two
carriers collided, so damaging the tracks of one that it had to be sent
back to Franleu. Two further sorties were made, both by different
routes, in which the enemy were driven back into the interior of the Bois
de Nevers. On one, Powell ordered his carriers to follow them up to
within 200 yards of the wood, at which point he was fired on by anti-tank
guns and mortars, and so hastily retreated to the village, arriving back
at about 6.30 am. In these three actions the Carrier Platoon had
suffered just one casualty, Sergeant McLean, who was hit in the head,
although all the carriers had been hit.

Once again, Powell ordered the men to dismount and return with
their guns to the left flank. There followed a curious lull in which the
only Germans spotted were stretcher-bearers using dogs to locate the
wounded in the corn; one actually approaching to within 200 yards of
where Powell lay, but was left unmolested because of his humanitarian
work. At 8 am, an enemy column of six trucks towing anti-tank guns
appeared crossing towards Powell and his men from their extreme left
flank, and then dug-in behind the slope to their front, facing the village.
Soon after this, Powell was relieved by Lieutenant Muirhead, the
Company Second-in-Command, with some Company Headquarters'

men, and he returned to Mons-Boubert to find the villages entirely surrounded.

* * *

For most of the early part of the morning the two platoons at the forward edge of Mons – 15 Platoon on the right under Second Lieutenant McLaren, and 14 Platoon on the left under Second Lieutenant Alan Orr-Ewing, the fighting patrol officer who had won an MC in the Saar – were left relatively unmolested. They had reported at 6 am that the enemy were advancing on their flanks but it was not until 9 am that a frontal attack was put in against them. Gradually these platoons were forced back into the heart of Mons, and at 10 am Orr-Ewing was brought in to company headquarters in Boubert, having been shot in the back and the leg by a machine-gun.

By 11.30 am, 15 Platoon had retired back into 14 Platoon's positions near the church in Mons, as the enemy were steadily advancing in hand-to-hand fighting through the houses. Soon after, Powell was sent back to the left flank – where the fighting had died down, to relieve Muirhead. Every time this position fired, it was greeted with a hail of incendiary anti-tank shells from the guns that had come up earlier.

Gradually the ring of fire was closing in on Mons, as mortars and shells battered the platoons near the church. It was clear that as the enemy worked round these platoons there was a danger they would be cut off from Company Headquarters, so, at about 5 pm, McLaren ordered his men to retire and form a final strongpoint around the headquarters in Boubert. But the situation was hopeless. Three times Captain Hewitt had sent messages back to Franleu, but there was no reply. There was only one option. He later wrote:

> I realised that the Coy was surrounded and the enemy could close in very easily, owing to the nature of the ground in the village. I decided to surrender and save the sacrifice of life that would have taken place.[6]

Because the company and the section of carriers had been captured in entirety, all the witnesses to the gallant deeds that day were either dead or soon in Prisoner of War camps. It was not until liberation in 1945 that Second Lieutenant Powell and Company Sergeant Major Milne were recognised by the award of an MC and an MM respectively.

While C Company was being gradually overrun, the rest of the battalion was faring little better. Soon after Private Malone arrived at Battalion Headquarters with the bad news from the Bois de Nevers, Major Young, commanding D Company at Catigny, rang through to say that his forward platoons were in contact with strong enemy forces. On going forward to confirm the reports with his own eyes, Major Young spotted armoured fighting vehicles (AFVs), horsed troops and infantry dismounting from lorries, at a range of 1500 yards. Like Second Lieutenant Moore he realised what a choice target these troops presented for artillery, and hurried back to his headquarters in a cellar in the centre of the village to request it. The line had been cut.

A despatch rider was sent instead, but within minutes of his departure, Company Quartermaster Sergeant Watson turned up in his lorry, with the windscreen shot away, to report that the Germans were already behind the reserve platoon in the nearby village of Arrest, and that they had occupied the crossroads and the château there, beside the company cookhouse from where he had come. He had also seen the despatch rider shot from his bicycle. Captain Jack Ritchie, Young's second-in-command, was sent back to Arrest to confirm this, and he returned with the wounded despatch rider, after having altered the position of the reserve platoon (17 Platoon under the recently arrived Second Lieutenant Green) to cover the company's rear.

At 6.30 am Major Young sent up the SOS for the first time, but there was no response. All the while, all three platoons were in action against forces whose strength Young estimated at over a battalion. Ammunition inevitably began to run out, and by this time the reserve ammunition truck at Arrest was in enemy hands. Within a few hours, with the enemy inexorably making ground, Young was forced into a decision:

> Further requests for ammo [from the platoons] were received ... As enemy were now in our rear, on our right flank and rapidly advancing on our left and front, I decided that as I could no longer make an effective resistance and hold my position it was my duty to extricate my [company] if possible. I decided to withdraw to St Blimont on our left rear and contact 8th [Argylls]. I sent orders to 17 [Platoon] to use direct Arrest–St Blimont road. This message was not received, as enemy elements had penetrated between them and [Company Headquarters].[7]

With his remaining two platoons, a brigade anti-tank gun and his headquarters personnel, Young evacuated Catigny at about 8.30 am. Before the last of the lorries carrying these troops had gone more than 200 yards, Germans were seen entering the village. By 9.30 am, Young and his men had reached the 8th Argylls' Battalion Headquarters in St Blimont. Young used the phone there to get through to Brigade in Belloy, and was instructed to defer to Lieutenant Colonel 'Hamish' Grant, the CO of the 8th Argylls, as it appeared that his company was the only remnant of the 7th Argylls. That Young had abandoned his positions without orders, leaving one platoon to its fate, was not discussed. The hopelessness of the piecemeal defensive line was such that only by acting on their own initiative could local commanders save their men. In this instance it was only a temporary reprieve.

Brigade was wrong in its assessment that D Company was the only fragment of the 7th Argylls left intact, but only just. All the remaining companies were under heavy attack and were clinging on by the skin of their teeth. Strangely enough, the unit in what seemed to be the most precarious position, B Company, holding the village of Saigneville on the banks of the Somme canal, was one of the later ones into action.

It was not until 6 am that a look-out at Company Headquarters spotted a German machine-gun detachment advancing down the Boismont road towards the village, followed soon after by a long line of infantry coming cross-country from the same direction. Harassing fire was opened against these targets, and at 7 am, when the main body of Germans had reached a ravine about 1000 yards west of the town, an artillery barrage was requested by Captain John Logan, the company commander. This proved highly successful in dispersing the attackers. Unfortunately, because the enemy could advance between the company strongpoints and quickly overrun the unprotected artillery, such a success was in isolation, and when a further shoot was requested soon after, Logan was informed that the artillery had withdrawn.

At 7.30 am, the sound of shooting was heard at Company Head-quarters from the direction of 11 Platoon, guarding the eastern approaches to the village. The platoon commander was Second Lieutenant Jim Atkinson, aged 28. (Later, in prison camp, he would devise the immensely popular Scottish dance, the 'Reel of the 51st', named after the division). An unconventional man, he had decided to reorganise his defensive system by placing outposts manned by two men between and ahead of his three section positions. In this way he hoped to fill in the gaps in his line. Occupying one of these outposts was Private Harry Pert, aged 21, from Alloa.

When the Germans attacked, Pert and his section realised that they were outnumbered and withdrew to the village. When they arrived, they discovered that the enemy had already worked their way in behind them. The section commander had no option but to continue the withdrawal, using gardens as cover. Before long, even this way was blocked and the section had to move back into the open. At the same time, the Germans appeared from the opposite direction, forcing the section to take evasive action by running into a barn. Pert recalls:

The door would be maybe five feet wide. All 11 of us were sitting in there.

Then there were a couple of shots and two of the boys were firing out of
the door into this wee yard. The Jerries were running past the door and
they can't have known where we were because they kept coming. A stack
of them were getting killed. Five of us were shooting out of the door by
this time. We couldn't miss.

Despite this last show of defiance, it was obvious to the section that
they were trapped. It took a small man who had been drafted into the
battalion from the Royal Scots to persuade the rest that the game was
up, and they trooped out of the barn with their hands up.

As 11 Platoon, and then 10 Platoon, came under attack, 12 Platoon,
defending the north-eastern approaches to Saigneville, could only
watch and wait. It was powerless to prevent the stream of German
infantry and transport crossing its front to the west because they were
out of range. After hearing small arms' fire start up from the other side
of the village, the platoon commander, Second Lieutenant John
Parnell, aged 20, tried twice to reach Company Headquarters for orders
with his batman, Private Halliday. Each time they were fired on and had
to retire. After what seemed like an endless wait, the platoon was
attacked. Parnell describes what followed:

> About a platoon of 30 or 40 came up over open ground and we held our fire
> and didn't make a sound until they got bloody close. They were about 50
> yards away when I shouted, 'Fire!', and there was an almighty crash. I used to
> tell my Jocks, 'Fire one round at a German and kill him!', and by jove that's
> what they did. The Germans suffered heavy casualties, many killed, and
> those that were left started surrendering in the middle of the field. As this
> was going on, my platoon sergeant, Wattie Livingstone, went out under fire
> to pull in some of the Germans who were badly wounded. He needn't have
> done it and I actually tried to stop him because I didn't see why he should
> sacrifice his life for a lot of Germans. But he did and he brought the German
> wounded back. The Jocks were incredibly good to them and started giving
> them drinks. This stood us in good stead for later on.

Not only was 12 Platoon surrounded, but the whole company by this
time had been cut off; a fact made plain to Captain Logan when a
machine-gun opened up on the village from a position near to the
Quesnoy road to the south. To cover this new threat the largely
administrative personnel of Company Headquarters and some pioneers
of the 7th Norfolks, armed only with rifles, were posted across the road.
But the defences were quickly crumbling. At 9.45 Logan received word
from a breathless runner that 10 Platoon under Second Lieutenant
Archie Orr-Ewing, a cousin of Alan, had been taken in the rear and
encircled. An hour or so later about ten Germans appeared 200 yards

to the north of Company Headquarters and Captain Logan took Company Sergeant Major Stevenson, and two other men to try and surprise them from behind. They failed. In the meantime, more Germans had infiltrated between them and the headquarters, and they were unable to return. Logan recorded:

> After a short time, in company with my CSM and one runner (Pte Muir), I crawled out to a tall cornfield about 200 yards south of my headquarters to lie up and observe. This was reached at about 1230 hrs. From this time onwards I heard very little firing apart from desultory shooting from the direction of 11 [Platoon] . . . At 1430 hrs about 10 men from 11 [Platoon] and [my headquarters] joined [us] in the cornfield. Private Muir was wounded in the shoulder and there was a considerable amount of firing on both sides. We were eventually surrounded and I instructed the men to put their hands up. This must have been at about 1500 hrs.[8]

A little after Logan had led his sortie from Company Headquarters, Jim Atkinson pitched up looking for orders. He found Company Quarter Master Sergeant Edwards lying dead in the road, and the building deserted. As he made his way back to his remaining men, Atkinson had a brainwave. He picked up a chain he had seen lying in a yard, and dragged it up and down the road to simulate the sound of a tank. If this worked, it was only a temporary respite. Atkinson recalls:

> I realised by early afternoon that if we had not been relieved by then, we weren't going to be. I was pinned down by fire when two shots hit me. One knocked my tin hat off, so that I had no protection, and left a scar on my forehead. At that moment I threw my hands up, rolled, then kept quite still. I had been taught this by a Guards' sergeant before the war. The idea was to make the enemy think he had hit you. It worked. The man who had fired at me was sitting behind a fence, and as he half stood up I aimed and fired at his chest and he disappeared from view. Then a chap on his right, who I hadn't seen before, started to climb up on a dyke in a hurry, but luckily I reloaded quickly and his face disappeared in a blur of red. He can't have been more than 50 yards away.

Minutes later, realising the game was up, Atkinson shouted 'Kamerad, I surrender!' and stood up. To his surprise, a senior German officer got up just a few yards away and shook his hand. Then he blew a blast on a whistle and stretcher-bearers materialised out of nowhere to deal with the wounded. After organising this the officer walked back over to Atkinson and spoke to him in perfect English:

> First he asked me how we had managed to kill so many of his men. Then

he said, 'Your young companion over there has done a lot of damage!', pointing to John Parnell's positions. He told me he was a Saxon and started talking about his dead men: 'I know their wives, I know their families, and I know their girlfriends. I come from Scottish ancestry. We should be shooting the communists, not each other. Well, if this is the Scottish troops the war goes on for four years. I congratulate you!'

By three in the afternoon the only troops of B Company still in action were those of Parnell's 12 Platoon. Following their bloody repulse of the German advance, there had been a lull in their area. As the firing had also died down in other areas of the village, Parnell assumed that the rest of the company had capitulated and decided to try and escape with his platoon, taking his wounded and the fit Germans with them, but leaving the enemy casualties.

> It was a pretty unwieldy bunch and we had only gone a matter of a hundred yards before we were surrounded by Germans all pointing their rifles at us. It was then that our prisoners told our captors that they had been looked after properly and we were treated accordingly. With hindsight, I should probably never have tried to take my platoon out then and there. I should have lain low and hidden until night and then got out. But the lack of communication was a killer.

The decency of the German commander was again displayed when he rounded up the unwounded remnants of the company in the village church to hear a service of remembrance for the fallen. At least 35 Germans had been killed, as against only seven Jocks.

Despite its position, set back behind its rifle companies, Battalion Headquarters in Franleu was in action as early as 4.15 am because it lay astride the route of the main German thrust north of Abbeville. Realising that his company strongpoints had been bypassed, 'Copper' Buchanan had to act fast if Franleu was to hold. Captain Alastair Irvine Robertson, commanding HQ Company, was given the task of organising the defence of Battalion Headquarters which was housed in a large two-storey brick building that served as the village school. He managed this by taking the Bren guns off the remaining six carriers and setting up a chain of posts, while one of the school's cellars was set up as Battle Headquarters. Regimental Sergeant Major William Lockie was given charge of the left hand posts, while Company Sergeant Major Dyer took over the right. Buchanan then phoned through to A Company, in reserve two and a half miles away at Quesnoy, and told it to make for Franleu without delay.

Captain Glen Handley, A Company Commander, was the first to leave in his pick-up truck, closely followed by the company Bren gunners in the cook's lorry. Handley left orders for his reserve platoon under Second Lieutenant Haig to start marching immediately. The remaining two platoons needed time to withdraw from their forward positions and did not set off for another hour. Unfortunately, Handley did not know the exact location of Battalion Headquarters, and stopped at a cross-roads to look at his map. As he did so, he was shot in the back by a sniper and mortally wounded. At 7 am, after a march of two and a half miles in full kit, Haig's platoon reached Franleu and was quickly put into positions to the front of the school.

It was already obvious to 'Copper' Buchanan that his battalion was in desperate trouble. At 5 am he had phoned through to Brigade at Belloy to ask for support, and was told by the Brigade Major, Scott-Elliott, that the only reserve available was a platoon of 1st Kensington machine-gunners. Shortly afterwards the line went dead. At 6.30 am, a battery of the 17th Field Regiment at Ochancourt were asked to fire on some Germans, spotted by an observer in the church steeple at Franleu, who were massing in a small wood 500 yards north of the village. This shoot was carried out with some success, the accuracy of the shells causing the enemy to scatter in panic, but when a repeat was asked for soon after, the reply was that the battery had been instructed to withdraw.

By this time, a heavy and accurate mortar barrage had been opened against the school. In response, the 3-inch mortar detachment returned fire, frequently silencing the German mortars, and firing until all its ammunition, 140 bombs, had been used. The Mortar Officer, Captain Forbes-Hendry, despite being hit in the knee by shrapnel early in the morning, had continued to direct operations.

Shortly after 7 am, Captain Handley was brought in to the school. Soon after, more wounded arrived. They had originally been directed to the Regimental Aid Post, located 100 yards south of the headquarters. The news was bad: The Medical Officer, Lieutenant Mackenzie, could not be found. 'Copper' Buchanan was mystified:

> I sent a Runner to the RAP . . . to confirm this report or fetch the MO. The Runner reported on his return that the RAP had been evacuated, and that there was no sign of the MO or his Orderlies, or of the Ambulance, MO's Truck or medical pannier.[9]

In his report on the action, Buchanan wrote:

> The lack of medical assistance was a very severe handicap throughout the day, as an increasing number of severely wounded men came into the HQ area, no stretchers being available, no dressing beyond the ordinary field dressing and no one present with any medical knowledge. The day was

excessively hot and airless and the personnel and wounded at [the school], which faced due South, suffered considerably from the heat which was ... increased when German shells set fire to the outhouses in the yard. The Chaplain, MacInnes, who took charge of the wounded, did splendid work, repeatedly going out in search of water under heavy fire and any assistance he got was from unskilled men who should have been in the firing line. Many of the earlier wounded could also have been evacuated had the ambulance been available and possibly some lives would have been saved.[10]

In Mackenzie's absence, Padre MacInnes had to care for the physical as well as the spiritual well-being of the men, a role for which he was only partially equipped. By his untiring, selfless and gallant acts of 5 June, MacInnes proved the value of a good army padre and after the war was awarded the Military Cross.

At 8.30 am, the two remaining platoons of A Company, under Lieutenant Donald Fisher, arrived at the outskirts of Franleu, along with a platoon of 7th Norfolks who had been billeted with them in Quesnoy. By this time, German penetration into Franleu had cut the road from Quesnoy and these platoons were forced to take up a position on the east side of the village, with A Company's headquarters located in some farm buildings near to the road. Not long after their arrival, Captain Irvine Robertson appeared in a Bren carrier with some ammunition and orders to clear a wood between them and Battalion Headquarters. After completing this task successfully, in the course of which Second Lieutenant Diarmid Macalister Hall was wounded in the arm, the survivors of the two platoons returned to positions around the farm buildings.

For the remainder of the morning, the school in Franleu remained under constant mortar and small arms fire. Attempts by the enemy to establish vantage points in houses close to the school were only repulsed when small patrols, led by Regimental Sergeant Major Lockie and Company Sergeant Major Dyer, used grenades to bomb them out. The Vickers machine-gun in support of the 7th Argylls, manned by two men of the 1st Kensingtons, was silenced by snipers, but a patrol, again led by Lockie, managed to retrieve the gun and brought it into action from another position. One carrier under Lance Corporal Currie did some good work patrolling the streets, clearing out snipers and bringing in the wounded.

At noon, the tide, slowly but inexorably, began to turn. First, one of the two battalion ammunition trucks, concealed in an orchard, was set on fire. Then, more German mortars were brought up and the intensity of the bombardment increased, repeatedly hitting the top floor of the school which had to be evacuated. Two hours later, a shell burst directly outside the entrance to the Signal Office on the ground floor of the school, injuring everyone inside with the exception of the CO. The casualties included Major Ossie Younger, the Adjutant, who was hit in the face and lost an eye, Captain Irvine Robertson and Second Lieutenant Charles Mackie. The latter was saved from serious injury by the bowl of his tobacco pipe, which was shattered when it deflected a piece of shrapnel. All the wounded were taken down to the cellar of the schoolhouse which had been turned into a makeshift aid post. But the biggest blow of the afternoon was when a shell hit the reserve ammunition truck at the back of the school, setting it on fire and for a while making any movement in the vicinity extremely hazardous because of the constant explosion of ammunition.

While the Jocks of the 7th Argylls were fighting for their lives, Brigadier Stanley-Clarke at Belloy was trying desperately to organise some relief. As soon as it became clear that it, and the 8th Argylls to its left, were in serious difficulty, Stanley-Clarke managed to persuade General Fortune to release the 4th Black Watch from Divisional Reserve and by 7 am the battalion was on the march from its billets in Le Plouay to the rear of the area held by 154 Brigade. Also on the move in the same direction was a detachment of 12 French tanks, accidentally left behind by Perré's *Groupement* at Les Alleux.

The plan was for the 4th Black Watch to support the 7th Argylls in Franleu, as well as occupying the villages of Feuquières, Fresseneville and Valines to the rear, so as to form a new line by linking up with the 1st Gordons on the right and the 8th Argylls on the left. By 2 pm, D Company of the 4th Black Watch and the French tanks had arrived in Valines, one mile behind Franleu. The CO of the Black Watch, Rory Macpherson, had already received orders to counter-attack with the French tanks towards Franleu, but no attempt was ever made. To this day, survivors of the 7th Argylls accuse the 4th Black Watch of leaving them to their fate. Writing much later, Macpherson explained the implications of the late arrival of the French tanks and their lack of clear orders. He went on to say that, without this support, he considered that an advance towards Franleu over one mile of flat ground covered by two-foot crops 'was not on and it was not attempted'.[11]

The truth is that Macpherson had both the troops and the tanks but he did not feel the operation was worth the risk, and he may have been right. After all, enemy elements had already infiltrated well to the rear of Franleu, and some had even got behind the 4th Black Watch and were approaching the River Bresle. As it was, D Company avoided being trapped in Valines that night by the skin of its teeth; a last minute withdrawal was ordered during which the Captain Thomas Fothringham, D Company Commander, won the Military Cross, as did two of his platoon commanders, Second Lieutenant Lord Glenorchy and Lieutenant Donald Mirrielies. For the same action, Lance Corporal Melville was awarded a Military Medal for returning to the German-infested village to rescue a wounded man.

With the cancellation of the counter-attack, the Franleu garrison was doomed. The troops were running out of ammunition, they had not had a proper meal for 24 hours, they were exhausted by hours of combat, and casualties were mounting. By 4 pm, Lieutenant Ross had been killed and both Lockie and Dyer severely wounded. At about this time, Second Lieutenant Haig, the only fit officer, apart from Colonel Buchanan, reported that his remaining men could no longer hold their positions. Buchanan decided that the only solution was to shorten the perimeter and he sent a runner with a message for A Company to close on the school. The runner failed to contact Lieutenant Fisher and reported, erroneously, that A Company had retired.

From the information available, it was obvious to Buchanan that Franleu was indefensible. He, thus, gave permission for anyone who wished to escape. Second Lieutenant Haig was the first to take up the offer, and, with the remaining ten fit men of his platoon, he managed to break through to the British lines. Despite his wounds, the Intelligence Officer, Second Lieutenant Charles Mackie, was also willing to take a chance:

> I was down in the cellar with the wounded when, in the afternoon, the CO said, 'Well, those who think they've got a chance of getting away can try.' My sergeant had managed to get the water truck – which had earlier been hit – started up, and he got me out along with my batman. A water truck is really a big container with little room for passengers; because of this, there were only eight of us, most of my section, on it. The sergeant drove but I knew the way because I had come up with the CO a few days earlier. We drove westward and only stopped once to clear a barricade of carts and things from the road. Then, just as we came round a corner, there was a German machine-gun! They weren't expecting us, luckily, and the gun wasn't manned. We went as fast as we could and as we passed they hit one of our chaps, who fell off, but we couldn't stop. Then we were away.

One other truck, crammed with wounded, including Captain Forbes-Hendry, the Mortar Officer, and two Bren carriers also managed to escape. Although a few men were hit, the opposing fire was relatively light, and this was undoubtedly because the German guns were facing in the opposite direction, expecting a counter-attack.

At about 6 pm, 'Copper' Buchanan gave instructions to Padre MacInnes – who had volunteered to stay with the wounded crammed in the cellar – to surrender the garrison while he, an artillery spotter named Second Lieutenant Thomas, and two NCOs tried to escape on foot. They did not get far. While crossing some open ground at the edge of the village they were fired on by a machine-gun which pinned them to the ground. Under cover of this a group of Germans came over and took them prisoner.[12]

The defence of Franleu was not yet over. Unknown to Colonel Buchanan, the remaining two platoons of A Company were still holding out in the eastern outskirts of the village. After Macalister Hall had withdrawn his platoon back towards Company Headquarters in the afternoon, Lieutenant Fisher had decided to hold the area around the farm buildings as an all-round position. As there was no water available, cider, found in a cellar, was used to quench the men's thirst. Other than one half-hearted foray, the Germans ignored A Company until nightfall.

At 11 pm a bizarre incident occurred that shook Diarmid Macalister Hall from his slumber in the haybarn serving as an aid post.

> I was wakened by the sound of a galloping horse followed by a burst of fire. I later found out what had happened. A German horseman had been galloping through the village from our rear in the dark, quite unaware of our presence, and had been fired on at point blank range by one of our Bren guns. Amazingly, as happens in war, the bullets missed – the rider lost one of his nine lives – and the horse went into the barrier we had across the road, throwing the rider, who was then captured by the sentries.

The rider turned out to be an artillery officer who had been on his way back from a forward observation post. Papers on him indicated that Franleu was now two miles behind enemy lines.

As dawn broke on the 6th, more and more German troops could be seen from A Company's positions advancing past Franleu. Fire was opened on them, causing many casualties, but this only served to bring attention to A Company's nagging presence and throughout the day an increasing number of enemy troops joined in the siege. By the afternoon, incoming mortar fire had become intense, and, at 4.30 pm, a determined attack was put in, finally repulsed with many casualties.

Ammunition, not surprisingly, was nearly exhausted and, shortly before 6 pm, the battered, hungry and thirsty defenders were greeted with the sight of a single, unarmed Jock walking towards their positions. Diarmid Macalister Hall could not believe what he was seeing:

> I was standing at the door of the farmhouse facing a wood when I saw a Jock walking down out of the wood towards me. I couldn't think what he was up to and I shouted, 'Run, you bloody fool, or you'll be shot!' I didn't know where he had come from, maybe from another platoon or company somewhere else. He just kept walking and he was holding something white in his clenched fist. When he got to the door I said, 'For god's sake, get under cover!' He said, 'I've already been taken prisoner. The German commander asked me to tell you that unless you surrender he'll open up with all he's got. You've got five minutes to give him an answer.' This was five minutes to seven and I spent a worrying time waiting until Donald Fisher made up his mind to surrender. As we left the farmhouse I noticed the Vickers machine-gun with both its gunners dead beside it. When we were brought before the German commander he said, 'Your man got back just in time. I was about to open up.'

5 June was described in the 7th Argylls' War Diary as the 'blackest day in the history of the battalion', although 'the great traditions had been upheld and much glory was added to the battalion's history'. On this day alone, 23 officers and 500 other ranks were killed, wounded, or taken prisoner.[13] From this point on, the 7th Argylls ceased to exist as a separate formation in the 51st Division. As well as the decorations already mentioned, Major Younger, Captain Forbes-Hendry and Lieutenant Fisher all received the Military Cross, and Regimental Sergeant Major Lockie was awarded the Distinguished Conduct Medal. Curiously, there were no medals for Colonel Buchanan, Second Lieutenant Parnell, or Company Sergeant Major Dyer, all of whom had done particularly well.

* * *

The Battle of the Somme began for the 8th Argylls at 4.30 am on 5 June when 14 Platoon of C Company, commanded by Second Lieutenant Jimmy Mellor and dug-in around the village of Pendé, opened fire on advancing German cavalry, backed up by infantry. Fortunately, there was an artillery forward observation officer at Pendé, and Mellor was able to use his telephone line to pass the news on to Company Headquarters, a mile to the rear in Tilloy.

Within an hour, C Company's 15 Platoon, positioned in a small wood 500 yards to the right front of Tilloy, had also reported a major German attack. Although this wood was deserted at night, a platoon would occupy it at first light, dragging a field telephone with them. The platoon commander, Second Lieutenant Bruce Cheape, was so impressed with the formation of the German advance that he almost forgot his own peril:

> I had three or four men lying hidden on the front edge of the wood and I kept the rest of my chaps in the middle under such trees as there were, completely out of sight. I would change the men in front every hour or so. While the spinney was very exposed, it did enable us to observe a large area of dead ground with a German held ridge in the distance. There was an even smaller clump of trees 200 yards to our front with the ridge perhaps 1200 yards further away. It was from there the German attack came. As far as one could see to either side, there was a rank of German infantry supported by a few armoured vehicles, then another rank of infantry, more vehicles then a third rank of infantry. All in open order, some ten yards between each soldier. They advanced in very good formation through waist-high growing crops.
>
> The next thing we noticed was a cavalry patrol of about six riders come up to the small clump of trees and dismount. I could see them looking through their field glasses in our direction. I ordered the men not to fire because I didn't want to give away our position. They disappeared out of sight for a while and the next we saw they were cantering across our right flank heading directly towards Tilloy. We opened fire at about 250 yards distance and bowled them all over. One of them started firing at us, lying down behind a dead horse. We fired back and that eventually stopped. I then reported over the telephone what was happening and was told by Company Headquarters to come back. We withdrew and succeeded in getting back to the edge of the village without being fired on.

Cheape arrived with his platoon in Tilloy at 8.30 am. Two and a half hours earlier, Colonel 'Hamish' Grant, the CO of the 8th Argylls, had arrived at C Company Headquarters. On being informed that 14 Platoon at Pendé was very hard-pressed, he had given permission for it to withdraw to Tilloy. Under cover of accurate artillery fire, directed from St Blimont, Mellor's men were able to disengage intact and reached Tilloy shortly before 15 Platoon. All the while, artillery fire had been directed at the German advance, causing much slaughter. However, by 8 am the battery concerned began to retire from St Blimont and the attack continued unhindered. The numbers were beginning to tell and, as Tilloy was in danger of being surrounded, Captain John Inglis, C Company Commander, gave the order to move back to St Blimont. By this time, all communications with Battalion Headquarters and the artillery had been severed, and Inglis had to act on his own initiative. His decision, undoubtedly correct, contrasts starkly with the point blank refusal of some of the 7th Argyll company commanders to move back without orders, resulting in inevitable encirclement.

While C Company was on the march, events were moving fast at Battalion Headquarters in St Blimont. Reports had come in that its other two forward companies were under attack, and at 9.30 am Major Young arrived with his two platoons from Catigny. These men were put into a position on the east of the village, alongside D Company of the 8th Argylls under Captain Tress. Soon after, St Blimont came under mortar attack and a number of wounded, including Captain Tress, were added to those already sent back from other companies to the Regimental Aid Post run by Lieutenant Murray.

At 11 am, alarmed at the speed of the German advance, Brigade Headquarters gave orders to shorten the 8th Argyll's defensive line. But the new line of Brutelles–St Blimont–Nibas was soon considered untenable, and within an hour it had been changed to one further back. A and B Companies were now to occupy Hautebut, C Company Belloy, D Company Escarbotin, and D Company of the 7th Argylls were to take up a position between Escarbotin and Friville. Just as Battalion Head-quarters was packing up to leave St Blimont for Tully, at 12.30 am, C Company marched in.

Within an hour, C Company were on the move again to take up their new position at Belloy, the original site of Brigade Headquarters, which was in the process of moving back to Dargnies. Also on the move, towards Escarbotin, was D Company, now commanded by Lieutenant Roderick Mackenzie. So too was D Company of the 7th Argylls, which had received orders to move to Nibas after all, because a section of the 8th Argylls' Bren carriers under Second Lieutenant Freddie Lawder was still holding on.

When D Company arrived in Escarbotin, 16 Platoon under Second Lieutenant Peter Douglas, the grandson of the 19th Earl of Morton, was given the task of holding a large manor house in woods on the edge of the village. Unfortunately, as Corporal Jock Cairns, a member of the platoon, later recorded, the Germans were already in position there:

> Little did we know that halfway to this house there was a sunken road held by German infantry. Our platoon sergeant led us in extended order, and then halted as we neared a large haystack. He ordered McGluskey to climb to the top and to observe what he could, which he did, and Eddie shouted, 'The woods are full'. The enemy opened up with automatic fire and he fell wounded to the bottom of the stack. The Bren gunner of my section was killed in this opening of the action, and I took over the Bren. As I was changing magazines, a long burst from one of the enemy machine-guns shattered the butt, and I received one of the bullets in my right shoulder.

Our sergeant shouted for us to move back and, as I reached the rear of the haystack, I came across McGluskey, his right shoulder and arm shattered. All this time the enemy mortars were plastering the area, wounding and killing our platoon. I pulled Eddie by his ankle with my arm, having to unhook his shattered arm bone which he had caught in the long corn. He was yelling with pain and his blood drenched me. Amidst this inferno, Lieutenant Douglas had crawled out, despite the heavy fire from enemy rifles and machine-guns, and grabbed Eddie's ankle. Eddie was now unconscious. 'Well done, Cairns, I'll take over now' he said, and that was the last I remembered.[14]

Cairns, too, had fallen unconscious and when he awoke that evening, he heard German voices nearby. Realising he was behind enemy lines, he began to crawl back in the direction of what he thought must be safety. Luckily for Cairns, he bumped into another member of his platoon, Geordie Scott, who was lightly wounded and who had also been left behind. Scott found a wheelbarrow and, despite the pain, began to push Cairns in the direction of the River Bresle, assuming the British lines must have reformed along the way. It was not until night of the 6th that an exhausted Scott reached the bridge at Beauchamps, after a journey of five long miles. He was just in time; a few minutes later and the bridge was blown by the Royal Engineers. Both men were safely evacuated to Britain. For some reason, Scott's selfless action was never recognised with a medal.

By early afternoon of 5 June, C Company was in position outside Belloy, D Company, despite the setback to 16 Platoon, was holding nearby Escarbotin, and D Company of the 7th Argylls had arrived in Nibas. Yet within two hours, Young had ordered his company and the section of carriers to withdraw. He later justified this decision in his report on the action:

> Nibas was in a hollow surrounded by thick woods and was quite untenable by my available force, and also, as the enemy were using the main road to our left with large columns, I accordingly decided that I was serving no useful purpose there, and withdrew to Escarbotin, which I reached about 1700 hrs.[15]

Soon after Young and his small force reached Escarbotin, Colonel Grant arrived to say that the line Belloy–Escarbotin–Fressenneville had to be held, and that contact should be made with the 4th Black Watch to the right. Because Major Young was the senior officer in the village, he was given overall command of both companies, the carriers and the platoon of machine-gunners. After Colonel Grant's departure, Young sent out Second Lieutenant Lawdor in a carrier in an attempt to link up with the 4th Black Watch, but he returned with the news that enemy action had prevented him from getting beyond Fressenneville and that there was an unmanned gap of three miles to their right, including the main Ochancourt–Woincourt road.

Once again, despite orders to the contrary, Young decided to move back. He later wrote that this decision was influenced by a report from one of his despatch riders that C Company at Belloy had already retired. This was not true, and it is inconceivable that the despatch rider would have made it up – after all, there were only 500 yards between Escarbotin and the nearest C Company positions. The first Captain Inglis knew of a withdrawal was when Major Young sent a message across at 9.30 pm stating that he considered the position untenable and that he and his men were going to move a mile back to Woincourt. It was this information that caused Captain Inglis to take the decision to retire his men, and not vice versa.

The men at Escarbotin were the first to move. At 10 pm, the carriers under Second Lieutenant Lawdor went ahead, followed by Captain Ritchie and Company Headquarters, and 18 Platoon, with Young and the remaining men bringing up the rear. On approaching Woincourt at around 11 pm, Young was met by a despatch rider from battalion with orders that he and his force return immediately to their former positions. By this time, Lawdor had reached Battalion Headquarters at Yzengremer, and had told Colonel Grant of Young's intentions. Horrified that Young had again disobeyed orders, Grant sent the despatch rider to rectify matters. Young never saw Ritchie again; the latter was put into positions at Woincourt on the orders of Brigadier Stanley-Clarke.[16]

Back at Belloy, arrangements were well underway for C Company's withdrawal. The move had been timed for 11.30 am, but 15 Platoon, the furthest away, was late and there was a delay. These few minutes were crucial because they allowed a despatch rider from Woincourt the time to arrive and deliver the message that Young's force was returning and that C Company was to remain at Belloy. Captain Inglis later wrote: 'Had the DR been ten minutes later, it is very doubtful if contact would have been made'. As it was, platoons were returned to their old positions in the grounds of the château to await their fate.[17]

Apart from their vast numerical superiority, the Germans had one big advantage. As attackers, they were able to choose the timing of an attack, and so usually got a good night's sleep. The Highlanders, on the other hand, were on the defensive and could not afford to be taken unawares. By the morning of 6 June, the bleary-eyed defenders were both hungry and exhausted. At 7 am, the first attack was put in against 15 Platoon, holding the outskirts of a farm, covering several roads, about 400 yards east of the château grounds. The platoon commander, Bruce Cheape, had been over at company headquarters in the château and was on his way back when the assault began:

> As I was making my way towards the farm through a rather scrubby orchard attached to it, a German motorcycle combination went whizzing down the road behind me and an absolute storm of fire came down on our position. I saw to my horror that my platoon was falling back in some disorder across the orchard towards me. There was a lot of machine-gun fire and mortar bombs going off and there seemed absolutely no point whatsoever in advancing into it, so I brought my men back to the edge of the road where there was some cover. One carrier in support of us managed to run itself aground on one of the apple trees. I sent another carrier back with two wounded men on it. Soon we all retired into the immediate château perimeter.

Unfortunately, another of the three carriers in support of 15 Platoon had also had to be abandoned, and this was the one carrying some of the reserve ammunition. Within an hour of the attack beginning, the men holding Escarbotin were also withdrawn into the château grounds. As Captain Inglis later wrote: 'After this, it may be said that we were not really holding the roads. We were really only an island of resistance, causing nuisance value and occupation of enemy troops surrounding the château.' As the attacks on the château itself continued through the day, approximately 170 men were holding out against a force estimated at 1500. On Major Young's arrival at the château, Captain Inglis offered him command of the whole garrison. For some reason, Young declined and Inglis remained in charge. By midday, with casualties mounting and the men obviously weak from lack of food and sleep, Inglis decided to sound out the officers as to the next move. But because the perimeter was constantly in action, this could only be done piecemeal, as Bruce Cheape remembers:

> During the lulls, and as no platoon headquarters was by now more than 100–150 yards away from the château, all the officers got orders to go back, in turns, and discuss the predicament with Captain Inglis. He worked on the somewhat unmilitary system that we were in a pretty unpleasant hole and we might as well have a council of war. He was an officer that consulted rather than simply ordered. When it was my turn to go back, Inglis had with him his second-in-command, Lieutenant Cameron, Major Young, and Lieutenant Mackenzie who was commanding D Company. By this time we were all aware that the chances of getting away were pretty small, and the likelihood of getting relieved was getting less and less.

As it was generally accepted among the officers that after the night of 6 June the men would no longer be fit enough to break-out, it was agreed that some men should attempt to escape that evening. Inglis was in favour of D Company going, but both Lieutenant Mackenzie and Major Young stated that they would stand by C Company. In the end, it was decided to send back just two men with a message for Battalion Headquarters.

The first man chosen was a Private Rennie of the Intelligence Section attached to C Company. He had already tried to get a message through early that morning by motorcycle and had been apprehended by a German sentry. He had managed to escape and returned to the château. On being asked who he would like to accompany him, he chose the intrepid Second Lieutenant Peter Douglas of D Company. This request was turned down because it would have meant Douglas abandoning his platoon. Instead, Corporal Michael of Cheape's platoon, a professional stalker and therefore ideally suited to the task, volunteered. The two men set out at 10.20 pm, managed to evade the German picquets, and set a course for the south. Unfortunately, the German advance had continued much further than they expected. After several close shaves, they finally reached the town of Le Tréport, held by the 6th Royal Scots Fusiliers, in the morning of 8 June. They rejoined the remainder of their battalion two days later.

By the morning of 7 June it was just about all up for the defenders of the château at Belloy. Tanks and armoured cars had been brought up by the Germans the night before, and by 7 am the familiar mortar barrage was begun, supplemented by field guns. The only food available that day, found in a storeroom of the château, was one cooked preserved egg and a lump of sugar per man, with the lucky few also getting a mouthful of cocoa. After an infantry attack was repulsed in the morning, there was a relative lull until about 3 pm when a particularly intense mortar bombardment of more than 20 bombs per minute opened. Captain Inglis recorded the last few minutes of the defence:

> Previously, we had coped with mortar bombardments by moving the positions of the platoons and in some cases bringing them right into the château. This had been fairly effective, and kept casualties comparatively low, but this last bombardment was so searching that platoons were almost all finally driven into the château itself and casualties at this stage were very heavy and it was obvious that ... it was just a matter of time. A quick decision was therefore made ... and the order to 'Cease Fire' was given.[18]

Bruce Cheape was devastated. For a young man whose father had won two DSOs and had commanded the 7th Black Watch at Beaumont

Hamel, the Highland Division's finest hour in the First World War, this was a shameful end:

> Later on in the war nobody was unduly surprised when fairly large bodies of troops were cut off, surrounded and eventually captured. But, at the time, being taken prisoner was a rather shameful happening unless you were wounded. Even so, we were becoming less and less efficient and our chances of survival were becoming less by the hour. We had started off as two companies less some casualties, say 180 strong, on 5 June. By the afternoon of the 7th we only had an effective strength of less than half that.
>
> After we were captured, the German officer in charge saluted Captain Inglis and said, 'For you the war is over but I salute you as a gallant enemy. Are these all the men you have?' He had ambulances in for the wounded very quickly. I was the youngest officer there and the Germans sent me off with six of our men as a burial party. The German troops had retired to a clump of trees to the side of us and one of the Jocks, a chap called Willie Kemp, said to me, 'I've got a grenade in my pocket. I'll throw it at them and we'll get away!' Quickly, I snatched it and threw it into the grave we were digging. He said, 'Why did you do that?' I replied, 'If you'd have thrown that grenade, they'd have killed every one of the survivors!' He was a wild boy.

Willie Kemp's impetuosity did not end at Belloy. A week later, he and two others from C Company, Lance Corporal James 'Ginger' Wilson and a Corporal Macdonald, escaped from the prisoners' line of march with the help of a French boy and his mother, who hid them and gave them clothes. In a little over a month, by walking, cycling and hitching lifts the three men reached the Spanish frontier. On one occasion, they were picked up by a German Army truck, but were mistaken for Belgian refugees. A more serious crisis arose when they were arrested for failing to produce identification papers. By only speaking Gaelic, they managed to defeat the attempts of eight different interpreters to uncover their identity. They were finally released when, after being asked by their exasperated interrogators to indicate their homeland on a large map of Europe, Willie Kemp pointed to North Russia. After catching a boat at Gibraltar, they steamed into Gourock on 28 July, some of the first escaped POWs to make it home. For this remarkable achievement, all three were awarded the Military Medal.

The gallant defence of Belloy was finally recognised after the war when Captain Inglis, Second Lieutenant Mellor, and three other ranks were awarded the DSO, the MC, and MMs respectively. Second Lieutenant Lawder, who with his section of carriers had made it through to Battalion Headquarters at Yzengremer on 5 June, was also decorated with an MC.

* * *

By the morning of 6 June, Lieutenant Colonel 'Hamish' Grant was trying to digest the unpalatable news that his battalion, to all intents and purposes, had ceased to exist. He knew that his C and D Companies were still holding out, but that the Germans had bypassed them in strength. He had not heard from his two companies on the left, A and B, since the previous morning. As far as he was concerned, the battalion was now effectively HQ Company, made up of the Anti-Aircraft Platoon, the 3-inch Mortar Platoon, the three remaining carriers, and a motley collection of signallers, clerks, pioneers and orderlies: a grand total of just 140 men.

Yet A and B Companies were still very much at large, although they had had a trying day. A Company, in positions around the village of Sallenelle to the west of St Valéry-sur-Somme, had been attacked early in the morning. At 7 am, Sergeant Whayman, the Intelligence Sergeant, arrived in the village in a carrier with orders from Colonel Grant for the company to withdraw through B Company, a mile further back in Lanchères, to Brutelles. But Captain Lumley-Webb, an ex-Regular who had taken over command of A Company on 3 June after Captain Maxwell-Macdonald had been wounded, was reluctant to leave the village until 7 Platoon under Second Lieutenant Malcolm, in positions a mile to the north of Sallenelle, had come in. By 9 am there was still no sign, and Captain Webb finally decided to withdraw. But as Company Headquarters and the survivors of the remaining two platoons were leaving, 7 Platoon appeared. A little over three hours later, the company was hard at work preparing positions in Brutelles; it had already sustained nearly 40 casualties, having lost most of 8 Platoon and some of 9 Platoon.

While A Company was on the move, Captain James Taylor, commanding B Company at Lanchères, received orders to withdraw his men to Hautebut as part of brigade's plan to shorten the line. The one complication was 10 Platoon, a good three miles to the north, holding the village of Le Hourdel on the mouth of the Somme estuary. A truck was sent to deliver an order for this garrison to fall back, but it had to abandon its mission when it ran into Germans on the way. There was nothing left but to leave without 10 Platoon. Thirty minutes after A Company had retired through Lanchères, Taylor's men set off on the three mile march to Hautebut.

At 4 pm, Major Lorne Campbell arrived in Brutelles. For many men in the battalion, he, rather than 'Hamish' Grant, should have been commanding during a war. Although a Territorial, he was that rare breed of natural soldier with powers of leadership only enhanced by his imposing 6'3" frame. He also had an impeccable military pedigree: his father had commanded the 8th Argylls, while his uncle, Vice Admiral Gordon Campbell, had won a VC (turning down a second in favour of another man) and a DSO with two Bars in the First World War.

Campbell had been sent up to Brutelles by Colonel Grant with orders for A Company to move even further back to Woignarue, a village off the main coastal road about a mile south of Hautebut. The men set off immediately on what became a particularly hazardous trek across country because German armoured cars were on the road south from Brutelles. Lieutenant James Campbell, the company second-in-command, recalls that much of the move was done on hands and knees, crawling through ditches, an experience worsened because 'it was a beastly hot day and we got covered with ticks'. When these weary troops eventually reached Woignarue, they were horrified to discover it already occupied by Germans.

Campbell decided to continue the march south, and to try to prevent further enemy incursions by occupying Ault, on the coast, and Friau-cort, two miles inland. Orders to this end were sent to B Company, but after a reconnaissance towards Friaucourt had revealed that the Germans had passed through it in the direction of Eu on the River Bresle, Campbell realised that he was cut off and ordered both companies into Ault. Once there, they found a platoon of 6th Royal Scots Fusiliers and 15 French marines in residence, so they joined them in positions around the lighthouse on cliffs above the town. That night, Campbell managed to use the Fusiliers' telephone to get a message through to Divisional Headquarters. He was told that the line was still holding and to hold on until further orders. None came because, shortly after, the line went dead.

In the early morning of 6 June, Second Lieutenant Moncur miracu-lously arrived with the remaining men of 10 Platoon who had been assumed lost in Le Houdel. Although one of his sections had been cut off and captured, Moncur had managed to work his way down the coast with the rest, before laying up in a farm outside Ault. But this good news was dampened by the realisation that Ault was by now well behind enemy lines. Since the previous evening, German transport had been rumbling down the nearby road from St Valéry towards Eu, while the sound of fighting had gradually receded. After consultation with both company commanders, Campbell decided to attempt a breakout that night. Although in direct contradiction of orders from division, this initiative was the last hope for A and B Companies, as Major Campbell later explained in a report on the action:

Rather than be bottled up in Ault and wait for ultimate suppression, which seemed inevitable, it seemed better to make a final attempt at getting back to our Div. with at any rate the prospect of a final effort in the open instead of in a trap.[19]

With the decision to move taken, the only wait now was for nightfall. It was to prove an eventful day. First, at about midday, a German car was shot up by some men of B Company as it approached Ault, and two German officers, one wounded, were captured. As well as possessing some valuable maps, the officers were armed to the teeth: a Belgian light machine-gun, numerous other small arms, and even some knuckle dusters, made up their personal armoury. A little later, a second German car arrived at the beach and its two occupants, unaware of the danger, got out to swim. Then followed an episode of pure farce. On spotting the swimmers, the French marines opened up with their ancient 75mm gun, the first shell missing by a street and only served to knock the gun from its mounting. By drawing such obvious attention to the lighthouse defenders, the Marines ushered in a period of sniping from a nearby farmhouse.

Then, at 8 pm, just as Major Campbell was giving out orders for the move, the Germans opened up. Instead of an infantry assault, they were content to bombard the lighthouse area with tank cannon and machine-guns. In response, Campbell withdrew the men into the comparative cover of the lighthouse compound and only three men were wounded. But the fire was too much for some of the defenders, Captain Taylor recorded:

> The effect of this fire ... on the French Marines was electrifying. Those who were in a house on our left rushed towards the Germans with cries of 'Kamerad' while those who were behind the lighthouse made off towards the shore at great speed, stampeding a few of our men with them.[20]

These few men were in fact a sergeant and 20 Jocks, the best part of a platoon. They later redeemed themselves by working their way back through to the British lines at Eu.

At 11.45 pm, the break-out began. At the head of the column Lorne Campbell placed three fighting patrols of section strength, led by Second Lieutenant Mackinnon on the right, Second Lieutenant Moncur on the left, with Campbell himself in the centre with map and compass. The remaining men followed behind: B Company, Royal Scots Fusiliers, A Company, in column of threes. A total of around 200 men. The fit German prisoner was also taken, guarded by a Jock with fixed bayonet and orders to use it at the first sign of betrayal.

The obvious route was four miles straight down the coast to Le Tréport which they knew had been held the night before by the 6th Royal Scots Fusiliers. But Campbell, rightly, had other ideas:

> Le Tréport seemed the route the enemy were most likely to try and block, so we decided to avoid it and make our way south across country avoiding villages and woods. The subsequent experience of the men who got through to Le Tréport showed that we were right.[21]

The plan was to march the whole way on a compass bearing of 146 degrees, but with two changes of direction at right angles to the bearing to avoid suspected trouble spots. Thus, the column would march on the bearing until 500 yards south of the St Valéry–Ault road, then 1,100 yards at right angles to avoid Ault station, back on the bearing to bisect the villages of Friaucourt and St Quentin to the Abbeville–Eu road, 1,000 yards at right angles to avoid Méneslies, and finally back on the bearing to the Bois de Bouvaincourt. Campbell hoped to reach the wood, and with luck British troops, before daylight. The key to the plan was the change of direction, which had to be made at exactly the right place. To solve this problem Campbell had two men with him counting their steps to give him a rough idea of how far they had gone.

The move went smoothly enough the first night, but the tank attack had delayed the departure a crucial couple of hours and by dawn on the 7th the column had only reached the western edge of Méneslies. To avoid moving by daylight, Campbell ordered a search for a suitable hide and it was Captain Webb who eventually found some scrub cover on the south face of a valley. Campbell was convinced that a German spotter plan had seen them as they looked for a hiding place, and his temper was not improved when Captain Webb reported that, on a recce towards Dargnies, he had been fired on by a German sniper.

It was a particularly unpleasant day for the column. Two hundred men lying without moving for 15 hours in scrubland covered in gorse bushes. As the sun blazed down, a lack of water became the biggest torture and most survivors of the march remember this first, rather than fear of death or capture. The most nerve-racking moment came when four motor-cyclists stopped on a road above the prone Highlanders, and were soon joined by six officers who surveyed the country through field glasses. Luckily, they failed to spot anything amiss.

Nightfall brought a relieving change of temperature and the chance to stretch stiff limbs; it also brought decision time. As there was still no sign of the front line, Campbell opted to make for a crossing on the River Bresle. Le Lieu Dieu was chosen because it was small and, if held by Germans, might not be too difficult to take. To reach it and avoid villages on the way, no less than three compass bearings were needed. The march began at 11 pm, and within an hour disaster beckoned. As the fighting patrols were approaching a road, they were challenged in German and soon after fired on by some sentries who then ran off. No one was hit but the game was now up. The remainder of the night was one of excruciating suspense. A spotter plane kept coming over, while parachute flares were constantly fired from all the villages on the route, and the odd rifle shot. Near Embreville, the column passed very close to a German artillery battery under fire and narrowly missed being shelled by its own side.

As it was getting light, the column were nearing the top of a ridge overlooking the River Bresle when they were challenged by a group of men who shouted 'Hallo!'. Thinking they might be French, Lieutenant Mackinnon shouted back '*Amis!*' and the column came to a halt. Major Campbell then chimed in, '*Êtes vous Francais?*', but was met with a stream of German. On hearing this the prisoner shouted to his countryman for help and was promptly bayoneted by his escort. Machine-guns immediately opened fire, but the column was soon over the ridge with no casualties. Leaving Captain Webb to form a rearguard, the main column continued on down towards the small village of Le Lieu Dieu directly below it. Realising they might have to fight their way through, Major Campbell formed up B Company for an attack and sent Second Lieutenants Mackinnon and Moncur forward to reconnoitre into the village. They reported that the near end was clear, and the column moved on. By good fortune, the Argylls now found themselves between the two front lines with the early morning mist covering their movement. Without delay, they pushed on, most crossing the Bresle by the wreckage of two blown bridges, while some waded over. Once across, the only danger was death by friendly fire. Second Lieutenant Mackinnon volunteered to go forward with his patrol at great personal risk, and it was he who made contact with a picquet of the 4th Black Watch.[22]

Major Lorne Campbell had accomplished the most remarkable feat of the campaign. He had led 200 men, long since given up for lost, on a march of 14 miles behind enemy lines, moving only at night and relying solely on his compass reading ability. No less than seven changes of direction were necessary, a mistake at any one of which could have been fatal. Only three men had been lost, almost certainly through falling asleep and being left behind.

It is generally accepted by those on the march that Lorne Campbell was the only man of the battalion who could have got them out. Captain

Taylor concluded his report of the action with the words: 'Our safe journey through the German lines can be solely attributed to the fine leadership and brilliant compass marching of Major LM Campbell.' For his efforts, Campbell was awarded the DSO, while Captain Webb and Second Lieutenant Mackinnon were each given an MC, and Sergeant Whayman an MM.

At the relatively late age of 38, Campbell had given the first hint of the great soldier he was to become. In 1942, when commanding the 7th Argylls in the reformed 51st (Highland) Division during the Battle of El Alamein, he won a Bar to his DSO. A few months later, he crowned his career by winning a Victoria Cross at the bloody Battle of Wadi Akarit in Tunisia, thus becoming one of only four members of a Highland regiment to be awarded this medal during the whole of the Second World War. He finished the war as a Brigadier, a rank rarely attained by the Territorials.

8

Withdrawal to the Bresle

While the brunt of the German attack against the 51st Division on 5 June fell against the luckless 154 Brigade, the neighbouring brigades were also in action. In a particularly hazardous position were the 1st Gordons, facing the left flank of the Abbeville bridgehead along the Cahon valley. Elements of their A Company were the most vulnerable, holding the village of Gouy in sight of the Somme Canal.

The left-hand unit of the company, huddled in small weapon pits to the front of Gouy and just a few hundred yards across flat, marshy land from the canal, was 7 Platoon under Second Lieutenant Ran Ogilvie. As dawn broke, the view ahead of 7 Platoon's positions was obscured by a thick summer mist, and for a time the only indication of an attack was the sound of shelling and small arms fire from the direction of 154 Brigade on its left. Then, slowly and silently, ghostly figures began to penetrate the fog from the direction of the canal. Ran Ogilvie recalls:

> My Bren guns opened fire, in short bursts at first, which gradually grew in volume as the rifles joined in. I can well remember the hesitancy of those little groups of the enemy, some making for the little cover that there was, or disappearing back into the mist, others, the machine-gun groups, going to ground, their bullets spattering up the turf around us.
>
> Artillery and small arms fire had now started towards A Company's right rear, some distance away, growing with intensity with the minutes. We later learned that an attack in force had been launched from the Grand Bois de Cambron – scene of the previous day's successful, later aborted, attack by B and C Companies, and their subsequent frustrating withdrawal. Now the enemy attack was being faced by B and D Companies, with C Company in reserve, the latter having suffered fairly heavy casualties on the previous day. A Company, not directly involved in this new attack from the Grand Bois sector, was not only facing an attack from the direction of the Somme, but had a major attack now developing on its immediate left flank in 7th Argylls' sector, but completely out of our view and contact.
>
> As the mist started to clear, firing grew in intensity as the battle developed along the whole front, especially on A Company's left and left rear, and it seemed to us that the 7th Argylls were being attacked in strength and that the attack was making penetration. It also seemed that,

at this early state, we were on the fringe of the attack, rather than being in the forefront.

As the fire-fight intensified, it also, quite suddenly, developed on our immediate front, as parties of infantry started to move towards my platoon positions. We were now under heavy small arms and mortar fire. I left my weapon-pit to move over to a section Bren gun post, to direct fire onto an enemy machine-gun which was giving us some trouble. At that moment, a sudden mortar concentration came down on the short stretch of open ground that I was crossing. Fortunately, the ground was fairly soft and the force of the explosions tended to go upwards rather than sideways. I never flattened myself so quickly! Shortly afterwards, Number 1 of the Bren, Private Bremner, received a bullet high in his chest. He was spitting up a little blood but, as the bullet entered high up, and he was leaning forward on the gun, I hoped that the bullet might not have caused any serious damage to his left lung. He was able to walk and I immediately sent him back, on foot, to Company Headquarters at Cahon for evacuation. I later learned that he had died from his wound.

I temporarily took over as Number 2 of the Bren while Piper Robbie, Company Piper attached to 7 Platoon, moved over to take Number 1 and continued to engage the enemy. I spotted an enemy post which was giving us trouble and took Robbie's rifle. Fortunately, I was a good rifle shot. My first two shots only made the two machine-gunners change position, from where they reopened fire. I then engaged them again and, as they neither moved nor fired again, felt certain that I had dealt with them successfully. Unfortunately, shortly afterwards, Robbie collapsed beside me, killed by a bullet through his forehead.[1]

At about this time, 11 am, a runner arrived from Captain Stuart Aylmer, Ogilvie's company commander in Gouy, with a message that the company was being withdrawn and that C Company were moving up to cover the withdrawal of 7 Platoon. Ogilvie had to move fast if he was to make the company rendezvous in Cahon, the village housing Battalion Headquarters. Unfortunately, the incoming fire had increased in intensity, while a new frontal attack had begun on Ogilvie's positions, making it impossible for his men to leave their slit-trenches and withdraw over open ground without covering fire. Then, with time running out, supporting fire began to come from a small bluff to the left rear of 7 Platoon. Ogilvie, assuming it was C Company, gave orders to thin out. Without warning, and before the withdrawal was complete, the firing stopped and 7 Platoon was left to cover itself, with small groups firing while others moved back.

Making good time, Ogilvie and his men arrived in Cahon for the rendezvous but were dismayed to find it empty, not even a guide had been left. All Ogilvie knew was that the battalion was withdrawing to the line of the Abbeville–Le Tréport road, three miles away. The noise of firing was still coming from both flanks and it was clear to Ogilvie that the survival of his platoon was in the balance. He later wrote:

> Only a narrow corridor of retreat was left to my platoon – along the line of the railway running back from Cahon and east of Franleu (now surrounded). If I withdrew the platoon to ground on either side of the railway line, which was in a cutting as far as I could see, I might find myself involved in a dangerous fire-fight with the enemy on my now unprotected flank. If I used the railway line, and the enemy reached it and saw my platoon withdrawing along it, I could be dangerously enfiladed by machine-gun and mortar fire and suffer heavy casualties. I took a gamble, and decided to use the railway and to get in as much distance as I could moving fast, with sections on alternate sides of the line.
>
> I don't know at what time I reached the Abbeville–Le Tréport road – over four anxious miles from Gouy – but at the road I was met by the CO, Harry Wright, relieved, and sent to rejoin my company a short distance back. We were lucky to have got out of a very tight corner, and without further casualties.[2]

Only later did Ogilvie discover that the short-lived supporting fire had come not from C Company but from a section of Second Lieutenant Basil Brooke's Carrier Platoon. C Company, the unit that had been so successful in the attack the previous day, had indeed been sent up as the reserve company to help get A Company out, but it had never arrived at Gouy. Second Lieutenant Charles Barker recalls the very hurried nature of the operation:

> We had no large scale maps, so we didn't know exactly where A Company was. Our company had been withdrawn from the Grand Bois the previous evening and the route we were to take had not been reconnoitred. To launch a company without proper reconnaissance or fire support is most unusual, but the desperate situation made this the case. I don't think we even had the three company trucks carrying our extra ammunition, picks and shovels with us. They would have followed us up later.
>
> After leaving the village of Cahon we had gone about 300 yards when suddenly we came under the most intense mortar fire, caught completely out in the open. Of course we took to ground. As we looked ahead, there were Germans moving across to the left, and on our right flank they were pouring out of the woods. There was no way the company could go forward. Donald Alexander, the company commander, decided we had to go back to the village and take up a defensive position there.

To effect the withdrawal, the company split into two. Half the men under Captain Alexander tried to get back under cover of a small gulley to the right and were cut to pieces. Severely wounded by mortar fire, Alexander was picked up by Lance Corporal Groves and Private Knight who tried to get him to safety. But suspecting he was finished anyway, and would only cause his two bearers to be captured, Alexander ordered them to leave him. He died in captivity but his grave has never been found.

Barker and the remainder of the company went to the left, and had more luck. Although hit in the leg by mortar fragments and temporarily deafened by explosions, Barker was able to make it back to Cahon with 21 other survivors. On the way, he tried to help another man who had been hit, but had to leave him as he was too heavy. He stuck the man's rifle in the ground, placing his tin hat on it, in the hope that the carriers might pick him up. Barker was the last survivor from C Company to reach Cahon. He was met by the Second-in-Command of the battalion, Major Hutchins, who told him to move back to the Abbeville–Le Tréport road. The other remnants of C Company had already left. They were guided in their withdrawal by Private Tom Copland of the Intelligence Section who, before moving forward with the company, had been given a map reference by the Intelligence Sergeant to make for after the rescue attempt. Copland is convinced that, without this reference, the survivors would have been captured. Barker and the other wounded were evacuated, finally sailing for England and safety on 19 June. He narrowly missed being put aboard the hospital ship SS *Lancastria*, which took a bomb in the funnel and went down with 5,000 lives.

Unbeknown to the survivors of A and C Companies, the action by the Carrier Platoon on 5 June was undoubtedly the biggest factor in their deliverance. As soon as it was appreciated that the Germans were advancing up the left flank of the battalion, through ground that should have been held by the 7th Argylls, the carriers were sent across. First the Carriers' Officer, Second Lieutenant Basil Brooke, posted two sections of three carriers each on high ground to the left of the railway track, then he sent his remaining section up a sunken road to aid the withdrawal of the companies in action on the right. Although all three carriers were lost to mortar fire, this action was a success. But as the Germans were approaching Cahon, Brooke was ordered by his CO to retire. This was easier said than done:

> I had left one of my other two sections of carriers at a building that looked rather like a windmill without sails, up on some high ground on our left flank. I though they would be alright there because they had an all round view. Anyway, when I was told to bring the carriers in, I had no radio link, so I had to take the order myself.

When I arrived, I pulled in underneath this building, but there was no sign of my section. Suddenly we realised the whole place was full of Germans and as they opened fire I shouted to the driver, 'Let's get out of here!' He shouted back, 'We can't. They've blown off a track. We've got to run for it.' I retorted, 'You two make for the road at the far end of that field.' I wanted to give them a head start before I dropped a couple of grenades in the carrier and followed them. This I did, leaping out of the carrier and running like hell.

As we ran, they shot the driver, Duncan. My batman, Henderson, who was a huge great chap, stopped to go back for him when I shouted, 'Leave him, come on!' He went back anyway. The noblest thing in the world but in doing so he was shot dead. There was I about 30 paces on with little chance of escape and my best pals being shot; I too went back for Duncan. I lifted him up and saw he had been shot several times through the right arm and the side. But he could use his left hand and his legs to a certain extent. I hurled him up and we ran with me supporting him. Bullets were all around us and how we weren't shot I just don't know. We had so far to go, I quickly ran out of breath and had to lie down on the ground for a rest. At last the firing stopped.

Brooke struggled on with Duncan for some time until he reached the road south from Cahon. By sheer luck they managed to flag down the last truck to leave, and in it rejoined the battalion on the Abbeville–Le Tréport road. Despite Brooke's gallant efforts – for which he was awarded the MC – Duncan died in a French hospital. Of the ten carriers that went into action that day, only one returned and it could only steer to the right. It was subsequently sent back to be repaired with a Private Sims driving, and neither was ever seen again.

By late afternoon, the Germans had reached the Abbeville–Le Tréport road and the position that the 1st Gordons had taken up nearby, covering woods over a front of 3,000 yards, was in danger of being outflanked. After a visit to General Fortune at his Battle Headquarters in Martainneville, Brigadier Burney and Colonel Wright obtained permission for the battalion to withdraw that night to high ground north-west of Gamaches on the River Bresle. Before dawn they were in position.

* * *

The decision to withdraw a battalion was usually taken at short notice because of the poor communications and the large distances involved, and this often left another with its flank undefended. So it was with the 1st Black Watch, holding from Lambercourt to Toeufles, when the 1st Gordons began to retire on the morning of the 5th. Captain Bill Bradford later recorded:

Owing to the way the withdrawal was carried out, our left flank was left completely exposed. As soon as I saw what was happening, I went and told Brigadier Burney because I knew he hadn't meant this to happen. I wanted to tell him to leave one company forward on our left and to swing their battalion back pivoted on that. He came back but was too late to alter it.

From Battalion Headquarters at Miannay, Bradford and his CO, Colonel Honeyman, could clearly see the enemy moving up on the left. It was only vigorous action by Second Lieutenant Angus Irwin's Carrier Platoon, who moved to engage them, that prevented the battalion from being outflanked. With Brigadier Burney's permission, Honeyman withdrew his men back a couple of miles in the afternoon, leaving a rearguard of two companies – one in Miannay and one in Toeufles.

The jittery state of some of the men during such a fluid battle is illustrated by two incidents. First, an officer lost his nerve taking orders for withdrawal up to A Company, and returned without completing his task. Bradford was forced to take the same orders up himself, on a motorcycle, but when he reached the positions he was shot at by a Jock from a distance of just a few yards, and fortunately missed. Bradford was more irritated at this evidence of poor marksmanship than he was at almost having his life ended. Then, when D Company, holding Toeufles, were attacked, one of the first to be killed was popular Corporal Spalding. This so demoralised some of the men of his platoon that they picked up his body and started back with it. An officer met them and returned them to their positions.

By nightfall, the whole battalion had disengaged and was withdrawn over five miles from its original positions to Vismes-au-Val, where Headquarters 153 Brigade had been until that afternoon.

* * *

For the battered companies of 152 Brigade, 5 June afforded no respite. By 5 am, an attack down the *Route Nationale* had developed against the Camerons holding Villers. Second Lieutenant Slater's mixed platoon on the right of the village fought with great tenacity but within two hours had been overrun. At one point, Slater and Lance Corporal Walsh, the sole surviving NCO of a platoon of D Company that had attacked the previous day, crawled out to an isolated shell-hole in an attempt to bring fire to bear against an assault from the rear. As Slater later reported, Walsh, using a Bren gun to 'great effect, displayed immense coolness and a total disregard of his own safety right up until the time when he was killed by shots through the head at almost point blank range from a Schmeisser'. Slater and his remaining men were subsequently captured. In a letter to Major MacLeay, written in POW camp, Slater recommended Walsh for a posthumous medal, citing his 'exemplary courage and determination'. The letter concluded with the words: 'I cannot pay too high a tribute to this boy's efficiency, gallantry and continual thought for his men's welfare and I trust that it may be possible for this to be, in some manner, officially recognised'. Sadly, Walsh's family got nothing to assuage the grief of his death.[3]

When the attack came in, Second Lieutenant David Ross was visiting Company Headquarters in the farmhouse at the bottom of the village, and by the time he had made it back to his platoon at the top end, it was obvious that the original positions could not be held. He ordered two of his sections to join 15 Platoon in the White House, the former Company Headquarters across the road and a little further forward than the farmhouse. Ross then carried on to give the same instructions to his last section, on the left of the *Route Nationale*. Arriving there, he found Second Lieutenant John Anderson of the 4th Seaforths, who had crawled back on his elbows during the night after being shot in both legs the previous day. Sergeant McLean and Lance Corporal Black wrenched a door off to use as a makeshift stretcher, while Ross and some other men fought off a small attack. Unfortunately, the door broke and after a brief debate on whether it would be wiser to leave him, Anderson was dragged to safety.

Within minutes of Ross and his party reaching the White House, it was under heavy attack. Salvation came in the form of an artillery bombardment, so severe that it caused the attackers to retire. Amazingly, the White House remained unscathed. The bombardment had been requested by battalion as the only way to stop the enemy advance up the *Route Nationale*. This assessment had been made by Colonel Cawdor after hearing Captain Ross's report, given in person at Huchenneville, that his men could not hold the attack. It was a cold-blooded decision because there was every chance that the defenders of Villers would be hit; by good fortune they were not.

The lull in the assault, provided by the shelling, gave David Ross the opportunity to make contact with Company Headquarters in the farmhouse, where 20 men under Second Lieutenant Cavaye were still holding out. They had beaten off a strong attack, during which Company Sergeant Major Fox and Lance Corporal McCuish both distinguished themselves. Ross then sent Lawder, the man who had bravely made contact with the farmhouse, back to Huchenneville for orders. He returned with the news that the village was deserted. Absolved by this of his duty to hold on, Ross collected all the 60 or so survivors together and ordered a withdrawal down the *Route Nationale*. Doors were used as stretchers for the wounded, each one covered with a mattress and carried by six men using rifles as struts. Despite regularly swapping, such was the strain of carrying the stretchers that the men were soon exhausted and the pace was slow. If Private Lawder had not found some proper stretchers in the woods opposite Huchenneville, the wounded might well have had to be left.

By early evening, the exhausted column, made up of C and D Company men, some 4th Seaforths, and even some machine-gunners, arrived at Limeux, still held by the 2nd Seaforths. Ironically, for all their heroism, only one of the defenders of Villers was decorated for gallantry: David Ross, who was awarded the MC. John Anderson won a similar award for his part in the attack on the previous day.[4]

During the night of 4/5 June, A Company, supported by the handful of B Company men, had remained in their dangerously advanced positions on the edge of Tourbieres. But spirits had been high ever since Battalion had telephoned through the previous evening to inform Captain Tweedie that a company of the 5th Gordons would relieve his command before dawn.

Company Quartermaster Sergeant Gregor Macdonald, the man who had gone forward in the attack and who therefore knew the exact position of A Company, was given the onerous task of guiding up B Company of the 5th Gordons. As he was being briefed by Lord Cawdor himself, in the Château de Huchenneville, Macdonald could not help noticing the haggard look on Cawdor's face. When he realised that he was being asked to take a relief up to A Company's exposed position, he wondered if his CO was cracking up under the strain and voiced his doubts. Cawdor dismissed them by insisting that he was following brigade orders. With a strong sense of foreboding, Macdonald left:

> I rejoined B Company, called for two volunteers and was immediately joined by Corporal Maclean and Private MacGlynn. We got half a loaf and some cheese from the ration clerk, and as a great favour were given a tin of 'bully' by one of the colour sergeants. As darkness fell we made our way down the Limeux road to the Map Reference where we found the Gordon company waiting. Their commander, Captain Usher, suggested that he and I and his Sergeant Major should lead the column while the two Camerons would take up the rear. We kept to the grass verge and were forbidden to speak . . . It was apparent that the enemy were occupying many positions commanding the road and we were very lucky indeed to find a clear way back.

The relief column arrived at A Company's positions at 3.30 am, just as dawn was beginning to break. On being informed of the orders to move his company back, Tweedie surprised Macdonald by insisting that it was far too dangerous to cross the open ground in daylight and that they would wait for nightfall. Macdonald repeated that the CO had ordered their immediate withdrawal, but Tweedie was adamant. His one concession was to allow Macdonald to attempt to make the return trip if he wanted to. Without hesitating, Macdonald collected Maclean and MacGlynn and set off, successfully reaching the château later that morning despite being shot at three times.

By delaying his departure, Tweedie had effectively written off his company. At 9 am a German attack came in from two sides, and although beaten off it enabled a host of snipers to get into positions from where they caused many casualties through the day. Tanks were also brought up by the Germans to support the assault. Private Iain Mackinnon, a runner with B Company of the 5th Gordons, remembers how ineffective the anti-tank rifles proved:

> There were several attacks made on the orchard during the day of the 5th from both infantry and tanks, and the only thing we had to fire at the tanks with was the Boyes anti-tank rifle. It was useless. It might have been okay for getting a despatch-rider on a motorbike, but not for tanks. During one attack, a tank went right over the top of the slit trench I was in.

Gradually, more German troops moved up until by nightfall the position was surrounded. Tweedie's gamble that darkness would offer the best opportunity for withdrawal had failed. It was estimated that 800 Germans were involved, with mortars, anti-tank guns and tanks. Before stand-to, Tweedie sent two men, Lance Corporal Ross and Private Ross, to report their predicament to Battalion Headquarters at Huchenne-ville. The two never returned. They did manage to reach the château, found it deserted and were captured on their way back to A Company to report this.

As day broke on the morning of the 6th, the bombardment of mortars and shells started again. Defence was now pointless and a conference of all the officers was held. Taking into account the heavy casualties – about half the Camerons' strength and a third of the Gordons – it was agreed that to hold out longer would only result in more loss of life as firing nearby had long since died down and there was little chance of a counter-attack. Before giving the order to surrender, Captain Usher went to talk to his men. Private Bobby Shand recalls his words:

> Usher called us up and says, 'You've three options. First, run for it.

Second, surrender. Third, fight it out. What do you think?' So one chap went up and said, 'Well, you've led us all this time, and we'll do whatever you say.' And everyone agreed. 'Well,' he says, 'there's no hope, we're surrounded which you know, so the only thing we can do is surrender. Back to your positions.' Then the boy went out with the white flag.

   When they were marching us out, we were passed by truck loads of Germans, and one officer leant out of his truck and said, 'We'll be in London in a fortnight!' A little wee devil called Curly replied, 'The longest fortnight ever you'll live!' We were devastated. We had thought we might be killed, or wounded, but never, never, prisoner of war. Yet still he could say that.

Captain Tweedie also offered his men the opportunity to escape that morning, but no one was reckless enough to accept. At 11 am, Tweedie and Usher formally surrendered their companies and another disastrous chapter was written in the history of the Highland Division's 1940 campaign. Again, despite a gallant defence, the inadequacy of a defensive line made up of far-flung strongpoints was demonstrated.

Battalion Headquarters of the 4th Camerons had left Huchenneville at midday on 5 June, ordered by 152 Brigade Headquarters to positions at Les Croisettes, a short way back. Also involved in this move were the remaining companies of the 5th Gordons, in a hide a mile to the north-east of Huchenneville. Worried about his B Company, 'Sailor' Clark sent a despatch rider to Huchenneville to find out whether it had been told of the withdrawal, but by the time he arrived the Camerons had moved out. Once at Les Croisettes, both battalions received new orders to continue their move back: the 4th Camerons to St Maxent and the 5th Gordons to Huppy.

   By daybreak of 6 June, the 4th Camerons, since joined by Second Lieutenant Ross and the survivors from Villers, were in positions on the railway line behind St Maxent. Such were its casualties over the previous two days that it now comprised just two companies: one made up from the remnants of B, C and D Companies, and the other from HQ Company personnel. The 5th Gordons, considerably stronger, had by now also been moved back to the same place and were holding the railway line from the right of the Camerons to the edge of the village of Cerisy-Beleux.

* * *

Despite the apparent hopelessness of the positions occupied by the infantry battalions of the 51st Division on the morning of 5 June, none were as futile as the four mile front that the 1st Lothians were expected to hold, on high ground overlooking the River Somme. With two of their fighting squadrons in the line – A on the left and C on the right – and B Squadron in reserve, the density of men at the front was an absurd 40 per mile. The Lothians did have one advantage over the infantry, though; their tanks and carriers were equipped with wireless.

Shortly after 4.15 am, C Squadron's posts at Bray were attacked. Within 15 minutes, Major Jimmy Dallmeyer, commanding A Squadron, had despatched a troop of carriers to assist C Squadron. Second Lieutenant Lawrie, commanding the posts in Bray, later told Dallmeyer that without these men the German advance could not have been held up. But Dallmeyer may have later regretted sending the carriers because at 5.30 am his own positions were attacked.

A Squadron was holding 2,000 yards of ground with just 65 men. Its front was made up of two strongholds: Squadron Headquarters on the right edge of Tourbieres; the remaining 20, supported by a troop of carriers under Second Lieutenant Bobby Dundas, over a mile to the right, and three-quarters of a mile from Bray. Dallmeyer would have preferred to have occupied the wooded ridge to the rear of his positions, but heavy shelling had made this impractical. The two tank troops and most of the carriers of the squadron were in reserve, some way back.

The Germans' attack was put in against the left of the squadron, down the road from nearby Mareuil, and must have taken an advance post by surprise because no shots were fired from it. Forming a cornerstone, literally, in the squadron's defences was a disabled French tank. It had broken down in an earlier battle but its crew had stayed to man its main armament and machine-gun. In a report of the action, Dallmeyer recalled the shock the advancing Germans got when they saw the tank:

> As the Germans rounded the corner they caught sight of the French tank. There were two men in front. The leading man put up his hands, the second man shot him in the back. We shot the second man. The Germans retreated and some made their way through the houses and back gardens up the ridge on the north side of the valley, others towards the Somme. Once established there, they opened fire with mortars and machine-guns.[5]

Realising that the point of the attack was now on his flank, Dallmeyer sent a despatch rider to order Second Lieutenants Dundas and Chambers to move at once to the left sector. By 8 am, Chambers and Dundas arrived with their men, but Dundas' troop had been attacked and only one carrier survived. As the squadron was out of wireless

communication with Regimental Headquarters, Dundas was immediately instructed to make for RHQ, in a hamlet just behind Bray, to
request a counter-attack against the German push. Before long, Dundas
returned with Colonel Ansell's regrets that a counter-attack was not
possible and that Dallmeyer should hold on at all costs.

By midday the German fire had slackened, and Dallmeyer took the
chance to reorganise his defences, abandoning the leftmost positions as
the French tank had by now run out of ammunition after excellent
work. All phone lines had been cut and wireless communication, via
Dundas' carrier, was still not getting through to Regimental Headquarters, so Dundas was once again sent to report the situation and ask
for orders.

While they were waiting for him to return, Dallmeyer decided to lead
a patrol of 15 men up the hill to the back of his positions to find out
what had happened to two small parties he had sent up earlier to spot
any German flanking movement. Dallmeyer recorded:

> The hill was covered with low growing bushes and saplings affording
> excellent cover and it was not a pleasant task advancing with a rifle at the
> alert expecting a burst of Schmeisser fire at any moment, nor was it made
> any more pleasant by finding the body of Lance Corporal Baillie almost
> at once. He had evidently been killed at short range. Sergeant Cormack
> and Trooper Queen were also found dead ... Then Schmeissers opened
> on our left and at the same time machine-guns opened fire from the ridge
> across the valley. Those on our right flank could do nothing so we
> returned to squadron headquarters and, on our arrival, found Lieutenant
> Dundas with three carriers and two tanks and orders to withdraw if
> possible.[6]

The two tanks, under the command of Second Lieutenant Addie
Thorburn-Brown, had been ordered up by Colonel Ansell to help with
the withdrawal. Dallmeyer asked Thorburn-Brown to cover the Mareuil
road with one tank, while Bobby Dundas went in the other to effect the
escape of the remainder of the patrol, who were still pinned down.
Sergeant Jack Allen, commanding the second tank, recalls Dundas
commandeering it:

> Lieutenant Bobby Dundas said to me, 'Jack, I've got a patrol cut off, I've
> got to borrow your tank.' Well, we were short of a tank, it had been lost
> in front of the Maginot Line after we changed over, and we only had two
> tanks. So I said to my gunner, 'You get out. I'll go with Bobby Dundas, I
> don't trust this rascal!' Well, instead of just going up to the ridge he
> ordered the tank over it. As we were coming down the other side through
> scrub and brushwood, I said, 'Bobby,' I knew him from home so I didn't

call him Sir, 'If Jerry's across in that wood we're a sitting duck coming down this hill.' I'd no sooner said it than we got hit. The first shell came in and blew me out of my seat; the next one brought us to a halt.

I was hit for six, I thought I'd lost my right eye because I had a split next to it and the blood kept rushing in. I was also a bit concussed, but I struggled to my feet and got a hatch open to let the smoke out. I could see Bobby, slumped on his seat. It was obvious that he was dead. I struggled to get out and fell over the side. As I was picking myself up, the driver, Boyd, was getting out. Then a machine-gun started up so we ran round the back of the tank and into a field. I stopped to tie a hanky over my eye, I couldn't see where I was going, and when I moved off again Boyd was 20 yards ahead. I had just got through a hedge when another machine-gun opened up from my left. I dropped in the grass, which had just been cut, but Boyd was about ten yards away on my right and made it into some long grass. He managed to crawl off but I was pinned down.

However gallant, Dundas had made a grave error by ordering the tank over the cover of the hill and down the open slope beyond, and it cost him his life. Allan was captured that evening, unable to move, but Boyd made it back to A Squadron's positions. This action had some success though, all but two of the patrol it had gone to extricate managed to return.

Dallmeyer then set about organising the withdrawal. So many on each carrier and so many in between. The only men who had not been called in were Second Lieutenant Lord Brackley – heir to the Duke of Sutherland – and his party holding a house nearby. A signal of four loud bursts on the whistle would indicate a sudden evacuation. But as the preparations were being concluded, a lethal bombardment of high explosive came down. Major Dallmeyer recalls:

After each burst I heard groans. Finally it stopped. At least three men had been killed and about 15 wounded. Two carriers were loaded and sent off southwards towards Bray and were told to take the first road to the right and there to await us. Whilst the last carrier was being loaded and the wounded attended to, the Germans appeared at very close range running and firing Schmeissers. One Bren started firing and I told Thorburn-Brown to protect our withdrawal by advancing down the road and when he had seen us round the corner 500 yards away, to follow us. We did not see his tank again. Somehow all the wounded and all the guns were got away, there were nine in the last carrier, and off we went. Halfway to the corner, I realised that the party from the house was not with us. The signal had been given, but either because the shelling had driven them to ground or the noise of the firing was too loud, they did not hear the whistle. It was too late to return.[7]

Brackley and his men were captured; Thorburn-Brown's tank was knocked out, and its commander killed. The rest of the squadron, by using a small track through the woods behind the original right sector of the defensive line, and with a certain amount of good fortune, escaped, and finally, after a trek of ten miles, rejoined the regiment that evening at Oisemont, in positions on the railway line to the right of the 2nd Seaforths. A Squadron's casualties were a hefty 40 out of 65 men, including two officer's killed and one captured. In comparison, C Squadron's losses of one killed and two taken prisoner were negligible. B Squadron, in reserve, was unlucky enough to lose Second Lieutenant Tighe and three men to a direct hit from a shell.

* * *

After the failure even to dent the Abbeville bridgehead the day before, the successful German advance of 5 June was a bitter pill for General Fortune and his staff to stomach, at their Battle Headquarters in Martainneville. With just one battalion, a handful of French tanks, and the composite tank regiment from the 1st Armoured Division, Fortune was hardly equipped to plug the gaps in his line. It was not the victory of German arms that had made those gaps; they were already there. The fault was the overlong front that his division was defending, made necessary by the imbalance of Allied to German divisions still in the field.

As reports of German incursions came in, Fortune threw in his reserves. First, the 4th Black Watch and the French tanks were sent to relieve Franleu and stabilise the line behind the 7th Argylls. They could only manage the latter, and even then too late to prevent some German troops from reaching the Bresle and, after being shot up by a troop from the composite armoured regiment, crossing the river and taking up positions behind the division in the Forêt d'Eu. As well as being used to patrol parts of the River Bresle, elements of the composite regiment were sent to hold Dargnies.

But these were piecemeal efforts, and could not prevent a general withdrawal of the division. Oddly enough, the French 31st Division, starting the day in the Moyenneville–Béhen sector, faced very little pressure until the afternoon, but had to retire with the Highlanders to avoid being outflanked. By evening, Fortune had received permission from General Altmayer at Tenth Army Headquarters, located way to the south at Lyons-la-Forêt, to move back during the night to the line Oisemont – railway to Vismes-au-Val – Aigneville – Feuquières – Woincourt – St Quentin.

Unit locations by the morning of 6 June were as follows: From

Oisemont to the *Route Nationale*, the line of the railway was manned by 152 Brigade with the 1st Lothians, 2nd Seaforths, 5th Gordons, and 4th Camerons holding from right to left. In reserve were the 4th Seaforths at Ramburelles. The French 31st Division was next, guarding the railway to the edge of Vismes; 153 Brigade then took up the line to near Hocquelus, with the 1st Black Watch on the right, and the 1st Gordons on the left; 154 Brigade at this time was little more than the 4th Black Watch, holding a dangerous salient with three companies covering from Hocquelus round to Fresseneville, although a platoon of 7th Argylls was at Woincourt and the headquarters personnel of the 8th Argylls were dug-in at Yzengremer. The men of the 6th Royal Sots Fusiliers, pioneers with no specialist infantry arms such as carriers or mortars, were still on the River Bresle from Le Tréport to Eu.

Despite the permission to withdraw to a new line – General Weygand's original instructions had been that there was to be no retreat from the Somme–Aisne line – Fortune was still a worried man. In just two days fighting he had lost the equivalent of over four infantry battalions in casualties; even in the charnel-house of the First World War this would have meant immediate relief. At midnight on 5 June, Fortune sent a message to Marshall-Cornwall at Tenth Army Headquarters asking him to intercede with Altmayer on behalf of the 51st Division. First, Fortune wanted the option to move back to the anti-tank obstacle of the River Bresle the following evening. Secondly, he wanted a reduction in his front of 50 per cent, citing as reasons the 'very trying and tiring' time on the Saar, the lack of 'a real night's rest for six weeks', and the 'sheer murder' of holding the 19 mile stretch. The response, received at the new Divisional Headquarters at Helicourt in the early hours of 6 June, was only partially favourable. Altmayer's Chief of Staff, de l'Orme, agreed to the withdrawal, but only on condition that the River Bresle was then held at all costs. Furthermore, the division's new front would stretch from Le Tréport to Senarpont, only a negligible reduction in length.

Although the new divisional line had only hastily dug defences and no natural anti-tank obstacle, it was a strong position with good observation and excellent fields of fire over the flat, open country to the north-east. Also of assistance to the defenders was the fact that the Germans did not seriously resume their attack until after midday on 6 June. This delay was in part due to the disruption caused by the number of besieged strongpoints still holding out behind German lines, but it was also part of a plan to allow the armoured divisions, attacking further south, time to encircle the left portion of the French

Tenth Army before it could retire south of the Seine.

There was some pressure in the morning on the left of the division's front. In 154 Brigade's area the remnants of the 8th Argylls at Yzengremer and the platoon of 7th Argylls at Woincourt had moved back by 8 am, covered by a squadron of tanks from the composite regiment, to Dargnies. From noon onwards, the 4th Black Watch was withdrawn from its dangerous salient and took up positions near to the River Bresle at Embreville and Hocquelus, while the men of the 7th and 8th Argylls moved back once again to hold the village of Incheville on the south side of the River Bresle.

The first determined attack of the day was put in against the 1st Lothians at Oisemont. On a slight hill, the town commanded flat, arable land for more than three quarters of a mile to the east, where some woodland began. B and C Squadrons were in positions holding the railway, right and left respectively. At dawn, General Fortune had personally rang Colonel Ansell to impress on him the importance of holding the position until nightfall. In theory, French cavalry units should have been dug-in to the right of the Lothians, but a patrol sent out to make contact searched for over seven miles and found nobody.

It was another beautiful, sunny day, and, for a few hours at least, you could forget that a war was on. Back at Regimental Headquarters, in a farm to the rear of the town, Ansell's despatch rider wrung the necks of some Aylesbury ducks and they were prepared for lunch. But the tranquil morning was an illusion, for the Germans were busily preparing an attack.

Number 6 (Carrier) Troop, commanded by Troop Sergeant Major Jimmy Hogarth, was in slit trenches on the right flank of the regiment, to the south of the town. Consequently, its right flank, which should have been covered by the French, was 'in the air'. There was an area of dead ground immediately to the front of the troop, but beyond that an excellent view of a main road leading diagonally across the front into Oisemont. In support, was a 25mm anti-tank gun from the Stornaway battery of the 51st Anti-tank Regiment. Hogarth, in the right of the two slit trenches, remembers the 'feelers' the Germans put out before advancing:

> About mid-morning we watched a black civilian saloon coming down the diagonal main road in front of us, up to a road block at the beginning of the village on our left front. It was stopped and turned back. This was obviously a 'look-see' by the Germans. Later a German motorcycle combination came down the road. It was fired on and quickly retired. Then a large eight-wheeled armoured car appeared, and also started to move back when it got near the road block. The anti-tank gun with us, by

common consent and common range speculation, opened fire on it, and, after bracketing it, hit it with the third round, leaving it on its side.

The time was now 4 pm and, within minutes, concentrated mortar and artillery fire had started against the Lothians' front, the prelude to the main infantry advance. Ahead of 6 Troop, the Germans came out of the woods and began to move across the open ground, well spread out in files of six men. Hogarth ordered his men to open up at a range of 900 yards, and they kept up a continuous fire until the barrels of the Brens were glowing red.

Also in support of B Squadron was a section of 7th Northumberland machine-gunners who did considerable execution. Its fire abruptly ceased when the barrage started and some *Messerschmitt* fighters started to strafe Oisemont from the air. Major Wattie McCulloch assumed the machine-gun must have been knocked out because, as he later wrote in his diary, 'it disappeared without so much as a "by your leave" or even the courtesy of a message'.[8]

At 7 pm, Ansell received word from Division that it was imperative to hold until midnight to give the infantry of the brigade time to withdraw. He was convinced his meagre force would have been overrun by then, but orders were orders and he started across the 400 yards of ground to Oisemont to give his squadron commanders the bad news. By this time the village was in flames, its oil tank blazing, its church flattened, and shell-holes pock-marking the main street.

To bolster the weary defenders, Ansell ordered up A Squadron and the tank crews from his reserve. It did not look as if the Germans could be held, especially as the flanking infantry had begun to pull out at 10 pm, but just as a number of the enemy reached the edge of the village, midnight struck and the regiment was able to move out. Number 6 Troop had to retire in its three carriers through the centre of Oisemont and Hogarth remembers his driver having to weave past and over an obstacle course of burning beams and debris. One of his carriers had been hit by shrapnel but it covered another 16 miles before it finally gave up the ghost. With the tanks of C Company covering the withdrawal, the regiment made for Blangy. In the early hours of the morning of 7 June they crossed the River Bresle and laagered in the Haute Forêt d'Eu.

For this heroic defence of the 'open' flank of the division, Colonel Ansell earned his 'Glory' nickname with the award of a DSO. Jimmy Hogarth got a DCM. Casualties were on the whole quite light, although Second Lieutenant Iain Lawrie of C Squadron had been killed by shellfire and three tanks were lost.

Holding the line to the right of the 1st Lothians, from Oisemont to Cerisy-Buleux, were the 2nd Seaforths of 152 Brigade. They too had had a peaceful morning, and Sergeant John Mackenzie of D Company even had time to buy some food and a pail of milk from a nearby farm, unaware that it was about to become embroiled in the storm of war. When the Germans debouched from the wood directly to the battalion's front, and started to move on Oisemont, the Seaforths, like the Lothians, had a good shoot. Mackenzie, in a position to the right of the battalion front, recorded the suicidal nature of the initial attack:

> The German infantry tried to assault on our right, coming on in waves and dying in mass formation. For hours it was mass slaughter, every Bren and (machine-gun) taking its toll. Roddy Graham [the Mortar Officer] and his mortars plastered the wood as the enemy emerged from it. It was the one occasion on which we really caught Jerry starting off on the wrong foot and we took full advantage. We had to put up with a lot from his planes, but B Company had all its riflemen firing at them and kept them at a good height. The attack on the right having failed, Jerry tried our left with no greater success, and towards 2030 hrs, in the failing light, started to infiltrate with 'Tommy-gunners'.[9]

At 6 pm, Colonel Barclay received orders to move back to the River Bresle, denying the enemy Cerisy-Buleux until 9.30 pm. This was later amended to 10 pm. As it was unlikely that all his sub-units would be able to disengage and form up as a battalion, Barclay ordered each company to move back independently and to rendezvous in the Forêt d'Eu. The time of withdrawal was later put forward again by Brigade to 9.30 pm, but as the battle was raging and it was difficult to move between companies, Barclay let the new time stand. This meant that when the 5th Gordons withdrew at the amended time, the Seaforths' left flank was exposed. Despite this, and even as the Germans closed on their positions, screaming like banshees, all companies were able to break off successfully. Major Godfrey Murray left last with the majority of D Company and a platoon of C Company after taking a bloody toll of the German vanguard. He and his party arrived at the Bresle at dawn, after the bridges had been blown, and were lucky to find a footbridge to cross. For this action, and good work later, Murray was awarded the DSO. Alec Ross, the Company Sergeant Major of C Company, also distinguished himself during the battle on 6 June, in which he was wounded, and won the DCM. He was evacuated, ultimately commissioned, and ended the war as a captain.

The whole withdrawal was covered by Second Lieutenant Bill

Cheyne's carriers, which did not leave the village until 10.25 pm with the enemy all around. They found the enemy on the bridge at the back of the village, blocking the exit, but drove them off with grenades. Two carriers from the section holding the right of the village were knocked out at this time by shellfire. The section commander, Sergeant Craig, sent his remaining two carriers ahead, and led the rest of his men back on foot without even a map or a compass. They turned up at the battalion rendezvous in the Forêt d'Eu at 11 am the following day. Oddly, neither Cheyne nor Craig were decorated.

While the main attack was being repulsed by the machine-guns of the 1st Lothians and the 2nd Seaforths, the battalions to their left were also managing to stand firm after a few early hiccups. The 4th Camerons at St Maxent were the first to be tested. Because the battalion was effectively down to two companies, its front was limited to positions in and on the edge of the village to the right of the *Route Nationale*. On the right flank were the 5th Gordons of 153 Brigade while a battalion of the French 31st Division was the other side of the main road. An international post, held by both the Camerons and the French, covered the approach up the main road.

At 4 pm, a direct frontal assault began against the right-hand company, a composite unit under Major Stanley Hill, the Battalion Second-in-Command. Initially, this was beaten back, but later, and possibly because many in the company were unfamiliar with each other, the right-hand Cameron platoon fell back without orders. This was spotted by 'Ginger' Gall, with his platoon of 5th Gordons, directly to the right of the Camerons.

> I could see the Camerons on my left scuttling away back. There was just one German vehicle of some sort in front. It wasn't threatening, and wasn't even in firing distance. The Camerons' headquarters must have seen these boys scampering and sent the carriers to get them back. I managed to intercept a section beside me, a Bren gunner and some others, and said, 'Where the hell do you think you're going. You come with me.' I repositioned them where I thought their positions were, then told the Bren gunner to fire in the direction of the German vehicle which withdrew. The lads I got hold of were shamefaced, but the rest had gone away. I still remember seeing this major with white hair, Stanley Hill I think it was, leading them back.

Thanks to Gall's quick action, and the work of a section of carriers who were sent up to support him, the line was secured until the errant

Camerons had been put back in position, and before the Germans could take advantage.

By 7 pm, the shelling and mortaring of St Maxent was causing many casualties and a German machine-gun had managed to get into position on the left flank of the village and was firing along the railway line, so cutting off the left company from Battalion Headquarters. The Germans had managed to set up this dangerous enfilade fire by forcing back the French guarding the Camerons' flank. At 8 pm, the Germans had reinforced the infiltrators on the left flank, and a heavy attack against the composite company was only stopped at 400 yards distance by desperate fire.

News reached Major Hill at 8.30 pm that the 5th Gordons had orders to move back an hour later. Starting at 9 pm, he began his company's withdrawal. Despite the presence of a French company preparing a defensive position 300 yards to the rear, Company Quartermaster Sergeant Gregor Macdonald remembers Hill's order as especially timely:

> We became aware of a massive build-up of German armour and infantry in the woods directly in front as we waited impatiently for instructions to withdraw. At last the order arrived, and as we prepared for departure, I sent Corporal Peter McIntosh to advise the French troops that we were withdrawing. Imagine our feelings when he returned to report that our allies had abandoned their prepared position and disappeared without trace. Before leaving, we planted six anti-tank mines around the level crossing, having obtained them from an RE section the previous day. During the evening, German shelling had set fire to a large expanse of forest two miles west of our position, and with this as a guide the 26 men of B Company set off.

Major MacLeay and his HQ Company had a more difficult task because of the troublesome machine-gun, but eventually a secure line of retreat out of the village was found. The Camerons in the International Post were brought back by Captain Ross. They stayed until 10.30 pm because their French comrades had orders to stay until then. Both companies crossed the River Bresle safely at Blangy, and marched from there into hides in the Forêt d'Eu.

Although the 5th Gordons fired an enormous amount of ammunition on 6 June – one machine-gun expending over 4,000 rounds – very little was at close quarters. The exception was during the withdrawal. Companies were ordered to move at 9.30 pm, while the carriers stayed a further 30 minutes to cover them. Unfortunately for the men of HQ

Company, a German machine-gun patrol had managed to work its way through the line and was covering the road they were supposed to move down. Lance Corporal George MacLennan, the medical orderly, remembers having to run the gauntlet:

> Bullets were coming through the hedge and no one knew where they were coming from because there weren't supposed to be any enemy near. We had to go down this road to a house at the corner where Major Christie and the Regimental Sergeant Major were lying. They were starting the men off, one after each other, with a few seconds in between. It was only a hundred yards but it seemed like a hundred miles.

By the time MacLennan reached safety, he had been hit by three bullets. Luckily, none had caused serious injury. One had hit the buckle of his gaiter, deflected through his boot and smashed the side of his ankle bone. Another had left a bright silver mark along the front of his helmet, while the third had passed harmlessly through his right hand pouch.

Covering the move back on the right of the battalion was Don Ritchie and a troop of his carriers. He had orders to support Captain Bill Lawrie's D Company until 9.30 pm, then to hold the position for a further 30 minutes to give the marching men time to get away. Ritchie decided to accompany the troop because he knew Lawrie was a bit edgy, a legacy of the Heydwald wood nightmare when he had lost most of his original company. This intuition was quickly confirmed. No sooner had he arrived with his four carriers at Company Headquarters, in a small farm outbuilding, then he was asked to return to Colonel Clark with a message from Lawrie that he did not think he could hold on until 9.30. Betraying his inexperience, Ritchie elected to take the message himself and set out on motorbike. He found Clark at a crossroads, studying a map and wearing nothing more protective than a soft cap, as dismissive of the flying shrapnel as a parent is of a tiresome child; ignore it long enough and it might go away. Clark listened to the message, and despite his exasperation calmly told Ritchie that the position had to be held, and that was why he had been sent up to help. Embarrassed by his gaffe, Ritchie returned, determined to make amends:

> So back I went and sent three of the carriers into the field in front to shoot up anything they could see. It was now about time for Bill Lawrie to leave, so he moved back with his company leaving just me and my four carriers. I realised that action in the carriers might result in them getting knocked out so I ordered the Bren gunners to dismount and arranged them in positions where we could put up a crossfire against any advance.

I left my driver and my batman in my carrier and I took the Bren gun out myself.

All the time they were shelling us, but I said, 'Ignore the shells, boys. Don't put your head down, that's what they want us to do.' They were hoping to rush us, and I knew damn fine they were coming through this long grass. I thought about setting it on fire but decided that was counter-productive as that would just create a smoke-screen.

Then I noticed that the opposition was going over to my right where the Seaforths had been, and that there was no firing from that area. So now we had a much wider field. I could see they were coming on, and as I looked at my watch I thought, 'What the hell do I do. If they get here before we're due to leave, do I sacrifice the section and carriers, or do I get out?' Fortunately I held on until the time, and immediately said, 'Okay boys, out!' There was a little shed just behind the position and I counted them there. One short. Then I heard a Bren, so I went back out but the bloody thing was firing at me. Suddenly it dawned on me that I had sent Sergeant Murray back with one of the wounded, which meant we were all there after all.

I was carrying the Bren and about 600 rounds of ammunition and, as I came out behind the shed, there was a section of Germans coming down the road, about 50 yards away. By the time I could have got the Bren into action they would have had me. But there was a corner, a wee turn in the lane, so I shot down it and got back to my carrier. The others had gone. I can remember my batman saying, 'Where the hell have you been, sir?' We didn't hang around.

Ritchie's nerve-wracking night was not over. He soon caught up with his section and was moving down a road towards the River Bresle when one of his men heard the tracks of a tank. Fearing it was German armour following up the withdrawal, Ritchie arranged his carriers into a road-block, placing his men on both sides of the road. His plan was to try and stop the tanks by blowing their tracks with grenades. As the clank of tracks grew louder, the Scotsmen held their breath, adrenalin coursing through their bodies, frozen in trepidation. Then a black hulk loomed out of the darkness and stopped. A voice called out, 'Where the hell are we?'

Recognising the Scots accent, Ritchie released a breath, recovered his voice and answered with a question of his own. 'Who are you?'

'Lothians and Border,' came the reply.

The gallant work of Ritchie's men, on both flanks of the battalion, had enabled the rifle companies to disengage successfully despite the proximity of the attacking Germans – as close as 50 yards in some cases. For his part, Ritchie was decorated with the Military Cross. After a four mile march, the battalion crossed the Bresle at Neslette, some 30 minutes before the divisional sappers blew the bridge. Taken by lorries to the Forêt d'Eu, the Gordons were welcomed back into 153 Brigade by Brigadier Burney in person.

Although they took the brunt of the fighting on 6 June, 152 Brigade exacted a timely revenge for the casualties they had suffered in a similarly ill-advised advance over open ground just two days earlier. The other two brigades and the French had also been attacked, but not with any great determination, and they escaped with very few losses. In 154 Brigade's sector, the composite armoured regiment did well in hull-down positions at Dargnies, deterring an attack and taking 40 prisoners.

By the early hours of 7 June, the 51st (Highland) Division and the French 31st Division were safely behind the River Bresle, but the move was not without its incidents. As the 4th Black Watch retired towards the Beauchamps crossing, they discovered that some Germans had beaten them to it. Fortunately, the battalion's anti-tank platoon, under Brigade control, had been sent there to help in the defence and it managed to drive the Germans off. At Ponts-et-Marais, a small village near Eu, Platoon Sergeant Major O'Neill of the 6th Royal Scots Fusiliers won a Military Medal for enabling the last-minute demolition of the bridge by sappers. Manning a post under machine-gun and mortar fire, O'Neill covered the demolition party and knocked out a light tank with an anti-tank rifle.

In general, the sappers did magnificent work: after waiting until all the troops were over, they had to go out, frequently under fire, to blow the bridges. At Eu, Sergeant Thornton of the 213th Field Company was in charge of the demolition. Faced with a sudden rush of Germans, he cut the length of the fuse to just a few inches, at great personal danger to himself, to blow the charge in time. He was awarded the DCM. At Beauchamps, sappers of the 239th Field Park Company captured three German motorcycle riders who rode into the village with the intention of directing traffic.

One unfortunate loss to the division, though, was Brigadier Stewart, commanding 152 Brigade. During an evening reconnaissance of the Forêt d'Eu, he was hit by shrapnel and had to be evacuated. Command devolved to Lieutenant Colonel Iain Barclay of the 2nd Seaforths.

* * *

General Victor Fortune had endured another tense day, wondering how long his men could survive the unequal struggle in which they were locked. During the afternoon, he received information from Tenth

Army Headquarters that the enemy had advanced well to the south and east of Oisemont, making a move back to the Bresle inevitable. It was this fear of being outflanked that had caused him to ask the Lothians to hold on until midnight.

Shortly after this news, Lieutenant General Karslake and Major General Beauman (recently promoted and his force designated a division) arrived. They found Fortune in his office in the new Advanced Divisional Headquarters at La Grande Vallée Château, three miles behind the Gamaches crossing. Karslake told Fortune that he had received instructions from London that the 51st Division would stay with the French, and, in the event of a withdrawal, would have to do so along its line of communication through Rouen. But even the order to move back across the Seine would have to come from the French, Karslake pointed out. Until it arrived, Fortune would just have to sit tight. At a stroke, the earlier arrangements made by Fortune and Beauman on 28 May for a move back into the Havre peninsula were null and void.

Disturbed by the news, Fortune voiced his opinion that the only way to save the division was by sticking to the plan to move back to Le Havre. Karslake agreed, telling Fortune that from information he had received an outflanking movement was likely. The problem as he saw it was that until General Brooke arrived, there was no BEF Commander with the right of appeal to the British Government. Fortune was shocked. He had always assumed that General Marshall-Cornwall had been sent out as *de facto* BEF Commander. In desperation, Fortune then asked how he could be expected to go on holding such a wide front when he had lost so many men and the rest were done in. After speaking privately to Beauman, Karslake offered a solution. 'A' Brigade from Beauman Division would swap with the depleted 152 Brigade, so allowing the latter some rest and more troops for Fortune to hold the Bresle position. If the 51st Division should retire to the Dieppe area, then the 2/7th Duke of Wellingtons, a Lines of Communication unit guarding the town, would also join the Highlanders. After what had already been said, this was small comfort. But thankful for any assistance, Fortune gratefully accepted and the two generals took their leave.

Aware, now, of the realities of the situation, Fortune decided to bypass Marshall-Cornwall and deal direct with Altmayer in a desperate attempt to save his beloved division. He sent for his French Liaison Officer from Tenth Army Headquarters and asked him to pass on a message direct to the army commander. He had two demands: he wanted his division to be relieved and placed in reserve, and he wished to relinquish command of the 31st Division. As reasons he cited his heavy losses, the exhaustion of his troops, and the difficulty of holding the wooded River Bresle. The liaison officer was shocked but agreed to pass on the request.[10]

Early the next morning, a reply arrived from General Altmayer in the shape of a message from Marshall-Cornwall. 'The Army Commander sympathises with the situation of your division', the British general wrote, 'but he much regrets that he has literally no reserve formation available with which to relieve you.' He, therefore, 'asks you to hang on to the Bresle line at all costs ... and to try to dislodge the enemy who have penetrated into the Forêt d'Eu'. Marshall-Cornwall went on to state that if it was still Fortune's wish, Altmayer had no objection to the 31st Division operating 'independently'.[11]

This was confirmation enough that Marshall-Cornwall's role was merely one of observation. He could only pass on the orders of Tenth Army Headquarters, and not even influence them. From now on, Fortune realised, he was on his own.

* * *

Despite his limited role, General Marshall-Cornwall had not given up his efforts to salvage the Highland Division. His mission was to advise the Imperial General Staff back in London of any French orders which might jeopardise British troops, and to this end he sent a telegram to General Dill on the evening of 6 June, before Fortune's request to be relieved had reached Tenth Army Headquarters. It read:

> Situation of the 51st Division is now serious. It has been fighting continuously for three days and has suffered heavy casualties. Has been forced to withdraw today to line of River Bresle from Gamaches to Tréport. Enemy infantry have infiltrated across Bresle into woods south of Eu... 51st Division is hardly fit for more fighting, and may crack if seriously attacked even on Bresle position. If politically undesirable to withdraw all British troops from front line I would urge that two more British Divisions with fighter support be sent urgently to France.[12]

Marshall-Cornwall had stumbled on to the real reason why the Highland Division could not be withdrawn. If the British Government wanted France to stay in the war it could not be seen to be deserting her. Indeed it would have to bolster her, and more divisions, if not more planes, were being prepared for embarkation to France. Furthermore, other events had already taken place that would make it even more impossible for the British to remove the Highland Division from French control.

On the morning of 6 June, General Spears had attended a meeting of the French War Committee in Paris. He was shocked, as he wrote

later, 'by the new line of approach' that Weygand's 'unflagging hostility
to the British led him to take':

> This time, General Fortune, commanding the 51st Division, was his
> target. He had, it seemed, fallen back without orders. It was quite
> intolerable. How could he, Weygand, conduct operations when such
> elements were included in his own reliable and disciplined forces? What
> had I to say? . . .
>
> General Fortune was behaving exactly as Lord Gort had done, as the
> British always did, he was now saying. 'I wish you to know that in my mind
> there is no doubt that General Blanchard was never able to obtain that
> the British Army should attack southwards. I am certain,' he went on,
> 'that the British Government ordered its Army to re-embark without
> informing the French Commander-in-Chief. Your General should be
> called "Misfortune".'
>
> . . . He was determined to link our alleged failure to support the French
> in the air to the pre-Dunkirk period. He was now literally yelling, in a
> high-pitched broken voice. 'What is happening in the air now is but a
> repetition of what happened in the north when the British refused to
> attack at Arras', he screamed . . . But there was something real and
> ominous under this spate of vitriol, and that was the clear indication that,
> before the fate of the present battle was cast, it was considered lost by the
> Commander-in-Chief and his excuse for this was British duplicity and
> delinquencies.[13]

Emerging from the meeting, shaken by Weygand's accusations,
Spears was taken aside by Marshal Pétain and told that the battle was as
good as lost because of the lack of reserves and the odds of two to one.
When Spears passed on an account of these two meetings to Churchill,
he only reinforced the latter's determination not to do anything further
to alienate the French political and military leaders, and give them an
excuse to seek an armistice. It had been obvious for some time that
neither Weygand nor Pétain had the will to continue the fight after
France fell, but Churchill was clutching at straws. All he could do was
pledge his support for the French and hope for the best.

That evening, General Dill formally notified General Georges of the
timetable for the arrival of more British troops. A brigade of the 52nd
(Lowland) Division would sail the following day but General Brooke,
the new Corps Commander, would not arrive for another week. Lord
Gort would resume command of the BEF when there were four infantry
divisions in France. Presumably with the warnings of Generals Karslake
and Marshall-Cornwall ringing in his ears, Dill also urged Brigadier
Swayne, head of the British Military Mission, to secure a line of retreat
for the 51st (Highland) Division across the lower Seine, where the new

BEF would concentrate, and not towards Le Havre. But anxious not to offend, Dill could only entreat the French High Command, not insist. Considering the anger already being expressed by the French at the Highland Division's withdrawal to the Bresle, and the new order to hold there at all costs, it was unlikely that this cautious approach would save the Scottish troops.

When General Karslake heard this news the following day, he sent a telegram to Dill urging him to send General Brooke without delay, otherwise the 51st Division was unlikely to survive. The reply was that Brooke could not arrive before 11 June at the earliest.

9

The Sickle Stroke

By the evening of 6 June, the swift advance of German armoured units to the south of the 51st Division was, as General Fortune feared, threatening to cut off the option of a withdrawal south of the Seine.

Spearheading the tank attack between Abbeville and Amiens was General Erwin Rommel's 7th Panzer Division, fresh from six days rest after trapping a French corps at Lille. For this feat, Rommel had been awarded the Knight's Cross by Hitler in person; now he was aiming to be the first German commander to reach the Seine. In the early hours of 5 June, Rommel's tanks rolled forward – as part of General Hermann Hoth's XV Panzer Corps of two panzer divisions and a motorised division – to attack units of the French X Corps holding the Somme between Hangest and Longpré. By an oversight, the French had left intact two railway bridges near Flixecourt, and Rommel's armour was able to use them to cross the canal. As night fell, the French had been pushed back and elements of his division had reached Montagne, eight miles beyond the Somme.[1]

Rommel's inexorable progress continued the following day, covering a further 12 miles south to the Poix – Aumale road. The other panzer division in Hoth's corps, the 5th Division, also made ground and was slightly to the north of Rommel's formation, while the 2nd Motorised Division was in support just behind. The XV Corps War Diary for 6 June reads:

> Avoiding woods, roads and adjoining villages and favoured by the gently undulating country practically free from ditches, the Corps advanced southwards across country, deployed with tanks in front and infantry in vehicles in rear.[2]

This policy of moving across country, avoiding barricaded roads and fortified villages, which could be reduced at leisure by the infantry following up, allowed a deep incision to be made in the French defences. A panzer division moving in this way, in extended order at speed, was an awesome spectacle. With a frontage of over a mile and a depth of 12 miles, the division was like an enormous lance: its steel-tip made up of tanks and motorcycle combinations, its shaft represented by motorised infantry and mobile anti-aircraft and field guns. And all the time supported by *Messerschmitt* 109 fighters and *Stuka* dive-bombers, the latter operating as a kind of airborne artillery.

At 9 pm on 6 June, Rommel went to Eplessier to discuss with General Hoth the plans for the following day. It was agreed that the corps would strike south-east towards Rouen, over 60 miles away. If successful, it would trap much of the French Tenth Army in the Havre peninsula, leaving embarkation as their only hope of escape.

Yet the fates had offered General Altmayer a chance to extricate the left portion of his army before it was too late. During the fighting on the 6th, an important Operation Order was found by the French on a dead German officer. It outlined the plan of advance for the XV Panzer Corps, stating that the area beyond the line held by the Support Group and Beauman Division was the objective for 7 June, with Rouen the target for the 8th. But Altmayer was unwilling to grasp this last opportunity to withdraw the divisions holding the Bresle south of the Seine because it would mean disobeying Weygand's inflexible orders to stand and fight to the last. Instead he made plans to try to hold the tank advance.

In the early evening of 6 June, Generals Beauman and Evans were called to a conference at Lyons-la-Forêt. Evans was asked by Altmayer to use his remaining 50 tanks, some only half-repaired, to bolster the men of Beauman Division holding the Andelle, directly in the path of the projected panzer attack. When Beauman asked Altmayer if there were any plans for withdrawing the 51st Division, he was told such a move was not necessary because his forces were preparing to counter-attack in the Poix area to seal the gap made by the panzers. Unimpressed with this promise, and pessimistic about their own tasks, the two British divisional commanders left the conference convinced that the Highlanders were doomed.

* * *

Although fears of an armoured breakthrough further south were never far from General Fortune's mind, most of his preoccupations on 7 June were with how to defend his own 13 mile front on the River Bresle between the coast and Gamaches. It was anything but an ideal defensive position. Marking the boundary between Picardy to its east and Normandy to its west, the Bresle was a relatively small river, in places only three feet deep with shallow mud banks. Even more ominous than this was the fact that it followed a densely-wooded course, allowing easy infiltration by an attacker.

Despite these inherent weaknesses, General Fortune had tried to make the best of the position. He had moved the French 31st Division to the right, in anticipation of being allowed to relinquish its command, and it extended the defences on the river to Senarpont. Beyond the 31st Division was the newly arrived French 40th Division, whose presence had made possible the small reduction in the Highland Division's front. The line was held by those units commanded by the division that had suffered the least. 153 Brigade was dug-in from Gamaches to the edge of what had been the bridge opposite the tiny village of Le Lieu Dieu, with the 1st Black Watch and the 1st Gordons up, right and left respectively, and the 5th Gordons in reserve in woods near Brigade Headquarters at Millebosc. The 4th Black Watch, still in 154 Brigade, then held to Incheville, with the combined company of 7th and 8th Argylls resting further back near Longroy. 'A' Brigade, from Beauman Division, had arrived at the Bresle the previous afternoon, and its 4th Borders was guarding the river to Eu, where the 6th Royal Scots Fusiliers was still in position as far as Le Tréport and the sea, with the composite armoured regiment in support behind.

Little pressure was exerted on the Bresle line on 7 June, but this was a mixed blessing. The Germans were deliberately slackening off the advance on this front to allow their panzers time to execute a sickle stroke and surround the left of the Tenth Army. Oblivious to this, the Jocks were grateful for a chance to have a decent feed and grab some much needed rest. It also enabled the smooth integration of some 900 reinforcements, mostly raw recruits, who had been ordered up from the Base Depot in Rouen by General Karslake. But there was still the problem of the 200 or so Germans who had crossed the Bresle and entered the Forét d'Eu, because they were a constant danger to the division's lines of communication. 'A' Brigade was given the tricky task of flushing out the interlopers, and during the hours of daylight men of the 4th Borders and a company of the 1/5th Foresters struggled through the dense woods. Owing to the difficult terrain, though, the pocket was still holding out by nightfall in the north-west of the forest. To help contain this sector, tanks of the 1st Lothians and the composite regiment were brought up.[3]

* * *

While the 51st Division was enjoying a day of relative calm on the Bresle, the armoured advance further south continued. Directly in the path of this thrust was the 1st Armoured Division's Support Group, still under General Fortune's orders and holding a massive 60 mile, east-facing front from Senarpont on the Bresle to Forges-les-Eaux. At Forges, the defences linked up with Beauman Division's 'B' and 'C' Brigades guarding the line of the Béthune and Andelle Rivers.

Holding a W-shaped position on the right of the Support Group's front, from Aumale to Forges, were the 2/6th East Surreys. This Territorial battalion had arrived in France in April, as part of the 12th Division, a largely untrained and poorly-equipped formation whose initial role was to guard the BEF's Lines of Communication. Towards the end of May, it was incorporated into 'Beauforce' (later Beauman Division), and on 3 June it took over from the 4th Borders as the infantry battalion attached to the Support Group. The same day, morale was dealt a severe blow when the CO, Lieutenant Colonel Burgess, was relieved of his command by General Karslake. His crime had been to request that his battalion be relieved so that it could complete its training and be properly equipped. Burgess's motive was the same as Buchanan-Smith's had been in the Saar. His men were mostly local Surrey men and he knew them off-parade as friends. He felt responsible for them and suspected that they were about to be asked to perform an impossible role. He was right.

The 700 men of the East Surreys were ranged along a huge front of 24 miles, the equivalent of just one man every 60 yards and with no defence in depth. They were backed up by anti-tank guns from a battery of the 51st Anti-tank Regiment, one every half mile. Their equipment was pitiful: no mortars, grenades, wireless, no artillery in support, and even the officers' pistols had been bought privately in France. Ammunition had been issued at a paltry 50 rounds per man, 500 for each Bren gun. With this they were expected to take on an armoured division.

At 9 am, the widely spaced posts of the East Surreys, grouped close to roads and villages, were attacked by the tanks of the 5th Panzer Division. The brunt of the attack fell on A Company, holding the first leg of the 'W' south from Aumale. Within hours most of the anti-tank guns had been destroyed and 8 and 9 Platoons had been virtually overrun, although Company Headquarters, a little to the rear at Rothois, had been augmented by some French mechanised troops. As before, the tanks did not hang around to snuff out all resistance. They forged ahead and left the cleaning up to the infantry behind. Not involved in the morning's fighting was 7 Platoon, on the edge of a forest to the east of Aumale, but by 4 pm a runner arrived to report that 40 tanks, backed up by artillery and infantry, had broken through immediately to the south, and the remnants of 8 Platoon had fallen back on Rothois. Second Lieutenant Redfern, 7 Platoon Commander, takes up the story:

> About 1700 hours, two Germans came down the road looking for mines and there was automatic fire on my left; shortly after Lance Corporal

Marriot and some of his men joined us, reporting they had been surprised by the enemy. Two lorries of German infantry then came down the road and we opened fire with the two pounder anti-tank gun, destroying both of them. Later, German infantry came into view and we forced them to take cover from our bren and rifle fire. They then tried to encircle us but we stopped them having arranged all round defence. Stalemate continued until 1900 hours when the Germans made use of some cover behind some refugees moving along the road and came round my right flank. Ten minutes later hand grenades were thrown, putting the anti-tank gun out of action with casualties to the gun crew, and firing started from the rear and both flanks. After refusing calls to surrender, they charged but stopped when they saw we had fixed bayonets. Machine-gun fire was exchanged until dark (about 2200 hours) when I emerged from my weapon pit to find four others, including my platoon sergeant, still alive. We saw to the wounded and left them food and water, then collecting the remnants withdrew towards Company Headquarters.[4]

As they moved back down a forest track in the direction of Rothois, Redfern and his band were challenged in German. One soldier panicked and shouted back, 'Don't shoot, we're English!' A grenade was the response, its explosion lighting up the night, and wounding Redfern in the leg. Realising that the way was blocked, Redfern whispered through clenched teeth to his batman to tell the men to move back 100 yards in the direction they had come where he would be waiting. They never arrived. Hobbling on his own, Redfern eventually managed to cross the River Bresle at a weir the following morning and bumped into a party of French *chasseurs* holding a road, narrowly missing the mines they had just sown. They sent him back to Rouen in a truck and he finally crossed the Seine at Evreux, much to the annoyance of some engineers who were about to blow the bridge. He reached St Nazaire on 13 June, and that night was evacuated back to Britain in a hospital ship. For his tenacious defence of the road to Aumale, Redfern was awarded the Military Cross.

By nightfall, the 2/6th East Surreys were still holding their ground, although all contact had been lost with A Company. But this was a technicality. The armour of the 5th Panzer Division had passed through with few losses, and it was only a matter of time before the East Surreys would be mopped up if they stayed where they were.

News of the tank attack against the Support Group reached Fortune's headquarters at noon. Appreciating that his lines of communication were in jeopardy, Fortune ordered two further batteries of the 51st Anti-tank Regiment to set up a series of tank stops from Foucarmont to Neufchâtel, a line facing south-east about 12 miles behind Aumale.

The position of the Support Group was now something of an anomaly. It had originally been posted as flank protection for the 51st Division during a possible withdrawal towards Le Havre. Not only was that move now out of the question, but the insertion of the 31st and 40th French Divisions between the Highlanders and the Support Group meant control was very difficult. In view of the need to keep a line of retreat to Rouen open, Fortune was persuaded by Brigadier Morgan, the commander of the Support Group, who happened to be visiting Divisional Headquarters at La Grande Vallée, to return it and the composite tank regiment to the 1st Armoured Division, which was moving into a position on the Andelle to try and stem the armoured avalanche. Morgan was sent back that night with the orders, but the Support Group, in his absence, had moved back into the Basse Forêt d'Eu, and he was unable to find them. Both Morgan and the composite armoured regiment made it to the Seine, but the Support Group remained with the Highlanders to the end.

The impressive gains made by the 5th Panzer Division on 7 June were surpassed only by those of Rommel's 'Ghost' Division. On that day, his 200 tanks swept forward more than 30 miles to the area around Saumont, just four miles south-east of Forges-les-Eaux. Elements of his reconnaissance battalion reached the banks of the River Andelle, near Sigy, seven miles further on. To be fair to the 5th Panzer Division, it had faced the task of breaching the British line at Aumale, while Rommel's men had not come up against any opposition worthy of the name; they would not encounter the Beauman Division and the tanks of the 1st Armoured Division until the following day.

But as far as the Tenth Army was concerned, this move was decisive. It was now effectively split into two halves, and to cope with this disruption Altmayer ordered a corps headquarters to be hastily set up to command the stranded northern half. General Ihler was put in charge of this new IX Corps, and under his orders came the 51st Division, the French 31st and 40th Divisions, and the remnants of the two light cavalry divisions, the 2nd and 5th DLCs.

In the evening, the small, spry figure of General Weygand himself arrived at Tenth Army Headquarters to hold a conference with Generals Altmayer, Marshall-Cornwall and Evans. He told them that the battle being fought by the Tenth Army was the 'decisive' one of the war and that, as no French reserves were available, all depended on the 1st Armoured Division holding the ten miles of the River Andelle from

Nolleval to Serquex. Evans took the opportunity to explain that his division no longer had any artillery, anti-tank weapons, or infantry, and, as such, it was unsuited for a defensive role. Weygand brushed aside this protest, but conceded that if the Andelle could not be held, then Evans could withdraw his tanks across the Seine in readiness for a subsequent counter-attack.

Following Weygand's departure, Marshall-Cornwall held lengthy discussions with Altmayer on the plans to repel the armoured advance and to safeguard the left of his army. In a telegram sent to General Dill late that night, he recorded his impressions:

> Have attended three hour conference at Tenth Army Headquarters after Weygand's visit. Regret I have lost confidence in ability of French leaders or troops to stop German drive to Seine. Only rear barrier is Evans' force of 50 tanks used as blockhouses on River Andelle. Have requested Tenth Army Commander to order 51st Division and neighbouring French Division to withdraw quietly to River Béthune, otherwise they will be trapped. German tanks already reached Forges les Eaux. Army Commander refused to do so without orders from higher authority. I suggest you come over and see Weygand immediately. Otherwise we shall have to evacuate 51st from Dieppe beach . . .[5]

By the early hours of 8 June, it was obvious to the British High Command and the War Office that the 51st Division was in serious jeopardy. British generals in France had repeatedly warned of the danger of encirclement, and the need to plan a line of withdrawal. But nothing had been done beyond vague requests. Now, even if an order to retire south of Seine was issued, it would be too late. Evacuation by sea was the only alternative, but no one was prepared to raise this scenario with the French for fear of fragmenting the Alliance. And it was a very genuine fear. Even the most Anglophile member of the French Government, the Premier Paul Reynaud, was beginning to show signs of believing Weygand's absurd claims that General Fortune was to blame for the most recent setbacks. In a telegram sent to Churchill on 7 June, Reynaud stressed the importance of the Highland Division's role which was to protect the road to Le Havre, so 'necessary to the existence of Paris'. He continued:

> I ought to tell you on this point that, although he has been placed under the orders of General (Robert) Altmayer, General Fortune withdrew the day before yesterday on his own initiative to the Bresle. Yesterday he allowed enemy elements to infiltrate to the south of the Bresle through the forest of Eu. When General Altmayer asked him this morning to drive out these enemy elements, he did nothing about it, and asked to be

relieved. General Weygand reminded General Altmayer that General Fortune was under his command and that he should obey the orders given to him. I would be obliged if you would see your way to confirming these instructions to General Fortune.[6]

If Reynaud was joining the hunt for a scapegoat, then the French really were standing at the edge of the armistice abyss, and it would not take much to push them into it.

* * *

General Marshall-Cornwall woke early on 8 June, and was surprised to find frantic activity. There was no sign of General Altmayer or his Chief of Staff, de l'Orme, and it was only by questioning a harassed staff officer that Marshall-Cornwall discovered the unpalatable truth. Tenth Army Headquarters had packed up and left Lyons-la-Forêt for Marines an hour earlier, at 6 am, and no one had even bothered to tell the British general. The activity was the departure of the rear party.

Almost speechless with anger, Marshall-Cornwall arranged for transport to follow General Altmayer and to lodge his protest in the strongest terms. But on arriving in Marines three hours later, he quickly understood that protest was futile. Altmayer was a drowning man, broken by the unfair struggle, and could no longer be relied on to command with any competence. The sudden move, initiated by him, had left his staff in chaos and communications with his two corps nonexistent. When pressed by Marshall-Cornwall to order the withdrawal of the IX Corps to the line of the River Béthune near Dieppe, he repeated the same old excuse: he could not do so without orders from the High Command. Realising further protests were pointless, Marshall-Cornwall set out for General Weygand's headquarters in Paris with the intention of using the priority phone line back to the War Office in London. At 1 pm he managed to get through, and spoke to a Lieutenant Colonel Isaac who took a message for General Dill. After describing what had taken place that day, Marshall-Cornwall got down to the nitty-gritty. 'General Altmayer is broken down and incapable of commanding,' he told Isaac. He went on to issue a dire warning, and his solution:

I consider the 51st Division in imminent danger of having its communications cut, and may have to be partially evacuated from the coast.

General Fortune should at once be released from French military control – certainly from that of Tenth Army – and given independent role of withdrawing his Division by successive lines to the Béthune and the Lower Seine, in contact with French 31st Division on his right ...

> Very doubtful how long Evans and Beauman can hold Andelle Line, and their flanks are threatened.
>
> Karslake should prepare [for destruction] all possible temporary bridges, boats and ferries over Lower Seine above and below Rouen.
>
> Situation in gap very obscure. 2nd French Armoured Division counter-attacked south of POIX at 2000 hours on the 7th and destroyed some German tanks, but failed to close the neck.[7]

Ironically, 40 minutes before this conversation, the War Office had sent a signal to Major General Howard-Vyse, its liaison officer to General Weygand, instructing him to inform the French Commander-in-Chief that 'unless orders were given soon for the manoeuvre of Allied wing', there was a 'grave risk of British troops being trapped'. He was also to represent in the 'strongest terms that evacuation between Dieppe and Le Havre cannot be contemplated'.[8] This was the War Office's response to Marshall-Cornwall's message of the previous evening, warning that unless the 51st Division was allowed to withdraw to the River Béthune it would be trapped. Given the plan for a new BEF to be concentrated around Le Mans, it follows that if the 51st Division was in danger, the War Office would want it to retire over the Seine in that direction. But on no account was it to be evacuated from the coast because that would be seen by the French as another Dunkirk, another betrayal.

The War Office's response to Marshall-Cornwall's latest warning – that the 51st Division 'was in danger of having its communications cut' and 'should at once be released from French military control' – was simply a repeat of its first unhelpful message. Howard-Vyse was instructed 'to press that any necessary withdrawal' by the 51st Division 'should be' in the direction of Le Mans, 'as already suggested.'[9]

At 5.15 pm, the Defence Committee met at Downing Street in London to discuss both Marshall-Cornwall's message and repeated telegrams from Reynaud asking for more fighter support. Among those present were Churchill, General Dill, Archibald Sinclair, the Secretary of State for Air, Air Marshal Pierse, the Vice Chief of the Air Staff, and Lord Beaverbrook, Minister of Aircraft Production. From the composition of the committee, it was clear that the request for planes was at the top of the agenda, with the fate of the 51st Division some way behind. After hearing a summary of Marshall-Cornwall's telephone call, Churchill ignored the implications and began to talk about Reynaud's request. There were, he said, 'two alternatives': They could 'regard the present battle as decisive' and throw in all their fighters in an attempt 'to bring about victory', but failure would lead to surrender. On the other hand, they could accept that while the 'present land battle was of great importance', it would not prove 'decisive one way or the other for Great Britain'. As long as Britain remained strong, Churchill emphasised, she could win the war and thereby restore France to her former position. Agreeing to French demands, he said, would only undermine Britain's safety. The conclusion was that the committee unanimously agreed to keep the five RAF fighter squadrons in France up to strength, while a further six could operate from Britain over France in co-operation with bombing raids.[10] In a draft response to Reynaud's requests, Churchill made clear his belief that the battle in France was as good as lost, but this did not have to mean the end of the war for either party:

> The additional fighter aircraft for which you press me cannot play any decisive part in this great land battle. They might give temporary relief and then they would be burnt up and cast away; whereas if not cast away they afford the means by which we expect to prolong the war until the United States comes in, or even indefinitely, thus saving not only ourselves but France. I understand your feelings and Weygand's and am doing my utmost to help, but there is no reason why you should give in if this battle goes against you, and certainly it must not be the end of the resistance of Great Britain for then all hope of final victory would be gone ...[11]

Presumably because this original message was considered too pessimistic, it was never sent. Instead, a short note, mentioning that Britain was giving all the support it could short of ruining its capacity to continue the war, was despatched. No mention of the 51st Division was made. In Churchill's eyes, Marshall-Cornwall's assessment of the military situation ignored the political reality. With French politicians and generals using every opportunity to accuse Britain of treachery, and the atmosphere becoming increasingly poisoned by Britain's refusal to send the fighters France had requested, how could the 51st Division be released from French control, let alone evacuated, without this being seen as the last straw?

There is no record in the minutes of the Defence Committee meeting as to whether or not any decisions were taken regarding the dilemma of the 51st Division. Perhaps this omission tells its own story. But was it a coincidence that, a few minutes before midnight, the War Office sent a signal to the Admiralty ordering that 'the blocking of Dieppe could be carried out forthwith, as it was probable that our own troops would be South of R. Béthune by first light 10 June'.[12] Despite Marshall-Cornwall's warning that 'the 51st Division may have to be partially evacuated from the coast', the War Office was still prepared to authorise the sealing off of its nearest point of escape.

* * *

Unaware of the unsavoury horse-trading taking place between the British and French governments, the men of the 51st (Highland) Division were enjoying another relatively peaceful day. The Germans to their front were making no great effort to pierce the Bresle line, content to let the panzers do the work further south. Once again, most of the fighting was confined to the north-eastern part of the Forêt d'Eu where the 1/5th Sherwood Foresters and the 4th Borders made another, unsuccessful, attempt to snuff out the infiltrators.

The only other battalion in action was the 4th Black Watch. It had already suffered a number of casualties from shelling, including many cases of shell-shock, because it had abandoned its entrenching tools during the hurried withdrawal to the Bresle and was not properly dug-in. At dawn, C Company, holding the high ground to the south-east of Incheville, was attacked and a number of Germans managed to infiltrate between 14 and 15 Platoons and into the dense wood behind. Undoubtedly, a factor in this was the accidental shelling of C Company's positions by, of all people, the Regulars of the 23rd Field Regiment, who were trying to ward off the attack. The gunners had made a slight error in line and it cost C Company about 25 per cent casualties in just a few minutes shooting. Colonel Macpherson, who requested the barrage, later speculated on the cause: 'Probably fatigue, possibly rather a stupid RA Officer attached to my HQ...'.[13]

In an effort to re-establish the line, 7 and 8 Platoons of A Company and a section of Second Lieutenant David Innes' carriers were sent up. The action was something of a fiasco. Captain Graham Pilcher, the Signals Officer, was wounded in the shoulder; Second Lieutenants Innes and Envy and many other ranks were killed, the former as he led a sortie from his carrier. Eventually, elements of both A and C Companies arrived at B Company's positions to the right. Only after Captain Thomson had rounded up these stragglers was he able to re-establish some semblance of a line.

The only other event of note this day concerning the infantry battalions was the relief of the Earl of Cawdor, CO of the 4th Camerons. At a morning interview with General Fortune, Cawdor was told that he was worn out and that he was being sent back to Britain to rest. He was indeed in bad shape, but it was mental rather than physical fatigue. A sensitive man from the noble family immortalised in Shakespeare's *Macbeth*, Cawdor was not best suited to the pressures of war. Like Buchanan-Smith of the 5th Gordons, he thought of the battalion as a family and was devastated by the loss of so many men on the Somme.

He was the last of the non-Regular COs, and his fate reinforced the argument of those who felt that, initially, all the battalions should have been headed by professionals. His replacement, Major Ronnie Mackintosh-Walker MC, a Regular Seaforths officer, had arrived the day before with the 900 reinforcements.

* * *

General Marshall-Cornwall's efforts during the morning of 8 June had not been entirely in vain. While at General Weygand's headquarters, he had managed to persuade the aged *Generalissimo* that it made sense to withdraw IX Corps over the Seine to fight another day, now that the counter-attack against the armoured breakthrough had failed. As communications between the Tenth Army and the IX Corps no longer existed, Weygand sent the order direct to General Ihler, in his headquarters at Bures. The problem, now, was time. If the panzers broke through the Andelle line – which was virtually inevitable – the horse-drawn transport of the French divisions would never be able to reach the Seine before them. The Highland Division, highly mobile due to its motorised transport, might have made it, but it was under French orders and on no account could it desert its allies.

During the afternoon of 8 June, General Fortune was called to a conference of divisional commanders at Ihler's IX Corps Headquarters to discuss plans for the withdrawal to Rouen. On the way, he was crossing a bridge over the River Béthune when he noticed that Royal Engineers, attached to Beauman Division, were preparing it for demolition. Realising it would be needed by his men for any withdrawal, he ordered them to leave it. This was just as well because Beauman Division had already destroyed a number of bridges on the same river, prior to their departure, without informing IX Corps.

At the conference, the assembled generals were told by Ihler that he had decided to move the Corps back in stages, holding the River Eaulne on 9 June, the River Béthune on the 10th, the River Varenne on the 11th, a line through the village of Tôtes on the 12th, and finally arriving in Rouen on the night of 12/13 June. If Fortune was frustrated at the snail's pace of this proposed move, he did not show it, but he must have realised that the panzers were unlikely to afford IX Corps anything like the time needed.

Hurrying from the conference, Fortune arrived at Melleville, 'A' Brigade Headquarters, at 6 pm in time for the divisional conference he had arranged to discuss the move with his commanders. His plan was for just two brigades to hold the 51st Division's share of the line, allowing the remaining two to leapfrog behind to the following day's position. In this way, only half the division would be in action at any time, while the other half could rest. For the first night, 153 and 'A' Brigades would move back to the River Eaulne, from near Envermeu to the sea, while 152 and 154 Brigades took up positions behind this on the River Béthune from one mile south of Martigny to Dieppe. Divisional Headquarters was scheduled to open the following morning at La Chausée, behind the Béthune.

With the carriers and the tanks of the 1st Lothians acting as rearguard, the withdrawal began at 11 pm and was carried out success- fully with most troops in their new positions by the morning of 9 June. 152 Brigade was already on the Béthune, having moved there on the night of 7/8 June. To conform with the new line, the brigade was shifted to the left to hold from Arques-la-Bataille to Dieppe. The 2/7th Duke of Wellington's Regiment was still holding the town of Dieppe, and from this time it came under 152 Brigade's orders. Two units that never made it back were D Company of 4 Borders and A Company of the 1/5 Sherwood Foresters. Located in woods near the Incheville crossing, they never received the order to move back and heroically managed to hold out until 13 June. During this time they captured a number of Germans, withstood all attacks and denied the use of the crossing to the enemy. Certainly, this confused the Germans and delayed the pursuit, but they rarely advanced at night and, because of developments further south, would have not have followed up hard anyway.

Apart from the two companies left on the Bresle, the only other troops to suffer because of the move on the night of 8/9 June were those of the 5th Gordons. Orders had arrived too late to enable the battalion to arrange its transport, and it had to march the 18 miles back to its positions on the River Eaulne in the dark. All equipment – including picks and shovels, arms and ammunition – had to be carried, and it was a very exhausted body of men that arrived at Bellengreville at 8.30 the next morning.

* * *

Even as General Ihler finalised his plans for the unrealistic four-day withdrawal of IX Corps to Rouen, the lightning progress of the XV Panzer Corps on 8 June had made them redundant. At the compar- atively late hour of 10 am, the tanks of the 7th Panzer Division moved off towards Sigy on the River Andelle. Faced with stiff resistance there from the under-equipped troops of Beauman Division, a ford was discovered a few hundred yards south and the first tanks crossed. At the same time, Rommel received a wireless signal from his reconnaissance troop saying that it had taken two bridges at Normanville, two miles further south still. With typical flexibility, Rommel broke off the fighting at Sigy and moved all his armour and men to the bridgehead. While most of the tanks continued the advance westwards, a force was sent north to Sigy which was taken in the rear at 2 pm, with the capture of 100 British prisoners. During this fighting there was no sign of the tanks of the 1st Armoured Division. In fact, Rommel had luckily chosen a weak spot between the remnants of the two armoured brigades, which could not possibly guard the whole front.

Further north, the 5th Panzer Division attacked the defences at Serqueux, just above Forges-les-Eaux, in the gap between the Béthune and Andelle river lines. Here the men of Beauman Division were backed up by some tanks, but the combined fire of artillery, mortars, dive-bombers, machine-guns and tank guns proved too much. The Germans even used captured French tanks to try to hoodwink the defenders, but this was hardly necessary. Most of the British infantry only had rifles. While some of the tanks had 2-pounders, the rest were armed just with machine-guns. The fight for Serqueux was an exaggerated microcosm of the Battle for France as a whole – a disadvantage in both numbers and equipment – but a microcosm none the less. With the inevitable shattering of the Andelle line, the usefulness of Beauman Division and the remnants of the 1st Armoured Division was over. Survivors from both formations made their way south and crossed the Seine that evening.

By 8 pm, Rommel's panzers had reached a crossroads five miles east of Rouen. He could easily have continued on and captured the capital of Normandy that night. But, convinced that his arrival would be expected, and the bridges blown the minute his tanks appeared, Rommel had earlier received permission from General Hoth to try the unexpected and storm the bridges over the Seine at Elbeuf, 15 miles to the south-west. Parties from his motorcycle battalion, supported by five tanks, were given the task, but the bridges were blown at 3 am when they were within a few hundred yards. That same night, the 5th Panzer Division reached the outskirts of Rouen. Ferries below Rouen were now the only means by which the French IX Corps could cross the Seine, and these were hardly suitable for such numbers.

* * *

As the net closed in around IX Corps, the British Government was at last making some attempt to salvage its troops. There were still 160,000 British soldiers in France, most of them non-combatants, and on 8 June the Admiralty was instructed to prepare plans – codenamed *Operation Aerial* – for their possible evacuation from the north-western ports. This was similar to Dunkirk's *Operation Dynamo* when suitable boats were rounded up days before the order to embark was given.

Trapped in the Havre peninsula, along with the 51st Division, were the 1,200 men of the British garrison at Le Havre and a number of Lines of Communication troops operating and guarding the numerous supply dumps. The evacuation of these men was likely to be far less damaging to Anglo-French relations than that of a fighting division, and Admiral Sir William James, Commander-in-Chief Portsmouth, was given the job of preparing for it. Although part of *Operation Aerial*, this was a separate task and was given a title in its own right – *Operation Cycle*. By the evening of 8 June, Admiral James had managed to collect together over 200 boats – 67 merchant ships and the rest smaller craft. This vast armada included everything from cross-channel ferries and Dutch *schuyts* to harbour tugs and small yachts. In anticipation of the order for evacuation, the boats sailed the following morning for Le Havre, escorted by destroyers.[14]

Operation Cycle was never intended to include the 51st Division. As far as the War Office was concerned, the French High Command had ordered the IX Corps to retire on the Seine, and the Highlanders would have to obey. But on the same day, the War Office decided to send two naval officers – Commander Elkins and Lieutenant Commander Elder – with a radio set and two signallers to join the 51st Division and so enable it to keep in touch with a destroyer, HMS *Wanderer*, operating just off the French coast. The initial plan was for these officers to arrange bombardments from the sea to impede German progress. But with the severing of communications between the Tenth Army and the IX Corps, the radio set would also enable the War Office to keep tabs on the Highland Division. The naval officers could fulfil another role: during his briefing by a Major Groves of the War Office, Commander Elkins was told that, if need be, he would be called upon to make arrangements for evacuation.[15]

10

The Net Closes

News that German armour had reached Rouen, causing the bridges across the Seine to be blown, arrived at the 51st Divisional Headquarters in the Château de La Chaussée via an unlikely source. At 7 am that morning, acting on advice from General Marshall-Cornwall that he should move back his heavy equipment, General Fortune had ordered the 110 slow-moving vehicles and 11 remaining 6-inch howitzers of the 51st Medium Regiment to cross the Seine at Rouen. After brushing with some German motorcycle troops on the way, the advance guard of the regiment arrived in Rouen at 10 am, just in time to see the last bridge go up. An attempt to use another crossing to the east was aborted when German motorised infantry were encountered. The Adjutant was sent back to La Chausée to pass on the news and to ask for orders, and it was the arrival of this officer, shortly before midday, that confirmed everyone's fears. The Germans were at Rouen and the only line of retreat, bar the impractical ferries, had been cut.

Shortly after, a staff officer sent by Admiral Platon, the French naval officer commanding at Le Havre, arrived at La Chausée with a similar message. According to Colonel Swinburn's diary, the message stated that 'the Admiral had orders to arrange embarkation from Le Havre if necessary, embarkation to be carried out by his orders only'.[1]

Taking the French naval staff officer with him, Fortune immediately set off for the IX Corps Headquarters at Bures to acquaint General Ihler with the news and to discuss the next move. By coincidence, Ihler was on his way to Fortune's headquarters. Once there he was informed of the situation, at which point, according to Colonel Swinburn, 'he showed great distress and appeared to consider that nothing could be done to extricate the Corps'. Shortly afterwards, Fortune returned and, seeing Ihler in this state, took charge. His plan was to make for Le Havre in four bounds, arriving there on 13 June. This slow withdrawal was necessary because of the French divisions' mostly horse-drawn transport, which could only cover 15 miles a day. With Le Havre 60 miles away, it would take them at least four days. Ihler accepted the plan in its entirety. The other four French divisional commanders, who had already been called to a conference at corps headquarters, were now summoned to La Chausée and informed of the changes.[2]

* * *

Perhaps the greatest tragedy of this campaign was that General Fortune chose the port of Le Havre and not Dieppe as his point of embarkation. After all, with panzer divisions already in Rouen by the morning of 9 June, it was inevitable that they would be able to reach Le Havre well before 13 June, or at the very least sever the IX Corp's line of retreat. Dieppe, on the other hand, was within a day's journey of the whole of the corps.

At least part of the explanation is that General Fortune had been led to believe that Dieppe harbour was unsuitable for embarkation. As early as 28 May, when embarkation was first discussed by Fortune and Brigadier Beauman, Dieppe was dismissed as an option because of bomb damage and mines at the harbour entrance. On 9 June, Colonel Swinburn wrote in the General Staff War Diary that the option of Dieppe was 'dismissed as impractical owing to the .... destruction of the harbour at an earlier date'.[3]

In fact, by 9 June Dieppe still had a partially functioning harbour. At 1.20 pm that day, the British Naval Liaison Officer in Paris sent a signal to the Admiralty in London confirming this. Part of it read: 'Dieppe is clear. Barge sunk near entrance and possible magnetic mines outside, but ammunition and all supplies can be landed at Dieppe though Havre better for heavy supplies'[4]. Another myth, fostered by many histories of the period, is that block ships had already been sunk in Dieppe's harbour, so making it unusable. In fact, according to Naval Intelligence's *Daily Summary*, the War Office order of late 8 June was not carried out until 3 pm on 10 June.[5] If boats big enough to land ammunition and supplies could use Dieppe, then it could certainly have been used to evacuate troops. There is no doubt that of the two harbours, Le Havre offered the best facilities for embarkation. But there should have been no question of choosing the 'best' harbour, it was a question of survival.

If General Fortune and his staff were unaware of the capacity that Dieppe's harbour still possessed, then it should have been made clear to them by the people who knew: the Admiralty and the War Office. It was not because the British Government was, more than ever, loath to interfere in military operations on French soil. Incredibly, despite the fact that the War Office already knew that German troops had reached Rouen, it was still urging the 51st Division to carry out Weygand's orders to retire south of the Seine. At 4.30 pm on 9 June, a signal from the War Office to General Fortune was intercepted by the British garrison at Le

Havre. The garrison War Diary states that the message reminded the '51st that their aim should be to break south of the Seine on the axis Dieppe–Rouen'.[6] Instead of doing everything in its power to extricate the Highland Division, the British Government was prepared to sacrifice it in the hope that it would stem the spate of Anglophobe sentiment and keep France in the war.

Yet, the duplicity of the Government does not fully explain Fortune's decision. After all, even without the use of Dieppe's harbour, there was still the option of evacuating men from the nearby beaches, notably at Pourville, a mile to the west. Had not thousands of British and French soldiers been evacuated from the sands of Dunkirk? This option was rejected by Fortune on the grounds that it would favour his own troops who were closer to the coast, and, more importantly, it was contrary to his orders.

After all, General Fortune was a career soldier, and as such imbued with a sense of staunch obedience to his superiors. In this case, his superiors were the French High Command, and they had not given him permission to embark from Dieppe. Instead, he had been ordered to retire over the Seine; an instruction that his own Government had backed up. Yet this order appeared to have been superseded by the message from Admiral Platon at Le Havre informing him that the Germans were at Rouen and that he, Platon, had new orders to arrange an embarkation from Le Havre 'if necessary'. If Fortune had been an army commander, with the right of appeal to the British Government, he might have felt, like Gort, that he had the right to save his men by disobeying orders and marching to the beach at Pourville. But he was only a divisional commander, and by this time was well aware that the discord caused by Gort's action made it all the more imperative that he was not seen to be contradicting French orders. It is not surprising, then, that Fortune, with the complicity of his nominal superior, General Ihler, decided to make for Le Havre.

The night before, Marshall-Cornwall had sent a message to General Fortune by despatch rider which confirmed from General Altmayer the order to retire on Rouen. Crucially it added: 'You may evacuate elements via Dieppe or Havre if possible. Enemy tanks have crossed Andelle line south of Serquex.'[7] Armed with this message, it is just possible that Fortune would have felt he had the authority to embark his men as best he could. Sadly, the despatch rider was prevented by the French from crossing the Seine at Rouen and the message never arrived.

* * *

Once General Fortune had made up his mind to make for Le Havre, the next problem was to arrange communication with London. This was necessary in order to inform the War Office of his intention and to keep it abreast of any changes in circumstances so that it could make the necessary arrangements. Whatever plans had been laid, Fortune must have secretly doubted whether the slow-moving IX Corps could beat two panzer divisions in a race to Le Havre.

Yet the division was still out of touch with Tenth Army Headquarters at Marines, there were no working telephone lines to either Le Havre or Rouen and the long range cipher transmitter – which could have sent and received messages to and from London – did not have the relevant code. The old one had been compromised by the capture of signals equipment in Belgium and a new one had not arrived. A day earlier, a cipher officer had been sent to collect it from the Headquarters of Beauman Division in Rouen, but on arrival there he was told that he would have to go on to the Headquarters of the BEF Lines of Communication at Le Mans. To add insult to injury, he was asked to collect keys for Beauman Division and the 1st Armoured Division. By the time he returned to Rouen, the bridges had been blown and there was no way through. As Swinburn later wrote: 'It would have been more practical if the rear formations had fed these forward to the fighting troops instead of the reverse'.[8]

All means of getting through to London were explored that morning, but one avenue raised considerable hope for a time. Rumour had it that there was an trans-channel underwater telephone cable that came ashore into a sea-box a couple of miles west of Dieppe. Second Lieutenant Andrew Biggar, the officer in charge of signals' cable, was eating his lunch in the small village of Le Bois-Robert when his CO, Lieutenant Colonel Thomas Murray, called to instruct him to report to Divisional Headquarters. Arriving at the château, he was ushered into Colonel Swinburn's office where he also found General Fortune and his Assistant Adjutant and Quartermaster General, Lieutenant Colonel Roney-Dougal. Wasting little time, Fortune explained to Biggar his mission:

> My task was to find the box; open it, by force if necessary and for this reason I was to take a party of men with me. Having opened it, I was to 'tee-in' to the line and make contact with the War Office in London, under their code-name. If successful, I had a message from the General to which an answer was required ... If all the above efforts failed, I was advised that there was a trans-channel cable which came ashore at Fécamp into a military exchange.

Despite an exhaustive search, Biggar's speculative mission failed. He finally arrived back at Le Bois-Robert at 4 am the following morning. Later, he described his inability to locate the cable as 'one of the greatest disappointments in my life'. Fortunately, during his absence, another means of contacting the War Office had been secured.

At 5.30 pm on 9 June, Commander Elkins, Lieutenant Commander Elder, and the two naval signallers arrived at La Chausée. They brought with them the invaluable Inter-Service Stencil, or cypher key, by which means they could receive and transmit messages to naval ships, the Admiralty and the War Office. Ironically, from this point on they used the Highland Division's wireless transmitter, as their own had insufficient range.

Half an hour after the arrival of these men, General Fortune held a divisional conference to explain his plan in the village of Arques-la-Bataille – the birth-place of William the Conqueror and now the headquarters of 154 Brigade. His commanders had assembled in the schoolroom that sunny evening, eager to hear the latest news. Rumours had abounded all day that the corps' line of retreat had been cut, now they were to get confirmation. Fortune began by outlining the events of the morning. The only route of escape now, he told his senior officers, was towards Le Havre. But because there was a likelihood that the Germans would arrive before 13 June, he was sending ahead a strong force that night to join up with some French troops already on the line Fécamp–Bolbec, about 20 miles east of Le Havre, through which the remainder of the corps would pass. The force would also reconnoitre an inner line of defence around Le Havre which would be held by a rearguard to cover embarkation.

Brigadier Arthur Stanley-Clarke, the 53-year old commander of 154 Brigade, was chosen to lead the force, which would comprise his own brigade, 'A' Brigade, the 6th Royal Scots Fusiliers, the 1st Kensingtons less two companies, the 17th and 75th Field Regiments, RA, 204 Battery of the 51st Anti-tank Regiment, RA, the 236th, 237th and 239th Field Companies, RE, and the relevant back-up troops. The name given to Stanley-Clarke's command was Ark Force. This was partly an anglicised version of the village in which the force was formed, partly a topical reference to Noah's Ark and embarkation.

Although nominally half the division, Ark Force contained units generally weaker in personnel, equipment and training than those taking part in the more leisurely withdrawal. All the Regular battalions, the armoured regiment and most of the anti-tank guns were to remain with the division; evidence in itself that it, not Ark Force, faced the toughest task. The method of withdrawal for the rump of the division was similar to that planned for the move to Rouen. Two lines would be held each day, parallel to each other and at right angles to the coast. Only now, the troops on the western line were as likely to see action as those on the east. However brave a face General Fortune put on, it could not fool his officers. Most felt as did Colonel Ansell, the CO of the 1st Lothians: 'We knew well we didn't have a hope of getting to Le Havre,' he later wrote in his autobiography, *Soldier On*.

* * *

A little after 8 pm, the naval section at La Chausée sent its first cypher telegram to the War Office. It urgently requested supplies of ammunition: 40,000 rounds for both 25-pounder and 40 mm Bofors anti-aircraft guns, and large quantities for small-arms. An hour later, another request for 10,000 anti-tank mines was despatched. Since its arrival on the Somme, the 51st Division had been drawing ammunition from the huge BEF dump at St Saëns, about 13 miles west of Forges-les-Eaux. But during 9 June, elements of the German 2nd Motorised Division had advanced from the south beyond the line of the Tôtes–St Saëns road, pushing back a battery of anti-tank guns and some infantry, and cutting off access to the ammunition dump.

A telegram informing the War Office and General Dill of Fortune's intentions was sent at 8.25 pm and received in London two and a half hours later. It read:

> Withdrawing with French Forces to Havre as crossings at Rouen blown. 51 Division on North. Force keeping north of St Saëns–Bolbec Road. Line to be occupied morning 10th, Dieppe–St Saëns. Speed regulated by French marching personnel. Essential to have maximum air support . . .[9]

A second, more detailed message was sent by despatch rider to Le Havre and telephoned through to the War Office at 8.45 pm. It outlined the plan of movement, including the role of Ark Force, and requested supplies of petrol and food for the French divisions. The message concluded with a proviso that is evidence of Fortune's underlying pessimism about the chances of reaching Le Havre. It read:

> If the enemy make a strong tank attack on the Southern flank the only thing I can do will be to pivot on to one of the ports between Dieppe and Havre in the hope that a certain number of men may be saved . . .[10]

The message ended with a request for 'maximum air support'. Such a request had been a continuous theme in the messages sent by the 51st Division since the opening of the Somme offensive. The massive air superiority enjoyed by the Germans at this time was a big factor in their success. The psychological disadvantage of knowing you could be attacked from the air with impunity at any time was felt by every Allied soldier. If the Highland veterans of 1940 are bitter about anything, it is the lack of air support. The Dunkirk evacuation was made possible by the use of every available RAF fighter, operating in relays, to create an aerial umbrella over the bridgehead. Troops of the 51st Division were lucky if they saw one fighter during their time on, and retreat from, the Somme. There were patrols over the division by the five squadrons in France, and even from planes flying from England. But these patrols were rare and, because the fighters were at the end of their flying range, often lasted only a few minutes and usually missed the enemy.

* * *

No sooner had the divisional conference at Arques finished than advanced elements of Ark Force were on their way to Fécamp, 40 miles away. The plan was for the force to concentrate in that sea town, and then to allot positions along the defensive line down to Lillebonne near the Seine.

Due to the sheer weight of traffic on the road to Fécamp, including vast numbers of refugees pushing their scanty belongings in carts and prams, the slower elements of Ark Force did not reach the town until midday. The whole force was travelling for a time in daylight, in tightly-packed convoys, and it was only luck that prevented it from being attacked from the air. Luck and the fact that the German bombing of Le Havre had set fire to huge oil containers, releasing great palls of smoke which spread for miles, and which, ironically, provided cover for the movements of Ark Force. Two companies from A Brigade – one from the 4th Buffs and one from the 1/5th Sherwood Foresters, again – did not make it to Fécamp. They were held up by the traffic congestion and lost their battalions. Hereafter they stayed under the command of 152 Brigade.

In fact, the men of these two companies were lucky to have made it even to Arques-la-Bataille. The plan was for all front line troops to be over the River Béthune by 2 am, when the bridges were due to be blown. 'A' Brigade and the 6th Royal Scots Fusiliers would then continue on their way, while 153 Brigade would take up defensive positions on the two lines scheduled to be held that day. Covering the withdrawal of the division, across the whole front, were the tanks and carriers of the 1st Lothians. Only when they were safely across were the Royal Engineers to be given permission to blow the bridges.

Commanding the important bridge at Arques-la-Bataille, over which

'A' Brigade had been scheduled to cross, was Captain 'Bim' Young of the 4th Seaforths. At first the traffic over the bridge was a deluge of military transport and refugees, gradually it became a stream, and then a trickle. As Young waited anxiously at the west end of the bridge, straining his eyes and ears into the still blackness for a sign of the 1st Lothians' armour, the deadline of 2 am ticked by. All of a sudden a Vauxhall sedan drove up with an authoritative officer inside who began to ask Young detailed questions about who had been over. When asked by Young who he was, he said: 'Don't you know I'm Staff Captain, 'B' Brigade?' As 'A' Brigade had already crossed, Young was hoodwinked into believing that 'B' Brigade might also be in the vicinity. In fact, most of the staff and men of 'B' Brigade were miles away, safely over the Seine, and this man was almost certainly a German spy.

Soon after the departure of this staff officer, a message arrived for Young with a request to delay blowing the bridge as long as possible because a company of Buffs was still on its way. Finally, almost three hours after the deadline, the exhausted Buffs arrived, shepherded in by the tanks of the Lothians. When all were safely across, the bridge was blown sky high. The huge explosion woke the commander of the 4th Seaforths, Shaw-Mackenzie, who noted in his diary that the time was 5 am, long after sun-up.

Years later, Young was having dinner with an ex-Buffs officer named Geoffrey Denne and their respective wives. The two men had met in POW camp, become firm friends, and often stayed with one another. During the meal they began to talk about their wartime experiences. 'There's a chap I owe an awful lot to', Denne began. 'He was in charge of a bridge and was told to blow it at a certain time. But he knew there were more troops coming so he held on, even though the limit for blowing up the bridge had long since passed. At last I arrived with my platoon and we got across safely.' His face showing obvious surprise and delight, Young replied: 'It was me! I was in charge of the bridge.' They had known each other for years and had never realised that both were involved.

* * *

As IX Corps was undertaking the first stage of its move back to Le Havre during the night of 9/10 June, information was received at La Chausée of a further advance by enemy tanks. General Fortune and his staff were now aware, as Swinburn later wrote, 'that if the Corps were to stand any chance of reaching Le Havre the withdrawal would have to be accelerated'. Hurriedly, a new plan was formulated. The east line would move back during the night of 10/11 June to the River Durdent, from the sea to Cany-Barville, thence along the railway line to Doudeville, and from there to Yvetot, while the west line would join up with Ark Force between Fécamp and Lillebonne. The Doudeville salient in the front line was necessary because the 31st and 40th French Divisions were not considered able to get further, whereas by using all its motor transport the 51st Division could travel greater distances.

The accuracy of the earlier reports was confirmed when a message reached Divisional Headquarters at 5.30 am that enemy tanks were moving northwards along the Tôtes–Dieppe road. It quickly dawned on General Fortune that if this attack was successful, through an area that should have been secured by French troops, it would cut off his headquarters and the portion of his division holding the River Béthune. An hour later the news was worse: eight enemy tanks were just six miles from La Chausée. When this second message arrived, Fortune was in conference with Major Parsons, a staff officer, and Captain Birch, a Royal Army Service Corps Supply Officer. They had been sent by Colonel Butler, commanding the British garrison at Le Havre, to offer any assistance and to arrange supplies of food and petrol for IX Corps. As soon as Fortune heard about the tanks, he told Parsons to get a message to Butler asking him to 'father' Ark Force when it arrived at Le Havre. He was then given a copy of the Operation Order for the withdrawal of the division to show Butler and the Navy, and was ordered to leave by the Assistant Adjutant and Quartermaster General, Lieutenant Colonel Roney-Dougal, with the words 'it's a matter of seconds now!'[11]

Two anti-tank guns were sent to block the advance of the German armour, while Divisional Headquarters hurriedly packed up and moved to Ouville-la-Rivière on the River Saâne where it was joined by a dejected General Ihler, accompanied by just one of his staff officers. Since hearing the news from Rouen the previous day, General Ihler, like Altmayer before him, had broken down and become incapable of command. From this point on, General Fortune was in effective control of the entire French IX Corps. But at 11.30 am, more disturbing news arrived at Divisional Headquarters, news that threatened to scupper the revised plans for withdrawal. It was received from a mobile wireless truck that had been sent earlier that morning to maintain contact with Ark Force. On the way it had run into elements of the 7th Panzer Division near Cany-Barville, on the main road to Fécamp, and only quick action by the wireless operator had allowed a message to be sent before it was captured. It simply read: 'Enemy tanks on route'. Confirmation of the presence of German troops between Ark Force and the remainder of the IX Corps then began to arrive from various noncombatant troops who had been ordered back early as part of the accelerated withdrawal. These groups made contact with the enemy at various points from Veulettes on the coast to Cany, part of the front line to which the division was scheduled to move that evening.[12]

At this point, the Highland Division was dug-in along the Rivers Béthune and Saâne, having completed the first stage of the original plan to withdraw back to Le Havre the night before. Four battalions were holding the line of the River Béthune from Dieppe to Martigny. From left to right they were the 2/7th Duke of Wellington's, the 4th Seaforths, the 5th Gordons, and the 1st Black Watch. About seven miles further back, on the River Saâne from the sea to Gueres, were the remaining three battalions: the 2nd Seaforths, the 1st Gordons and the 4th Camerons. The 1st Lothians were in Divisional Reserve at Longueil, near Ouville. As such, and because they were the most mobile unit, the Lothians were given the task of scouting towards Fécamp to ascertain the location and strength of the enemy. Colonel Ansell was given three intermediate lines, running south from the coast, to report back from: St Pierre-le-Viger, St Valéry-en-Caux, and the Durdent River. If only light enemy forces were encountered, they were to be cleared to allow a passage through to Fécamp.

The regiment moved off at 3 pm with two squadrons forward – C right and B left – and A in reserve. Despite delays caused by refugees and military transport on the roads, and the handicap of a lack of maps – B Squadron had just one, a Dunlop tourist road map – the first two lines were reported clear within the hour. Spearheading the recce on towards the bridge over the River Durdent at Cany-Barville was a troop of three Bren carriers of B Squadron under Second Lieutenant Baird. The troop had been brought up to strength by the addition of Troop Sergeant Major Jimmy Hogarth's one remaining carrier. Sergeant Charlie Foley's carrier was leading the troop, followed by Baird's and then Hogarth's, the latter two equipped with wireless. Hogarth takes up the story:

> We reached the crossroads at the top of the hill above Cany, and found the road block there clear. We carried on down the hill, first passing a dead French cavalry horse, then an RASC 30 cwt Bedford with its radiator smashed in, drawn in to the right hand side of the road. A little further down we passed an abandoned German light armoured car in the middle of the road. We proceeded slowly on down to the village expecting an ambush. The first and second carriers were level with the first houses on the right side of the road when the enemy opened fire with machine-guns. Mr Baird gave the signal 'tanks about' and all the vehicles withdrew safely. Luckily for us the German marksmanship was poor.

Second Lieutenant Baird ordered the troop back up to the crossroads where it took up a defensive position. After trying in vain to raise squadron headquarters on the wireless, Hogarth wrote out a message for his OC, Major Wattie McCulloch, and sent it back by despatch rider. Within half an hour, vehicles were sighted coming down the main road from St Valéry but they turned out to be Second Lieutenant Otter-Barry's No 5 Troop of carriers. Shortly after, Major McCulloch and his second-in-command, Captain Pat Turcan, arrived with squadron head-quarters and their two tanks, McCulloch's under the temporary command of Squadron Sergeant Major Alfie Upton. The total force at the crossroads was now six carriers and two tanks, but for some reason McCulloch chose to send the two tanks alone down to Cany to gather more information and, if possible, to clear the enemy.

Quite rightly, McCulloch decided not to lead the recce, but to send Captain Turcan instead. Less explicable is the change over of the tank crews. Corporal John Stevenson, the driver of McCulloch's tank *Bannockburn*, recalls the unwillingness of Squadron Sergeant Major Upton to accompany the mission:

> The Sergeant Major didn't seem to want to go into Cany and asked for two volunteers. Jimmy Hogarth and Charlie Foley, both from the carriers, stepped forward. Foley took over from the Sergeant Major as commander of my tank, and Hogarth took over as gunner in Captain Turcan's tank.

It may have made sense to include Jimmy Hogarth, because of his knowledge of guns and the fact that he knew roughly where the Germans were. But Upton had no good reason to avoid the action. Hogarth, for one, was surprised: 'I was busy sorting out the guns at the time, but I had thought Squadron Sergeant Major Upton was going to command the other tank'.

Before moving off, Sergeant Foley's tank was used to drag a dead French cavalry horse out of the way from in front of the road block. Then, with Foley's leading on the right hand side of the road, and Captain Turcan's 50 yards further back on the left, to give both a field of fire, the two tanks set off down the hill towards the village. Suddenly, near a roadblock of carts on the edge of the village, Corporal Stevenson spotted a German motorcyclist:

> We could easily have got him but the gunner, Trooper Wright, never fired. I was shouting, 'Fire!' as the German leapt on his bike, kick-started it first time, and raced off. Back came the reply, 'The bloody gun's not loaded!' I couldn't believe it; of all the things to happen in the middle of a battle.

Continuing on, the two tanks drove through the roadblock, over the bridge, which was still intact, and through the village until they came to a second barricade. While Foley's tank was bulldozing through it, Captain Turcan leant out of his turret and spoke to a Frenchman who informed him that Germans were just up the road. In the meantime, Foley's tank had got through the roadblock and was just leaving the village when it spotted a German six-wheeled armoured car about 400 yards ahead with a group of officers and men standing round it. Once again, Stevenson shouted 'Fire!', and again there was no response. Seeing the danger the Germans scattered down a side road, hotly pursued by the tanks. Jimmy Hogarth recalls the chase:

> The Germans all disappeared into woods on either side of the road. As our tank passed several motorcycle combinations beside a shed on the roadside, I fired on them and did considerable damage. Captain Turcan then ordered the about turn, making our tank the leading vehicle. We came back onto the main road and started down the hill towards the barricade. As we passed the armoured car we gave it a burst, but seconds later there was a crash inside the tank and it was filled with cordite fumes. An anti-tank gun had been set up on the left of the road and it hit us broadside at about 15 yards range. The shell penetrated the nearside between the driver and myself, level with my legs. My left leg was broken and I had shrapnel wounds in both legs. I shouted up to Captain Turcan, 'I'm hit!' He asked me if I could carry on and I said 'Yes'. I started firing the guns, but was a bit dazed and could not see what I was hitting. Meantime the tank was running down the road to the roadblock and gathering speed. Captain Turcan gave the order down the voice tube to the driver to slow for the block. There was no response. I saw through the telescope we were going to hit the house on the corner, and braced myself for the crash. As we hit it, the off-side front edge of the tank went through the wall. The turret and guns were jammed against the brickwork, while I was pinned inside by the gun-butts. Captain Turcan got out but I couldn't move.

Meanwhile, the second tank, Foley's, had also run the gauntlet of the anti-tank gun. Passing its stricken partner, it was skidding through the roadblock when it too was hit. Like Hogarth, Corporal Stevenson was badly wounded:

> I heard a big bang and my right leg was knocked off the throttle and the tank came to a halt. An anti-tank shell had gone straight through our armour, also hitting Sergeant Foley sitting up behind me. I am quite a small man and used to have to wind my seat right to the top; if I had been any taller that shell might have killed me. As soon as the tank came to a rest, the gunner, Trooper Wright, managed to get out and ran up the road. I got the hatch open and could see Captain Turcan jump from his

tank and run towards me shouting, 'Get out! Get out!' I replied, 'I can't, I've been hit!' He then helped me out and over to a shop on the corner a few yards away. Then he said he was sorry to leave me but he had to try to get away.

Leaving Stevenson, Captain Turcan made his way through the village, over the bridge, and had only got a few hundred yards away when, in broken country, a German popped up from behind a hedge just a few yards away and fired a burst into him from his *schmeisser*. The German walked over, and seeing Turcan badly wounded in the side said half apologetically, '*Krieg ist Krieg*'.

In the meantime, with some difficulty, Hogarth had managed to unclip his gun-butts. Uppermost in his mind was the fear of being caught in the tank as it 'brewed', like being roasted in an oven. He shouted down to the driver, Trooper Bainbridge, but there was no answer. He was already dead. By a superhuman effort, Hogarth then hauled himself onto the lip of the turret as quickly as his injuries would allow, swung his broken legs over the side and fell through a hedge into the garden of the house. Ten seconds later the tank burst into flames, cremating Bainbridge. The other tank 'brewed' shortly after, with Sergeant Foley still inside. As Hogarth crawled into a garden shed to hide, he could hear soldiers running and motorcycles starting up. Then machine-gun fire and mortar bursts mingled with the sound of the tanks' ammunition going up. When the noise died down, he tore some towels he had found into shreds to bandage his wounds and used a broom handle to splint his broken leg. With the assistance of two more brooms as crutches, he hobbled his way through the house, down some back streets, over the bridge and out of the village. Too weak to continue in the dark, he stopped at the damaged RASC truck, managed to start it but could not get it to move. Exhausted, Hogarth rolled himself in some blankets and a tarpaulin he found in the back and went to sleep in the ditch. The following morning he discovered why the truck would not move:

> A tow-rope on the front axle had got snared round the rear wheel, so I unhooked it, started the engine, and drove the truck up to the roadblock at the crossroads. After waiting there for an hour, some French civilians found me, put me on a cart and took me to their farm. They gave me coffee and bread and butter, then took me in a car to the main road. Two of the last lorries of the infantry were coming along. The second stopped and picked me up.

Corporal Stevenson was less fortunate. Lying semi-conscious in the shop, weak from loss of blood, he recalls a party of Germans coming in, seeing him and then leaving. It was unusual for German troops to leave badly wounded soldiers of the enemy untended; indeed Captain Turcan had been well cared for. Stevenson's bad luck was compounded when a French man came in later, and also left without helping him. It was not until the following day that he received medical attention from the local doctor, after he was found by a small French boy. It was too late to prevent gangrene setting in, and two days later his right leg was amputated at the groin by a German military surgeon. His wife was informed by the War Office that he was 'Missing presumed Killed' and remained in the dark as to his fate for a further 18 months.

C Squadron had fared little better to the north at Veulettes, suffering heavy casualties and ending the day with just three tanks and four carriers. The four bridges over the River Durdent that the regiment had been asked to secure, between Veulettes and Cany, were now all either blown or in the hands of Rommel's 7th Panzer Division. The escape route to Le Havre had been cut.

By 6 pm, General Fortune had still not heard definite news that the Lothians had failed in their attempt to secure the River Durdent. At 6.14 pm he sent a signal to the War Office and Admiral James which read:

> Isolated enemy AFVs have now intercepted my communications with Fécamp ... Corps plan tonight to move back to line of Durdent River to Cany thence Doudeville. Lothians clearing area between St Valéry and Fécamp. Am still under and in close touch with IX French Corps.[13]

An hour after the despatch of the 1st Lothians in the afternoon, the three battalions in reserve near the River Saâne – the 1st Gordons, 2nd Seaforths, and 4th Camerons – had been ordered by Divisional Headquarters to help the cavalry hold or secure the River Durdent crossings. Before departure, these battalions were ordered to jettison all baggage and equipment not essential for fighting, which effectively meant everything except weapons and ammunition, transport, food, and a haversack of iron rations per man. All personal kit had to go. Because of the need to find additional transport to fully motorise the battalions, they did not move off until late evening. By this time, news had reached Divisional Headquarters that the Germans held the Durdent crossings, but the intention was still to secure a line on the Durdent as part of a bridgehead for evacuation somewhere between there and St Valéry-en-Caux.

At 10.45 pm, Fortune sent a signal to Admiral James and the War

Office which read: 'Think possible that in this rapidly changing situation I might ask you to embark as much personnel as possible of my Division between St Valéry and mouth of River Durdent both inclusive. French Corps Commander has joined his HQ to mine'.[14]

It was only the personal intervention of Major James Grant, now Second-in-Command of the 2nd Seaforths, that caused the original orders to be modified. Arriving at St Valéry at 10.15 pm, the Seaforths were regaled with numerous reports of enemy forces between St Valéry and Fécamp. Armed with this news, Grant set off for Divisional Headquarters at Ouville, but owing to heavy congestion on the road did not arrive until around midnight. There he found General Fortune, Colonel Swinburn and three French generals, the latter sitting, as he wrote later, 'like three dummies on a sofa'. After making his report, Grant suggested that instead of trying to hold the line of the Durdent it would make more sense to hold a shorter intermediate line on the heights to the west of St Valéry. Fortune agreed and issued new orders for the three battalions to hold a line from Le Tot on the coast, two miles west of St Valéry-en-Caux, to the village of Néville, three miles inland. Thanks to the horrendous congestion of military traffic moving towards St Valéry, both British and French, the progress of the battalions involved was slow, and it was possible to deliver these revised orders before they reached the Durdent.

Circumstances had forced General Fortune by the early hours of 11 June to choose St Valéry as the main point of embarkation, and accordingly he made plans to secure a bridgehead. Writing later, Colonel Swinburn attempted to explain why St Valéry was picked, rather than the beaches at Dieppe:

> St Valéry-en-Caux was at this time being used for the evacuation of wounded and was thus known to the Navy. Further, it was well placed for the collection of the administrative echelons and the French, whereas the embarkation near Dieppe, apart from the Navy not being familiar with it, would give the British troops all the advantages which after Dunkirk and the tone of the wires from home [General Fortune] considered to be undesirable.[15]

If the British Government had intended General Fortune to appreciate the political repercussions of abandoning his French allies, then this comment shows that it had succeeded. Whether, at this late stage, the beaches to the west of Dieppe would have offered a better chance of evacuation for the 51st Division than St Valéry is debatable. Its troops were strung out between the two points, and the battalions holding the line of the River Béthune running south from Dieppe had been heavily

engaged during the 10th. What is certain is that even at this Eleventh
Hour, the French IX Corps, and with it the 51st (Highland) Division,
was receiving little practical assistance from either the French or British
High Commands, and through them their respective governments, to
extricate it from its predicament.

At 9.20 pm, in response to a request from General Weygand, Admiral
Platon, commanding at Le Havre, asked the British Admiralty to pass on
via General Fortune an order to General Ihler. It read: 'Withdraw upon
the Seine down stream Caudebec included ... High authorities will
prepare means of crossing.'[16] This contradicted Platon's earlier message to Fortune – that Platon had orders to prepare an evacuation from
Le Havre – and implies that then the Admiral had been acting on his
own initiative. Now, under pressure from Weygand, he had no option
but to pass on this revised version of the 8 June order for IX Corps to
retire over the Seine. In any case, Weygand had already asked the British
War Office direct to send the same order.

From this, it is clear that either Weygand was suffering from a
delusion that the IX Corps was still able to withdraw south of the Seine,
using the ferries below Rouen, or, more likely, that he was spitefully
unwilling to allow the British another embarkation from French soil like
Dunkirk. Whatever the motive behind the order, it had no chance of
being carried out. Such was the delicate nature of relations between the
Allies that London was not prepared to contradict this order, or allow
Fortune to. When Colonel Butler at Le Havre rang the War Office that
evening to inform them of this new development, he spoke to Major
General Percival, Assistant Chief of the Imperial General Staff. On
hearing that Weygand's order also forbade any evacuation by sea from
the Havre area, Percival told Butler that he had to comply with this, and
to make sure that Fortune did so too.[17]

Unaware of Weygand's order, Generals Fortune and Ihler went ahead
with the last-minute plan to create a bridgehead around St Valéry.
Fortune's original intention was that the British would hold the entire
three-sided perimeter, but this was slightly modified at Ihler's insistence.
Instead, it was agreed that the Highland infantry would hold the two
flanks, while the 1st Lothians and Ihler's own corps cavalry regiment,
the *Groupe Reconnaissance d'Armée*, would hold the southern edge. The
three battalions that had originally been earmarked to secure the
Durdent river would hold the western perimeter, while the four
battalions on the Béthune were the logical choice for the nearer eastern
face. These four had been heavily attacked during the day – particularly
the 4th Seaforths at Arques and the 1st Black Watch at Martigny – but

◀1. Lieutenant Colonel Harry Swinburn MC RA (from a photograph taken in Oflag IX A/H and sent to his wife. As GSO I of the Division, Swinburn was the linchpin of its operations. His immaculate diary, written up in his POW camp, was the principal source of accurate information used in the preparation of this book.)

▶2. Captain Bill Bradford MBE, Adjutant 1st Black Watch. (*For the story of his remarkable escape and distinguished service in the resurrected division, see Epilogue.*)

▼3. Members of C Company 7th Royal Norfolks at Bizing. (Front Row from left: Lieutenant R Gibson (KIA 1944), Second Lieutenant HJ Walker, Captain AD Colley (KIA at St Valéry) and RC Padre (POW). At rear: Sergeant Bunkle (POW), Company Sergeant Major (POW))

▲4. Second Lieutenant Johnny Rhodes MC, The Gordon Highlanders, on a billeting mission with Corporal Pierre Boudet (French Army) who so distinguished himself at St Valéry. (He has the unique distinction for a foreign soldier of having been formally accepted as a member of the Highland Brigade.)

5. At Boëncourt. A Bren gun team of the 2nd Seaforths (*Photo: IWM*)

6. Major CJ Shaw-Mackenzie MBE,
The Seaforth Highlanders, in full dress

7. Second Lieutenant 'Ran' Ogilvie,
The Gordon Highlanders

8. Second Lieutenants Diarmid Macalister Hall (right) and John Parnell, The Argyll &
Sutherland Highlanders, in Palestine after the war.

9. **On the Bresle. Men of the 4th Black Watch** (*Photo: IWM*)

10. Second Lieutenant 'Ginger' Gall MC, The Gordon Highlanders, gets married

11. Company Quartermaster Sergeant GG Macdonald, The Queen's Own Cameron Highlanders. (*Seen here as OC Anti-tank Platoon, the 2nd Camerons in 1943.*)

12. Second Lieutenant Jim Walker, The Royal Norfolk regiment (*for his daring escape from St Valéry he was Mentioned in Despatches. DSO 1945*)

13. Second Lieutenant Andrew Biggar MC, Royal Corps of Signals, in his POW camp

14. Troop Sergeant Major Jimmy Hogarth DCM, 1st Lothians & Border Yeomanry

15. Private Sandy Russell, The Queen's Own Cameron Highlanders

16. Lance Corporal George MacLennan, The Gordon Highlanders

17. Lieutenant Colonel Mike Ansell DSO and officers of the 1st Lothians & Border Yeomanry at an orders group. (*Centre: Lieutenant Colonel Ansell. Major Jimmy Dallmeyer is on his left. Major Wattie McCulloch is second from Ansell's right.*)

18. Cany-Barville 10 June 1940. Light tank Mark VIB '*Blue Bonnet*' after it had been knocked out.

19. **A Field Dressing Station at Huchenneville on the Somme** (*Photo: IWM*)

20. **Lieutenant General Sir James Marshall-Cornwall KCB CBE DSO MC** (*Photo: IWM*)

21. **Admiral Sir William James GCB** (*Photo: IWM*)

22. After the surrender on 12 June 1940. Generals Rommel and Victor Fortune in St Valéry (*Right: Harry Swinburn*) (*Photo: IWM*)

23. German troops in the main square at St Valéry (*Photo: IWM*)

24. The ruins of St Valéry after the battle (*Photo: IWM*) (*This, and Plates 22 and 23 were either taken by Rommel himself or with his camera*)

25. Privates Hugh Oliver MM and Neil Campbell MM, The Queen's Own Cameron Highlanders, after their heroic escape in an open boat. (*See Epilogue*)

they had managed to hold on until the assault was called off at 6.30 pm, due in no small part to accurate fire from the supporting artillery. It was with some relief that they jettisoned all excess baggage and set off, with the help of RASC trucks, towards St Valéry.

* * *

One man had been working feverishly to save the IX Corps, and with it the Highland Division. On the afternoon of 9 June, Admiral James had despatched to Le Havre a part of his hotch-potch armada, including nine destroyers, the bigger transports and the first flotillas of smaller boats towed by tugs and other bigger craft. There was no evacuation of British troops that evening because, he was told by the Admiralty, the French were taking precedence. But during the night, James' head-quarters received the signal from General Fortune which stated that if the Germans broke through then evacuation from a point other than Le Havre might be necessary. As he had no orders to begin the evacuation by the following morning, James decided to go to Le Havre to assess the situation for himself. After the pleasant coincidence of crossing in a Motor Torpedo Boat commanded by his son, James arrived in Le Havre at around 2 pm. He was greeted with the sight of the blazing oil tanks and the sound of numerous explosions as vital installations were demolished. Having dashed through a town choked with refugees, bad news awaited him at the British Military Headquarters. 'The situation was as bad as it could be', he later wrote. 'The French were giving way everywhere and our 51st Division would soon be forced on to the coast near St Valéry.'[18]

There was not a moment to be lost. 'I hastened to the headquarters of the French Admiral, who was the supreme authority in the area, and urged him to allow me to evacuate our soldiers before it was too late', James recorded. 'He was in a very excited state and was under the delusion that the French Army was disputing every inch; Weygand had ordered a retreat to the Seine and he could not give orders for evacuation.'[19] Failing to convince the French admiral, James grabbed the initiative. Returning to the harbour he told the senior naval officer to move all his craft to a position off St Valéry and await further orders. If there was to be a rescue attempt he wanted to be prepared.

His next move was to ring up the War Office and pass on the news that an evacuation of large numbers of troops from the St Valéry area might be necessary. On his return to Portsmouth that evening, he was handed an urgent message from the War Office, received by his staff at 8.15 pm, that threatened to undermine all his good work. As James noted in his official report of *Operation Cycle*, the message stated that 'the military situation had changed and that the French IX Corps, which included the 51st Division, had been ordered to fight its way south to the Seine, and therefore the only evacuation would be of stragglers and possibly of some formed bodies from Havre'.[20]

Like General Percival's telephone call to Colonel Butler in Le Havre, this was part of the War Office's attempt to prevent an embarkation unless it was ordered by the French High Command. James' immediate response was to call up General Haining at the War Office to reaffirm that embarkation was the only way out. Haining told him, as James wrote in his memoirs, 'that Weygand had assured them that the French Armies were conducting a fighting retreat to the Seine – and, which was worse, that as the 51st Division had been placed under French command, the War Office could not independently order evacuation'.[21]

At a time when only quick and firm action could save the 51st Division, the War Office, as ever, was preoccupied with the political repercussions of the Highlanders leaving French soil without French permission. Fortunately, Admiral James had already set the wheels of the evacuation in motion by ordering his whole rescue armada to sail for St Valéry that evening, and despite this conversation with Haining, he made no attempt to rescind these orders.

Apart from the political cost of an evacuation, there was also the material cost in terms of ships. This danger was illustrated by the damage done to three destroyers on 10 June. After receiving definite news that German tanks were advancing on Fécamp, Captain Tower, the British naval commander in Le Havre, instructed the Senior Naval Officer Afloat, Captain Warren, to prepare for a probable evacuation between Fécamp and Dieppe. Accordingly, Warren despatched three destroyers – HMSs *Bulldog, Boadicea,* and *Ambuscade* – to investigate the beaches between Fécamp and Dieppe with a view to embarkation. While investigating beaches near Fécamp at 3.30 pm, HMS *Ambuscade* was hit by shells fired from an artillery battery of the 7th Panzer Division, and put out of action. An hour later, the *Boadicea* was engaged by a separate battery as she picked up over 50 British soldiers of the 51st Division and some French from a beach near Veulettes. After the *Bulldog* had come to her assistance, both ships were badly damaged by Stuka dive-bombers and had to return to Portsmouth. The response of the Admiralty was to order Admiral James not to allow warships near the evacuation areas in daylight except for 'urgent reasons'.[22]

* * *

The Royal Navy, as much as the IX Corps, was surprised by the speed of the 7th Panzer Division's advance on 10 June. Rommel's orders that morning from General Hoth were to make a quick thrust through to the coast to cut off the escape of the IX Corps from Le Havre. His armour moved off at 7.30 am and, after travelling all out at an average speed of 30 mph, had reached the coast at Les Petites Dalles, 10 miles east of Fécamp, by mid-afternoon. Rommel, travelling as ever with the advance elements, was euphoric. He later wrote:

> The sight of the sea with the cliffs on either side thrilled and stirred every man of us; also the thought that we had reached the coast of France. We climbed out of our vehicles and walked down to the shingle beach to the water's edge until the water lapped over our boots ... Close behind us Rothenburg came up in his command tank, crashed through the beach wall, and drove down to the water. Our task was over and the enemy's road to Le Havre and Fécamp was closed.[23]

During the advance, Rommel had sent units of his 37th Panzer Reconnaissance Battalion to hold points on the River Durdent, including Veulettes on the coast. It was these troops that the 1st Lothians had encountered in the evening. This was a classic stroke by the arch-exponent of *Blitzkrieg*: although in relatively light numbers, these forces caused such disruption by their surprise arrival that after the failure of the Lothians, no further attempt to break through was made.

Ark Force in Fécamp had avoided being cut off by units of Rommel's reconnaissance battalion by just a matter of hours. The first Brigadier Arthur Stanley-Clarke knew about the advance of the 7th Panzer Division, in his headquarters at the *Hotel de Ville* in Fécamp, was when Second Lieutenant Bowring of 385th Battery, attached to the 1st Royal Horse Artillery, brought news that German armoured cars had attacked and machine-gunned a transport convoy on the Fécamp–Cany road.

In his written instructions to Brigadier Stanley-Clarke, General Fortune had stated that should enemy units intervene between Ark Force and the remainder of IX Corps, Stanley-Clarke was to act on his own initiative to save his troops. On hearing Bowring's news, this is exactly what he did. The majority of his force was ordered during the afternoon to move to a secondary line just two miles from Le Havre, between Octeville and Contreville. Only a scratch force was left on part of the original line, between Lillebonne and Breaute, and they had orders to withdraw if pressed. The 51st Division was now beyond the assistance of its comrades in Ark Force.

11

St Valéry

The Norman seatown of St Valéry-en-Caux could hardly have been less suitable for the embarkation of 25,000 soldiers. Set in a small, natural break in the 300 foot cliffs of the *Côte d'Albatre* that stretch from the Somme to Le Havre, it represents a bottleneck whose flanking beaches can only be safely reached through the town itself, and then only at low tide. Access to its small harbour from the sea is via a narrow entrance between two piers, while easy admittance from the land side is restricted to the southern approaches, as the cliffs overlooking the town from the east and west have steep slopes that were heavily wooded in 1940. For the attackers, though, the setting was ideal. The country around St Valéry, the *Pays de Caux*, is generally flat, open agricultural land, and in 1940 only the occasional sunken road linking the farms and villages hindered the swift movement of tanks to the top of the cliffs. Guns in position there would always dominate the town and threaten an escape by sea.

Captivated one stormy night in 1836 by the dramatic view from St Valéry's cliffs, Victor Hugo had composed his famous nautical verse, *Oceano Nox*. In honour of the seafaring men of Normandy, it begins:

> *Oh! Combiens de marins, combien de capitaines*
> *Qui sont partis joyeux pour des course lointaines.*
> (Oh! How many sailors, how many captains,
> have happily left for far-off journeys)

How readily the soldiers of the 51st Division would have jumped at the chance of joining this number by the morning of 11 June 1940.

* * *

The convergence of thousands of troops on St Valéry in the early hours of 11 June was necessarily a complicated manoeuvre; it was made chaotic by the indiscipline of the French. General Fortune had specifically confined his traffic to the coast road to allow the French marching troops a clear run into the St Valéry area from the south and south-east. But many of the French, panicked by rumours that the enemy were near, poured into the coast road from every side lane and track from Ouville onwards. Colonel Swinburn, given the task of organising the move, was exasperated:

> The ... congestion was ... aggravated by the fact that the French transport appeared to be a heterogenous collection from all their formations and was badly disorganised and no control existed. It would pay no attention to our traffic control staff and as a result the road was solid with vehicles head to tail most of the night ... It was broad daylight before units got anywhere near their positions on the eastern face and this stream of uncontrolled French transport continued all day adding much confusion in St Valéry and seriously affecting the troops in the eastern face who found great difficulty in distinguishing friend from foe when the latter started to make contact.[1]

To try and make some sense out of this madness, General Fortune and his staff stationed themselves in the early hours of the morning at the main road junction south-east of Veules-les-Roses, four miles east of St Valéry. That the commander of Britain's most famous fighting division had been reduced to the role of a traffic policeman is some indication of the desperate situation.

Outdoing the mayhem on the roads to St Valéry was the confusion in the town itself. Sergeant John Mackenzie of the 2nd Seaforths later wrote of the sight that greeted him at dusk on 10 June:

> The town had been badly smashed by an air raid and many houses were alight. Thousands of drunken French soldiers were looting cafes, shops and houses, blazing away at anything with their rifles. Someone took a couple of pot-shots at me as I was talking to the driver of a light tank which was guarding the road into St Valéry, sending me back to my truck in a hurry.[2]

The first troops into position on the morning of the 11th were those guarding the western perimeter of the bridgehead. Shortly after daybreak, the 1st Gordons – less C company, the Mortar Platoon and the Signals Section, which had become detached during the move – arrived at Ingouville, two miles south-west of St Valéry. Battalion Headquarters was set up in an orchard in the village, where it was later joined by C Company, while the three rifle companies were sent a mile further on to St Riquier-les-Plains, with the task of covering the St Valéry–Cany road. They were joined by D Company of the 7th Norfolks, which had been unable to reach its original rendez-vous two miles west of Cany.

At about the same time, the 4th Camerons arrived in the village of Néville, three miles south of St Valéry. After debussing and hiding the transport in an orchard next to the church, the battalion – consisting of three rifle companies since the arrival of reinforcements – marched off to its arranged positions at St Riquier. Finding them already occupied by the 1st Gordons, the CO, Major Mackintosh-Walker, decided to move his men to posts further south, on the fringe of a hedged field beside the road from Néville. They were supported by a French anti-tank platoon of one gun and a heavy machine-gun, and later in the day by two guns from the 51st Anti-tank Regiment under a Major Hicks. The 1st Gordons had got mixed-up during the move and had ended up holding the line to the north instead of the south of the 4th Camerons. When General Fortune visited the positions at 7.30 am he allowed the new arrangement to stand.

The 2nd Seaforths, the last of the three battalions allotted to guard the western perimeter, was on the cliffs to the west of St Valéry, still awaiting the return of Major Grant, at dawn on 11 June. He finally arrived with the revised orders from Divisional Headquarters at 5 am, and immediately the battalion began the dangerous daylight march to its position in the villages of Le Tot and St Sylvain, two miles west of St Valéry. Such a manoeuvre over open country – described by the Adjutant, Second Lieutenant Philip Mitford, as 'one of the most hazardous exercises we had done in our lives' – would not normally have been undertaken, but these were not 'normal' times. A French regiment, which had been ordered by General Ihler to thicken the perimeter between Le Tot and the sea, never arrived and so, by the morning of 11 June, the western sector was held from north to south by the following: 2nd Seaforths; D Company, 7th Norfolks; 1st Gordons; 4th Camerons.

Holding the southern face of the bridgehead, five miles south of St Valéry, were the remaining tanks and carriers of the 1st Lothians. A Squadron was on the right, linking up with the 4th Camerons near the village of Ocqueville; B Squadron was four miles to the east around St Colombe; C Squadron was on the outskirts of St Valéry itself. There was no sign of Ihler's cavalry reconnaissance regiment. Major Wattie McCulloch, commanding B Squadron, was not impressed with the French he did see that morning:

> There was no sign of the enemy but large numbers of French troops poured in. They were of every arm and even included a few tanks. They seemed to be dispirited and in a state of some disorganisation. A French General appeared and proceeded to attempt to bring some order out of the chaos but without much visible result.[3]

It was inevitable that the battalions destined for the eastern perimeter would be the last to arrive. They had been in action for most of the 10th and were the last to set off, they had the furthest to travel, and they faced the worst of the congestion. Under the circumstances, the 5th Gordons did remarkably well to reach their positions on the St Pierre–Yelon road by 5.30 am. In contrast, the 4th Seaforths did not settle into posts around Yelon until 11.30 am. By midday, the line from north to south was held as follows: a regiment of French gunners; 2/7th Duke of Wellington's Regiment; 4th Seaforths; 5th Gordons; 1st Black Watch.

* * *

Divisional Headquarters opened in the village of Cailleville, three miles south of St Valéry, at 4.30 am on 11 June, although a transmitter link with the Navy was not established until 6 am. General Fortune had much to ponder over during the first hours of daylight. With communications to Le Havre severed, the only rations left were those for the 11th, while all remaining ammunition available had already been issued to units. The French were even worse off, with severe shortages in small-arms ammunition, artillery and anti-tank rounds. Given these deficiencies, and the exhaustion of his men – who had been moving or fighting for over a month, and who had seldom had a full night's sleep during that time – it became clear to General Fortune that embarkation that night was imperative. At 8.45 am he sent a signal to Admiral James in Portsmouth, duplicated to the War Office, the Admiralty and the Captain Tower in Le Havre. It read:

> Intend to embark whole force to-night Tuesday provided sufficient ships and boat transport are available. If embarkation cannot be completed to-night propose continuing A.M. tomorrow Wednesday. Estimated numbers British (Corrupt Group) French at present 5,000 but may reach 10,000. Consider air superiority is essential to neutralise shore batteries. Jumping Ladders and Nets are required to assist embarkation.
> Time of commencement and beaches to be used will be signalled. Embarkation to-night considered essential owing to probability of attack and shortage of rations petrol and ammunition.[4]

Not long after the despatch of this signal, one was received from the War Office. It included a copy of Weygand's order of the previous day for IX Corps to continue to try to cross the Seine, and ended by reminding General Fortune of 'the importance of acting in strict conformity with any orders IX Corps commander may issue'.[5] Despite the fact that the War Office knew that the 51st Division was hemmed in to the coast, cut off from all forms of escape except by sea, it was still obliquely urging Fortune to co-operate with Weygand's absurd order that, if complied with, would inevitably lead to its destruction. Does this mean that Churchill and the British Government were not just prepared to sacrifice the 51st Division, but actually needed to, to provide a concrete example of its determination to stand by the French to the end? It seems possible. The loss of this division, so well-known to the French from the First World War, could have been seen as a means of wiping out the bad feeling caused by Dunkirk and the subsequent holding back of British fighters, and ultimately as a way of persuading the French to stay in the war.

If this was the intention, Fortune was unwilling to play ball. Unknown to the War Office, he had been the *de facto* commander of IX Corps since Ihler's breakdown on the 9th. It is unclear whether Fortune discussed this message with General Ihler, but he for one was not going to submit to such lunacy. At 10.10 am, the response to the War Office's signal was sent. Drafted by Commander Elkins and authorised by Fortune, it curtly dismissed Weygand's order:

> Physical impossibility Corps Cmdr [General Ihler] approach Seine. In same boat as me. Numbers Corps Cmdr estimates now 10,000 – British total 12,000 total 22,000. Air control of the enemy area round my bridgehead essential. To prevent free use of AFV. Men would like to see Hun bombed . . .[6]

The key request in this signal was a demand not just for air cover but air 'control'. Fortune knew only too well that without it any evacuation would be threatened from both coastal batteries and air attack. Despite this, the plea was largely ignored. Colonel Swinburn later wrote:

> The need for the maximum air support was felt to be so necessary to the success of the operation that the Divisional Commander sent a personal wire to the Chief of the Imperial General Staff asking that every effort be made to provide it. Despite repeated appeals, only the occasional British aircraft was seen over the Division from 5th June, whilst the enemy air was completely unmolested except for small arms fire and the 11 Bofors which had joined the Division from the Support Group whilst on the River Somme and which did some excellent work.[7]

At best this lack of air support can be seen as evidence that the British Government did not think the survival of the 51st Division warranted the risk of losing more priceless fighters; at worst it backs up the deliberate sacrifice theory. The next signal to arrive from the War Office, sent at 12.40 pm, only served to confirm the British Government's political priorities. It read: 'No evacuation to be carried out without French authority. Give information most suitable places for landing supplies.'[8]

* * *

Although no permission had been given for evacuation by the morning of 11 June, the Navy was busy making preparations. Admiral James' armada of over 200 boats had set sail for St Valéry during the night, and by 6 am two destroyers and the transport SS *Hampton* were lying off the seafront. Aboard the *Hampton* was Lieutenant Hemans, a Naval officer in charge of five beach parties who would go ashore and supervise any embarkation. Although with no definite orders, Hemans commandeered a motor launch and a cutter and landed at the harbour at 7.30 am. He was met by the 51st Division's Naval Liaison Officer, Commander Elkins, who was on the harbour mole making a preliminary reconnaissance for a plan of embarkation. After informing Hemans of the troop dispositions of IX Corps, Elkins instructed him to organise embarkation points and assembly places. He then gave Hemans his wireless frequency and call-sign and told him he would arrange for a transmitter to be set up on the mole, where Hemans would place a boat with an Aldis signalling lamp. If an evacuation was sanctioned, Elkins told him, it would begin at 10.30 pm. Leaving Hemans to his task, Elkins then went back to Cailleville.[9]

When Elkins returned to the harbour at 10.30 am, after having drafted the 10.10 am signal to the War Office, he told Hemans that General Fortune had definitely decided to begin the embarkation that night. The two Naval officers then agreed on the final plan of evacuation. British troops would embark from the beach to the east of the harbour entrance, and also from two points on the eastern mole. French troops, who were estimated in the same number, would use the west beach, a point on the west of the outer harbour and one at the entrance to the inner harbour. Once again Elkins left to update General Fortune, but when Hemans returned to where he had left his motor launch he found it had gone and all ships out of signalling distance.

During the morning, the boats off St Valéry had come under fire from a German battery sited on cliffs three miles to the west of the town and they had been ordered away from the coast. By midday this shelling was switched to the town itself, and then the beach. Still Hemans could not make contact with the boats. At 1.15 pm he decided that the only alternative was to set out in the cutter in the hope of being picked up. It was not until nine in the evening that he finally made contact with a British boat, the *Sir Evelyn Wood,* after drifting much of the day in a damaged French fishing boat that he and his men had boarded. Unfortunately, the *Sir Evelyn Wood* had no radio and he was unable to pass on the plan of evacuation to the Navy.

* * *

During the morning, it had become necessary for General Fortune to rationalise the command structure and artillery support for the two flank perimeters. The problem had arisen because the four battalions on the eastern perimeter had come directly from the front line positions on the River Béthune where they had been commanded by their respective brigade headquarters and supported by their brigade artillery regiment. Now, all these units were concentrated on the eastern face of the bridgehead. To solve this, 152 Brigade Headquarters was instructed to take over the western line, which contained two of its original battalions, while 153 Brigade Headquarters controlled the eastern line. Both headquarters opened in the early afternoon: 152 Brigade's on the St Valéry–Cailleville road, two miles from the town; 153 Brigade's at Blosseville. One battery of the 1st Royal Horse Artillery was also ordered to move to the western flank.

While these moves were being initiated, a German light reconnaissance plane appeared over Cailleville – a well-known sign that an attack was imminent. General Fortune decided to move his headquarters to a new location in St Valéry, where it would be more secure and from where the embarkation could be better controlled. A reconnaissance party was despatched accordingly. At the same time, he ordered the armour of the 1st Lothians to fall back two miles to guard the road in front of Cailleville. This was made possible by the arrival of elements of the French 5th Light Cavalry Division and the 31st and 40th Infantry Divisions, who had taken up a fragile line from the Cailleville–St Colombe road to near Houdetot, close to the positions of the 1st Black Watch.

By the time Fortune's reconnaissance party arrived in St Valéry, the shelling from the batteries on the west cliffs had begun, hitting both the *Mairie*, the provisional location for Divisional Headquarters, and the subsequent choice – a building near the station on the outskirts of town. Eventually, a large house was found on the west side of the inner harbour which was protected from the shellfire; Divisional Headquarters opened here at around 1.30 pm.

At about this time, Colonel Debenham, the CO of the 7th Norfolks, and his second-in-command, Major Johnson, set out to reconnoitre an inner defensive line about two miles outside St Valéry with both flanks on the cliffs. They were acting under orders from General Fortune, who intended to use this as a final perimeter before the evacuation was completed. The plan was for the 7th Norfolks to man this line by the evening, and then be supplemented by one company or battery from each unit arriving from the outer perimeter.

* * *

Pinning the Highland Division and the four dispirited and fragmented French divisions of IX Corps into a bridgehead just seven miles wide and five miles deep by noon on 11 June were five near full-strength German divisions and one motorised brigade. They included the 2nd Motorised and 5th Panzer Divisions, advancing from the south and south-east respectively, and the 7th Panzer Division, moving in for the kill from the west.

As a reward for their supreme effort the previous day, when they had advanced over 60 miles and cut off the retreat of IX Corps, taking hundreds of prisoners and two ports into the bargain, Rommel allowed his men to rest for most of the morning before resuming the attack. At midday, with about 200 tanks of the 25th Panzer Regiment leading, closely followed by the motorised infantry of the 6th Rifle Regiment, the 7th Panzer Division rumbled towards St Valéry, just six miles away. Directly in its path were the hastily prepared defensive positions occupied by the 2nd Seaforths, the company of 7th Norfolks and the 1st Gordons.

Nominally in command of the 2nd Seaforths on 11 June was a major from the 1st Seaforths, a short man apt to stutter and fond of wearing a monocle, who had been home on leave from Shanghai when war broke out and was consequently posted to the 2nd Battalion. After the injury to Brigadier Stewart and the promotion of Lieutenant Colonel Barclay to command the brigade on 6 June, this major, as next senior officer, had automatically taken over the battalion. But the strain of continual withdrawal had proved too much for this highly-strung man and his second-in-command, Major James Murray Grant, had become the *de facto* commander.

Recognising the vulnerability of the 2,500 yards of ground his men had to defend, gently undulating and mostly bare except for standing crops, Grant decided to concentrate the battalion in two strongpoints a mile apart – the tiny villages of Le Tot and St Sylvain. Made up of a series of interlocking farmhouses and orchards, both provided a measure of cover. Originally just one company, A, was detailed to garrison Le Tot; D Company was sent to join it at 11 am when the French regiment assigned there failed to materialise. A Company was put into positions in the front orchard, D in the one behind. At St Sylvain, B and C Companies were put into the two front orchards, right and left respectively, protected by nothing more than a low earth bank. Battalion Headquarters, HQ Company and the battalion transport were based in a small orchard at the back of the village, fringed on three sides by an earth bank and with a scrubby wood on the fourth. The Regimental Aid Post was established just inside the entrance to this enclosure in a lime-washed barn, criss-crossed with oak beams.

At 11 am, Major Grant decided to go in person to see General Fortune to request some artillery support. He was told that a battery of the 1st Royal Horse Artillery was being sent, and that some guns of the 51st Anti-tank Regiment would also move up. By 1.30 pm an artillery observation officer, Captain Nicholson, with a wireless was installed in Le Tot and an anti-tank officer, Second Lieutenant Burnett, had completed a recce to site his guns and had gone back to bring them up. Half an hour later, the defenders in St Sylvain were astonished when a squadron of French cavalry rode into their positions and said they were going to stay. Just 30 minutes later, and before Burnett could return with his guns, the tank attack had begun.

In his memoirs, Rommel talks of 'heavy artillery and anti-tank gunfire' greeting his tanks, forcing them to bear-off to the south-east. He goes on to say 'the enemy fire grew in violence and heavy batteries joined in.' Even allowing for exaggeration, it seems clear that the defensive fire from the 1st Royal Horse Artillery, directed by Captain Nicholson, had some effect. But it was like trying to hold the tide back with a sand wall.

At 2.30 pm, a breathless runner from A Company arrived at Battalion Headquarters with news that over 40 tanks were advancing on Le Tot. Almost simultaneously, a message arrived from C Company indicating an attack by 50 tanks on its left front. Major Grant recorded his memory of the first hectic minutes of battle in a diary:

> The Mortar Platoon was rushed out, with what little ammunition they had left, to the left of the Battalion HQ position, and opened fire. But within a few minutes the tanks had arrived all round Battalion HQ and were firing into us from three sides whilst mortar and [machine-gun] fire came in from the fourth side . . . With the limited tools we had available we had been able to scratch only narrow shallow cover in the earth banks. We had no [anti-tank] weapons except [anti-tank] rifles. The fire was intense and we suffered between 30 and 40 killed and wounded in this position within a few minutes. Three enemy tanks were knocked out by [anti-tank] rifle fire, the furthest out about 200 [yards], the nearest about 50 [yards]. It is thought that . . . the knocking out of these tanks saved us from being completely overrun, because after a few minutes, which seemed like hours, the main part of the attack swept on to St Valéry . . .[10]

According to Major Grant's diary, as soon as the first shell was fired, the French cavalrymen 'cut loose their horses and instead of assisting us in defending the position, the majority rushed about trying to find cover'. Later, when the firing died down, half of them crept away into the village and were never seen again. But taking over a section of the perimeter, the other half did fight well, especially when their commander was killed and his second-in-command took over.

While the majority of the tanks rumbled on towards the cliffs above St Valéry, a number were left to picquet St Sylvain, and a heavy shell and mortar fire continued to rain down on the Seaforths' positions. In the rear orchard, a number of vehicles had already been set alight, as had a cottage and the barn being used as the Aid Post. Second Lieutenant Philip Mitford, the Adjutant, had gone in to the barn to receive attention minutes before it was hit:

> I had been hit twice, by shrapnel in the foot and the head, and I thought I had better get something done. But there were so many people in the Aid Post that I decided to leave the doctor, McKillop, to carry on with the others and I left. Seconds later the barn received a direct hit from a heavy mortar. Quite a few were killed inside and McKillop was severely wounded – one leg was blown off and the other broken in three places. In spite of this he tried to direct operations and refused to be moved until the last man still alive had been rescued.

Tragically, the Medical Officer, 25-year-old Lieutenant Murdoch McKillop, and practically the whole of his staff had been either killed or wounded in the blast. The grisly and dangerous task of evacuating the burning barn was undertaken by a team of volunteers, using gates and doors to carry out the worst injured as there were no stretchers. The less serious cases were hauled out anyhow in a frantic effort to save them from being burnt to death. When it came to Lieutenant McKillop's turn, he asked to be left, realising his wounds were mortal and not wishing to endanger anyone else's life. His pleas were ignored, and he too was rescued, but he died later that evening. After personally checking that no one inside the barn was still alive, Major Grant called off the evacuation. At least eight dead soldiers were left to be burnt beyond recognition because, as Grant noted in his diary, 'owing to the flames and the enemy fire which was causing more casualties, it was impossible to get them out without further loss of life'. The surviving casualties were taken to an adjacent orchard where a new headquarters had been set up and the remainder of HQ Company had concentrated.

Almost as if the Germans had a spy in St Sylvain, the initial tank attack had been concentrated against the nerve-centre of the battalion – its headquarters position. Consequently, B and C Companies at the front of the village were relatively unscathed by the time the majority of the tanks had moved on. But soon German infantry followed up the attack, and mortar and tank fire began to be directed onto the front orchards. Sergeant John Mackenzie, now commanding 15 Platoon, was in the left front orchard:

> A light tank tried to work in a lot of Jerries armed with Tommy-guns but they didn't stand a chance against our Brens, going down like nine-pins ... we effectively put a stop to anything lighter than a tank moving between us and Le Tot.[11]

Another man in the same orchard was Second Lieutenant Colin Mackenzie, the man who had won a Military Cross in the Saar as a platoon commander but who was now the Intelligence Officer. Earlier, he had been to St Valéry to gather information about the evacuation and had arrived back just as the tank attack was getting underway, his truck being hit by machine-gun bullets in the process. Joining the perimeter held by C Company, he set about making himself useful:

> I thought I had better prime some Mills bombs in case German infantry attacked, and I was doing this when a bullet passed through the top of my tin hat and knocked me unconscious, although it didn't actually pass through my head. I didn't remember anything after that until I was woken by the screams of a very badly wounded soldier. By this time all the other troops that had been in this position had disappeared and I, presumably, had been left for dead. Somehow I got this soldier into the ammunition truck, which had been abandoned and I thought we might need, and drove it to Battalion Headquarters where the Regimental Aid Post was, only a couple of hundred yards away.

While Mackenzie was lying unconscious, Major Godfrey Murray, commanding C Company, deciding his position was too hot had withdrawn his men deeper into the village. Major Grant was suitably impressed by Mackenzie's gallant deed, especially as, according to Grant's diary, the 'truck was burning at the time and some of the ammunition was exploding'. As well as ammunition, the truck also contained a small quantity of water and a case of biscuits which, again according to Grant, 'enabled the [battalion] to fight on longer' and provided refreshment 'which was badly needed for the wounded'.

The first news from Le Tot reached Major Grant when Private George Dodd and Second Lieutenant Laidlaw arrived at the Regimental Aid Post shortly after the first tank attack, having dashed across the open ground between the two villages with a truck load of wounded. The two companies there had had an even harder time of it. In a smaller position with even less protection against tanks than St Sylvain, these men had been virtually overrun in the first attack, suffering heavy casualties. After the wounded had left, the two company commanders, Majors Ritchie and Fraser, decided that the position was impossible to defend and agreed to try and move back to an intermediate position on the cliffs above St Valéry. Unfortunately, as he made his way to the forward positions to ensure that the withdrawal orders were received, Major Fraser was surrounded by tanks and forced to surrender. Taken with him were Captain Hildreth (a reinforcement officer), Second Lieutenant Blair, and two platoons of D Company. Soon after, Major Ritchie was killed. Many of the remaining defenders managed to escape from Le Tot during the evening, but most were either killed or captured. A number lost their lives trying to work their way down the towering cliffs.

By evening, the battle at St Sylvain had died down considerably but German tanks were still ringing the village and any movement drew fire. Battalion Headquarters and HQ Company had since moved to a third position, in an orchard in the centre of the village which offered some measure of anti-tank protection but had practically no field of fire. The only means of observation was by sending out patrols. Just two trucks had been saved, and the mortars had been destroyed when they ran out of ammunition. As night was closing in, Captain Toby Tailyour, the acting Transport Officer, volunteered to try to reach St Valéry to ask for help in one of the two trucks. He was accompanied by Lance Corporal Everden. Despite being shot at on the way, badly wounding Tailyour in the arm, the lorry managed to get through but no help ever arrived.

A few minutes after Tailyour and Everden set off, the men at Battalion Headquarters heard the sound of firing. Assuming the truck had not got through, Major Grant called in his remaining company commanders for a conference. As Grant recorded in his diary, the factors discussed were as follows:

(a) We were cut off, and assistance from St Valéry problematical. (b) Ammunition was nearly finished. (c) Food completely finished. (d) Men and officers exhausted. (e) We could no longer fulfil our role of defending this approach to St Valéry. (f) We had 45 wounded, some of them very badly, no doctor or medical aid, and some of the wounded had already died from lack of attention. (g) A French civilian had been found in the village who volunteered to guide us to a way down the cliffs below which there was a path into St Valéry.[12]

Although no withdrawal orders had been received, it was known that evacuation was planned for that night. Not surprisingly, the company commanders were all for accepting the French civilian's offer and

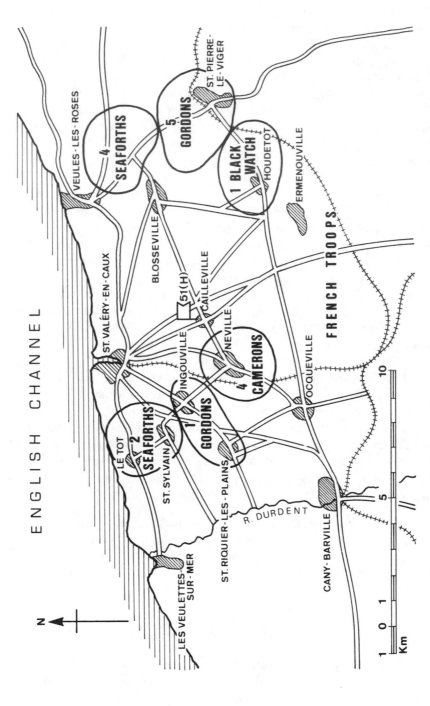

ENGLISH CHANNEL

VEULES-LES-ROSES

ST. PIERRE-LE-VIGER

4 SEAFORTHS

5 GORDONS

1 BLACK WATCH

HOUDETOT

ST. VALÉRY-EN-CAUX

ERMENOUVILLE

BLOSSEVILLE

CAILLEVILLE

51(H)

INGOUVILLE

NEVILLE

FRENCH TROOPS

LE TOT

4 CAMERONS

2 SEAFORTHS

1 GORDONS

OCQUEVILLE

ST. SYLVAIN

LES VEULETTES-SUR-MER

ST. RIQUIER-LES-PLAINS

R. DURDENT

CANY-BARVILLE

N

10

5

1 0 1

Km

Map 4. ST. VALÉRY-EN-CAUX : THE LAST STAND *(Based on a sketch by Second Lieutenant 'Ran' Ogilvie, The Gordon Highlanders)*

attempting to reach St Valéry. Unaware that A and D Companies had already left, four volunteers were sent across to Le Tot to inform them of the proposed move. As darkness descended, the wounded were put on doors and gates and the column formed up. But the difficulty of carrying the unwieldy makeshift stretchers, some needing as many as six fit men, slowed the column to a crawl and it was soon obvious to Major Grant that it could never reach the cliffs before daylight. He decided to return to the positions in the centre of the village, drawing B and C Companies into this smaller perimeter. The plan was to make a similar attempt the following night, leaving the wounded with a small party to surrender as soon as the rest had got away. The remnants of the French cavalry squadron were given a position across the road from the 2nd Seaforths perimeter but they disappeared during the night.

The three forward companies of the 1st Gordons, in a horseshoe position on the edge of St Riquier, were lucky. The flank of the panzer onslaught advanced narrowly to their right, straight over the top of D Company of the 7th Norfolks, in weapon-pits dug in a cornfield. Second Lieutenant 'Ran' Ogilvie, with his platoon to the left of the Norfolks, recalls that nine Boyes anti-tank guns were used against the thinner armour on the sides of the German tanks to no effect, even at ranges as short as 50 yards. After the tanks had moved on, Ogilvie was sent out with a patrol to assess the situation in the Norfolks' line. He found it largely unmanned, the carnage terrible. 'Heavy-calibre machine-guns had split heads open – torn bodies terribly; tank tracks had caught any man in the open,' he later wrote.[13]

Unfortunately for the rear elements of the 1st Gordons – Battalion Headquarters, C and HQ Companies and the Gordons' brigade anti-tank platoon supporting them – their position, in an orchard on the edge of Ingouville, lay in the path of the panzer attack. Second Lieutenant Jimmy Dunlop, commanding the three 25mm anti-tank guns, was the first into action:

> When the tanks advanced in sight of Battalion Headquarters they were almost at maximum range. I was with one gun which we had behind a haystack. When I went back to where the other guns were I found they had both been knocked out by direct hits from the tanks. Also, a mortar bomb had landed while some silly clot was filling up a truck with petrol, causing a fire which spread to the ammunition truck for the anti-tank guns. Luckily, we managed to get a couple of boxes off it which I took to the surviving gun. I left it in charge of a splendid sergeant who managed to get off quite a few shots, although it was put out of action soon after.

Luckily for the defenders of the orchard, it was ringed by a tall earth bank which the tanks could not penetrate and after a few minutes they moved on towards St Valéry. But during the remaining hours of daylight, German infantry infiltrated into the ground between Battalion Headquarters and the forward companies, effectively cutting off the latter. As darkness fell, a storm of lead and steel in the form of mortar and machine-gun fire ripped through the orchard at Ingouville, lasting 20 minutes.

When the fire died down, the wounded were moved across to a nearby chateau. The CO, Harry Wright, was now in a real quandary. He knew embarkation was planned for that night, but he had received no orders and he was out of contact with his forward companies. While runners were sent forward without success, he was forced to sit tight. Finally, at 2 am on 12 June, Captain Victor Campbell, Brigade Major of 152 Brigade, arrived at Wright's headquarters, after a hazardous journey, with orders for the battalion's withdrawal to St Valéry. Before leaving, Wright made one last attempt to get word through to St Riquier. The man chosen for the job was Jimmy Dunlop. Before he had gone 500 yards, he was hit in both legs by a watchful German. With great courage and the help of a child's bicycle, he dragged himself back to Battalion Headquarters where everyone was getting ready to leave.

Colonel Wright had no option now but to leave with the rest of his men. Earlier, two ambulances loaded with wounded had been shot up trying to reach St Valéry and it was now considered too much of a risk to take the worse cases with them. Some 50 badly wounded were left in the château, tended by the Medical Officer, Captain Altham, and some of his stretcher-bearers who volunteered to stay behind. With C Company leading the way, the remnants of the Ingouville garrison set off as dawn broke. At the head of the column, just behind Captain Freddy Colville, the company commander, was Private Tom Copland of the Intelligence Section:

> As we were marching in threes along this narrow road, a machine-gun opened up on us. We dived for cover in an orchard to our left but found it ringed with tanks. Captain Colville mounted the first tank we came to, his servant 'Taffy' Evans and I handing him grenades, the Captain lobbing them into the tank interior. He was successful twice but, at the third attempt, another tank opened fire on him and he fell dead at our feet. It was then a case of attacking the dug-in machine-gun nests, led by our French interpreter, Pierre Boudet. But he was severely wounded and 15 of us were captured shortly afterwards.

Bringing up HQ Company, some way to the rear, Major Hutchins heard the ambush and, taking his men by a detour, managed to reach the town, as did Jimmy Dunlop, who was driven in a truck, and Basil Brooke, who took a party in across country. Colonel Wright was less fortunate; following up with his headquarters' personnel some distance behind C and HQ Companies, he was unaware of the danger on the road and walked straight into the Germans.

All this time the forward companies were without orders and uncertain what to do. Intermittent fire had been directed against their positions at St Riquier throughout the night but no attack had been put in. At dawn, Captain John Stansfeld, commanding D Company, asked his trouble-shooter, ex-fighting patrol officer Johnny Rhodes, to try and get through to Battalion Headquarters to ask for orders. Stansfeld had sent back a number of runners during the night without success, and Rhodes was his last hope. Rhodes recalls:

> On the way I passed by A Company and Aylmer rushed out and seized me by the jacket saying, 'You stay here, we're in desperate danger!' I said, 'Now look, calm down.' I told him what I'd been ordered to do and I went on my way. Aylmer had decided that he was going to defend A Company HQ at all costs and so anybody who passed was called in. The place was absolutely full. That was what had happened to all our messengers. When I eventually reached Battalion HQ there was no one there.

Rhodes had gone to the original site of the headquarters in the orchard, and did not discover the Medical Officer and the wounded in the château nearby. Suspecting that the headquarters had moved back to St Valéry, Rhodes climbed into the CO's abandoned car and set off to inform the forward companies. After driving through a hail of fire, Rhodes roared into St Riquier in the bullet-riddled car and within minutes the company commanders were making arrangements to move back to St Valéry. Suspicious of Captain Aylmer's ability to get his men through safely, 'Ran' Ogilvie asked for and received permission to retire with his platoon independently. Shortly before Ogilvie left, he asked one of his look-outs, Private David Catto, to check the ground to the north for enemy posts. Seconds later, Catto was shot in the head and killed by a sniper. Without wasting any more time, Ogilvie and his men set off:

> We left the position and moved in open tactical attack formation across the open ground towards Ingouville. I moved with my ... HQ behind the rear section from where I could see my whole formation. 1200–1500 yards of open ground is a long walk, especially as we were under rifle and machine-gun and mortar fire all the way. By a miracle we reached cover

at the other end, unscathed, except for minor injuries . . . I had had to use
some rough language to keep the platoon moving forwards, for natural
reaction under fire is to 'go to ground'. In amongst trees at Ingouville was
a chaos of dead and wounded of C Company and Battalion Headquarters.
The Medical Officer and his team were working hard among the
wounded . . . We moved on.[14]

7 Platoon's luck continued to hold when they found three undam-
aged 15 cwt trucks complete with drivers in the middle of Ingouville.
Commandeering them, Ogilvie loaded his platoon and stationed
himself on the cab of the leading truck alongside a Bren gunner. For a
while, the trucks were unmolested and made good time as they hurtled
along the narrow road. It was too good to last. As the convoy topped a
rise in the road it was greeted with the heart-stopping sight of two tanks,
one 50 yards to the left, the other on the left verge 100 yards ahead. In
response to Ogilvie's yell to 'step on it', the first truck leapt forward but
at the same time the tank ahead fired. Slowly the truck rolled to a halt.
The shell had passed through the engine, shattering the driver's right
foot. Immediately, the two following trucks screeched to a halt, and the
contents of all three tumbled into a ditch on the right of the road.
Already in the ditch were an ambulance on its side, its wounded still in
it, two more trucks, and a number of soldiers firing at the tanks with
little result.

Realising that the situation was hopeless, and with no other officers
in sight, Ogilvie shouted 'Cease fire'. One of his platoon, a well-built
15-year-old called Private Gordon Holmes, who had managed to enlist
by lying about his age, continued to fire his Bren until Ogilvie cursed
him to stop. Holmes was destined to experience his 16th birthday in a
Prisoner-of-War camp. Ogilvie then started walking towards the nearest
tank, by now just 20 yards away, holding a white handkerchief in his left
hand and his captured German *Luger* pistol by the barrel in his right.
It was only as the tank commander leapt down to the ground to accept
the surrender that Ogilvie remembered with horror being told that any
prisoner taken with a German weapon would be shot. The tank
commander was obviously unaware of this offence, because he calmly
took the pistol, put on the safety catch and pocketed it without a
murmur.

Most of the remaining men of A, B and D Companies followed Ogilvie
and his platoon into captivity, picked up as they tried to make their way
to St Valéry and possible evacuation. One man, though, still lead a
charmed life. After informing the forward companies that Battalion
Headquarters had left, Johnny Rhodes set off for St Valéry in the CO's

car, accompanied by one of his men, Private 'Ginger' Simpson, who was manning a Bren gun at the back window. He also ran the gauntlet of the tanks on the Ingouville – St Valéry road, but by superior speed and good fortune managed to get through.

* * *

The success of the German armoured thrust in the afternoon of 11 June meant any attempt to embark large numbers of troops from St Valéry was virtually doomed to failure. By siting tanks and machine-guns, and later artillery pieces, on the high cliffs to the west of the town, the Germans commanded both the harbour and the beaches. The importance of the western cliffs, which directly overlook the harbour, had been appreciated by General Fortune earlier in the day and he had urged General Ihler to send a regiment to guard them; unfortunately only a few advance elements had reached them by the time the leading German tanks appeared, and they hastily retired. The inner perimeter being set up by the 7th Norfolks was also supposed to guard the cliffs on both sides of the town, but one of its reconnaissance parties had only just finished its task on the western cliffs when small-arms fire was heard and 15 tanks appeared on the top.

The response of the 7th Norfolks' CO, Colonel Debenham, was to form a Bofors gun detachment from elements of the 1st Armoured Division's Support Group into a roadblock. But this proved unnecessary because the German tanks did not need to take the risk of attacking the town to prevent an evacuation; from their position on the cliffs they could prevent this just as effectively. While Debenham was thus occupied, his Adjutant, Captain Jickling, sent the remaining four companies of the 7th Norfolks to their allotted positions on the inner perimeter line. But the jumpiness of the French, who were largely unofficered and who were firing indiscriminately, and the presence of the Germans, meant that the line was never complete, especially on the west of the town where it was established on the steep, wooded slopes. The line was thickened in the late afternoon by two platoons of 1st Kensingtons and one platoon of 7th Royal Northumberland Fusiliers. But these troops did not arrive in time to prevent some German infantry from working their way down through the orchards and gardens and reaching the edge of the town.

By mid-afternoon these troops, trained to infiltrate in small, NCO-led groups, were within a stone's throw of the large house serving as Divisional Headquarters. Fortune's staff were alerted to the danger when the CRA, Brigadier Eden, rushed in calling for volunteers to defend the house. Lead by Colonel Swinburn, a mixed bag of divisional staff, signallers and administrative troops managed to push the Germans back, right up to the fringe of the wooded area on the cliffs where the tanks could be seen less than 200 yards away. General Fortune missed the drama because he was away visiting troops on the perimeter. General Ihler, who had been with Fortune's headquarters for the previous two days, was also absent. He had regained some of his fight and was busy setting up his own headquarters on the other side of the inner harbour.

When the threat to Divisional Headquarters was first realised, Commander Elkins was advised to return to the beach to try and get in touch with the Navy, who had not yet indicated whether they could cope with 24,000 men, nor whether the suggested start time for the embarkation, 10.30 pm, was suitable. Elkins and Lieutenant Commander Elder had earlier set up a wireless on the end of the eastern pier, or mole, but had been unable to make contact. Now, with the German presence on the edge of the town and the likelihood that their artillery would soon be brought closer, Elkins was highly doubtful whether an evacuation could succeed. Before leaving Divisional Headquarters for the seafront, Elkins sent a short signal to Admiral James again asking for air support to neutralise the enemy artillery and air force.

Owing to shells landing in the business area of town on the east side of the harbour, Elkins made his way up the west side to the corner of the cliff, a couple of hundred yards from the start of the west pier. There he found a group of soldiers taking cover, and could see that both piers were under machine-gun fire. Accompanied by some soldiers – one of whom was the Assistant Director of Ordnance Services, Colonel Roth – Elkins edged round the corner and was shocked by what he saw:

> On the pier, beach and at the foot of the cliff, was a very large number of French soldiers, all of whom had apparently surrendered, but to whom I could not see. A figure on the cliff was calling in French and English 'Come up!' and many were doing so throwing aside their weapons.
>
> Men around me said 'Those are our fellows up there – don't shoot.' Others said 'Those are our fellows' and went up to join them.
>
> I walked towards the Frenchmen to find out what was happening, when I saw an unmistakeable German helmet at the top of the cliff less than a hundred yards away. I also saw the snout of a tank and what appeared to be a machine-gun on a tripod. I snatched a rifle from a soldier and ran down the pier and shouted to Elder on the other pier to destroy the cyphers. As I ran, the Germans opened fire with a machine-gun, but I was running very fast and they missed.
>
> I was unable to reach a small building at the end of the pier and

dropped down behind a heap of granite stones. The Germans called on me to surrender and when I remained where I was, fired into the stones, somewhat reducing the size of the heap.[15]

Spotting a German officer on the clifftop, Elkins fired off a hasty shot but missed. If he had been a better shot the German *Wehrmacht* would have been deprived of its most brilliant young commander, for that officer was none other than General Erwin Rommel who, typically, had joined his leading troops. In response to this affront, a machine-gun opened up again on Elkins' position, reducing still further his scanty cover, one bullet even ricocheting off his helmet. Once again, Elkins was called on to surrender, and as he weighed up the options he noticed Lieutenant Commander Elder on the east pier stand up with his hands in the air. Fortunately for Elder, the entrance to his pier was on the east side of the harbour entrance, still under the control of the British, and he evaded capture. Still Elkins was undecided. All the men around him had surrendered with the exception of a small group behind the pier lighthouse and another under the cliff, including the two RASC officers, one of whom had been wounded in the stomach. Other casualties were lying all about. Then, as Elkins still pondered his predicament, a most bizarre scene unfolded:

A highlander in a kilt ... appeared and, unfired at, walked down the pier to the lighthouse at the end and opened fire on the cliff top with a Bren gun. It was a very brave thing to do and I imagine he was killed. The few men near me shouted at him to stop because they still thought those on the cliffs were British.

Meanwhile, I was wondering what to do. I could see no chance of getting away nor of evacuation ... because the beaches and piers were now covered by enemy machine guns in addition to artillery fire.

The Germans now sent out two riflemen to the end of the cliff and against them my pile of stones afforded no protection. When called upon to surrender again, therefore, I complied, signalling to Colonel Roth as I did so. The wounded were taken up the cliff and one man only, hiding beneath the building on the pier, remained behind. I think he was wounded – in any case he refused to move. I gave myself up to the German General.[16]

If Elkins was nervous at having to surrender to the man he had just tried to kill, he did not show it. In response to a question from Rommel – whom he described in his report as a 'short active man, with a crooked smile' – as to why he had endangered his life by not surrendering at once, Elkins replied in faultless German that he was sure Rommel would have acted in the same way and could he have a drink because he was thirsty. A bottle of wine was immediately produced from a nearby tank. Soon after, Elkins was sent to join about a thousand prisoners who had already surrendered, most of them French, being guarded on the top of the cliffs. From this vantage point he could see a great number of German tanks to the south and west of the town, firing sporadically into the streets and houses, and behind them artillery batteries and infantry arriving in trucks.

During the early evening, Rommel sent a number of prisoners into the town under white flags. Their task was to inform its defenders that unless they surrendered, his division would begin an all-out bombardment of the town at 9 pm. Second Lieutenant Brian Hay of the 1st Gordons was approached by one of these emissaries. Hay had arrived in St Valéry with his transport section in the morning, and finding the inner defence non-existent had set up a series of positions in the centre of town using any man with a weapon who was willing to do as he was told. According to Hay, 'most of them, British troops that had only been in uniform a few months, were not'. Later in the day, Hay was taught a salutary lesson when he tried to shoot the lock off a door as he searched for food for his men. Unlike in the films, this bullet 'didn't have the slightest effect on the lock and instead whizzed round the room. It was a miracle it didn't kill one of us.' Shortly after this, at about 6 pm, one of Rommel's French messengers arrived at Hay's position under a flag of truce with a demand that everyone should surrender. Hay recalls:

> Well I spoke fairly adequate French so we discussed this and I said, 'It's nothing to do with me, I can't do anything about it.' He insisted, and I lost my temper so I walloped him with my revolver knocking him down into the mud in the side of the harbour. What could I do? I was a small cog and it wasn't in my power to surrender the Division – I didn't want to anyway. I don't know what happened to him. I suppose I was fairly hyped up with the pressure of the situation and when he came to ask me to do something so stupid I saw red.

At about the same time, a second French soldier sent by Rommel arrived at Divisional Headquarters. In General Fortune's absence, he was sent packing by Lieutenant Colonel Swinburn, who told him that the British had no intention of surrendering. Rommel's memoirs confirm these responses.

> It was mainly the British, though there were some French officers also, who turned down all idea of capitulation. They kept their men at it building barricades and getting large numbers of guns and machine-guns into position all round St Valéry and especially in the port area. Probably

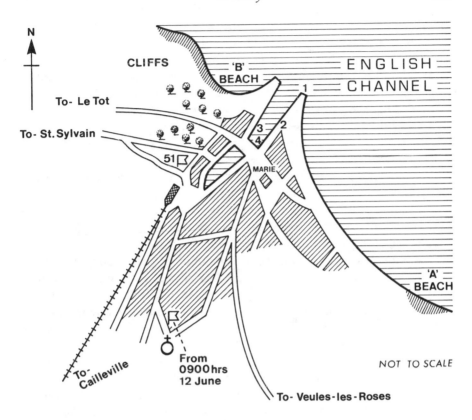

N

CLIFFS

'B'
BEACH

ENGLISH
CHANNEL

To- Le Tot

To- St. Sylvain

51

MARIE

'A'
BEACH

To-
Cailleville

From
0900 hrs
12 June

NOT TO SCALE

To- Veules-les-Roses

ALLOTMENT OF BEACHES etc FOR EMBARKATION

     BRITISH –   'A' BEACH, Nos 1 & 2 LANDING PLACES

     FRENCH   'D' BEACH, Nos 3 & 4 LANDING PLACES

Map 5. ST. VALÉRY-EN-CAUX : ALLOTMENT OF BEACHES FOR EMBARKATION
*(Based on a Sketch by Lieutenant Colonel HR Swinburn MC RA,
GSO I 51st (Highland) Division)*

the British were hoping to resume their embarkation during the night.[17]

True to his word, Rommel responded to the Allies' failure to surrender St Valéry by unleashing a heavy bombardment at 9 pm exactly. The combined firepower of his tank regiment and reconnaissance battalion was directed first against the entrance to the harbour and then to the north-western part of the town. At nightfall, the tanks were withdrawn, but the shelling of the town was continued by 88mm anti-aircraft guns, while infantry used machine-guns and rifles to keep up a harassing fire along the seafront.

As mad as it may have seemed to Rommel, with his guns trained on the beaches and harbour, it was still General Fortune's intention to attempt an embarkation that night. Divisional Headquarters had been out of contact with the Navy for much of the day, owing to Admiral James order at 1.30 pm for the warships and rescue armada to move six miles off the coast because of the danger from bombers and artillery fire. But Fortune had never given up hope of salvation, and he and his staff were doing everything in their power to be ready for embarkation by their proposed time of 10.30 pm.

Some time after 6 pm, the long awaited news that Admiral Platon in Le Havre had given permission for evacuation was received at Divisional Headquarters. It had finally been wrung from him at around 4.30 pm by Captain Tower, who had then set about informing all interested parties including the 51st Division, Admiral James, Captain Warren in HMS *Codrington*, and the War Office. At 6.15 pm, Admiral James confirmed Tower's signal by sending one of his own to Captain Warren. It read: 'Evacuation from St Valéry area is to commence this evening. All available transports are being sent.'[18]

Considering the proximity of the Germans, Fortune felt it necessary to emphasise to Admiral James and the all too hesitant War Office that time was of the essence. At 8.30 pm he authorised a signal which read: '. . . Consider to-night last possible chance of 51 Div. French authority given. Strength British 12,000 equal numbers French Total 24,000.'[19] One hour later, brief verbal orders were issued to representatives of all units of the 51st Division, giving times of embarkation from 10.30 pm onwards – the administrative units like the RASC being allotted the earlier times. All 51st Division troops holding the perimeter received these orders except the 2nd Seaforths and a portion of the 1st Black Watch, who could not be reached. For the rest, though, there was still hope; The Navy was on its way and tomorrow might see them back in Britain.

No such orders were ever issued to the thousands of French troops in and around St Valéry. When Colonel Swinburn went to see General Ihler in his headquarters at 8 pm to discuss embarkation times, he was told by Ihler that the boats would not come in and therefore there was little point in making any arrangements.

* * *

While Rommel's tanks were punching a hole through the frail defences of the western perimeter, the other sectors were still enjoying a relatively peaceful day as the other four and a half German divisions made a more leisurely advance. Finally, at around four, the eastern perimeter was bombed and machine-gunned from the air, causing casualties among the 5th Gordons on the St Pierre–Yelon road. This was soon followed up by hostile mortar and artillery fire, especially fierce on the positions held by the 2/7th Duke of Wellington's Regiment around Veules-les-Roses.

At 5.30 pm, a conference was held at 153 Brigade Headquarters in an orchard on the east side of the village of Blosseville. At the conference, Brigadier Burney told the COs of the four battalions manning the east perimeter that an attempt would be made to embark from St Valéry when the Navy arrived, but that this would probably not be until the night of 12/13 June. To prepare for this, he told them, all equipment and transport, other than weapons and one truck per company, were to be destroyed.

It was the British Government's refusal, without French acquiescence, to give its Navy the go-ahead that had resulted in this bizarre situation of unit commanders, even at this late hour, being uncertain as to when an attempt would be made to take their men off. Consequently, when the news that embarkation was to take place that night filtered through from Divisional Headquarters, it was too late for many units. Some did not reach St Valéry until well after dawn on 12 June, and some not at all.

The conference hastily broke up at 6.10 pm when positions held by the gunners of the 23rd Field Regiment just to the front of Blosseville were heavily shelled. Major Shaw-Mackenzie, the CO of the 4th Seaforths, set off to find a safe road on which to leave Blosseville for his headquarters in Yelon, when he was bumped into by a 30 cwt truck containing one of his 3-inch Mortar sections. Moments later, the remainder of the mortar platoon appeared with Captain Heffernan, the 152 Brigade Staff Captain. Heffernan told Shaw-Mackenzie that an officer at Yelon had issued orders to some of the 4th Seaforths' HQ Company to move back to Blosseville which was to be made into a strongpoint. Thinking that there must have been a change of orders, Shaw-Mackenzie returned to Brigade Headquarters to check, but Brigadier Burney assured him that there had not been. Intent on finding out the identity of this officer who was issuing orders in his absence, Shaw-Mackenzie rushed back to Yelon, taking the mortar platoon with him. He later wrote:

> On my arrival ... I found [Captain] Baird [OC HQ Company] in conversation with an officer I had not seen before. He said he was Major

Williams – Second-in-Command of 1 RHA. I asked him if he had given orders to my Battalion in my absence and what he meant by it! He seemed somewhat taken aback and said that I apparently did not know what the situation was. He explained that he had just come back from the west face of the perimeter and that here a heavy tank attack was in progress and that we were entirely surrounded on all sides. He said that our only hope was to concentrate in Blosseville, from a strongpoint there and fight our way to the coast that night. I asked him who had given these orders as I had only just come from a [Brigade] Conference. He said that nobody had given orders but this was his own idea![20]

At this point, Brigadier Burney arrived. After listening to the gunner officer's story, Burney seemed impressed and said he would go and find out about it. Five minutes later he returned, having had second thoughts, and said that Williams' version was nonsense and that the plan arranged at the conference would be carried out. Burney then left, as did Williams. Shaw-Mackenzie states in his diary that he never saw this gunner officer again, but that he learnt later that he escaped from Veules-les-Roses early the next morning with a battery of 1st Royal Horse Artillery and was awarded a DSO. In fact the officer who managed this feat was Major Mullens, commanding 385 Battery, and there is every reason to conclude that Shaw-Mackenzie got the names mixed up and that the officer who gave orders to his men was indeed Williams, not Major Mullens.

As the brigade conference at Blosseville was in progress, tanks of the 5th Panzer Division were moving into position to attack the 2/7th Duke of Wellington's Regiment near Veules-les-Roses. As they were advancing from a south-easterly direction, the tanks had to cross the front of the 5th Gordons and the 4th Seaforths.

The 23rd Field Regiment in front of Blosseville were told of this enemy column and their subsequent shelling of the road knocked out a number of vehicles, including some tanks. But the majority got through, and from 6 pm onwards a tank attack was put in against the 2/7th Duke of Wellington's guarding the northern stretch of the Veules-les-Roses–St Pierre road. Eventually piercing the line in a number of places, the tanks rumbled on towards St Valéry and the defenders managed to hold on.

Units of the 1st Black Watch, in positions near St Pierre-le-Viger, were also in action. The defences at this time were being manned by just two companies, A and B, one section of carriers, and some French cavalry, who had joined them a couple of hours earlier. This fragmentation of the battalion was the result of a brigade order, received at 1 pm, to reconnoitre a new line between Gueutteville-lès-Grès and Cailleville. In preparation for a probable withdrawal to the new line later in the afternoon, Colonel Honeyman had moved back his C, D and HQ Companies to an orchard near Houdetot, one mile to the east of St Pierre.

Shortly after 4.30 pm, when Honeyman left for the Brigade Conference, A and B Companies were engaged by mortar and machine-gun fire. As it was expected that a withdrawal would commence at 5 pm, the position, especially that occupied by B Company, was not properly dug-in. Even more unfortunate was the fact that the best trench had been used for burying Platoon Sergeant Major Royle, a Warrant Officer who had been killed when one of his own men went berserk. Gradually, the vulnerability of these positions to shell and machine-gun fire began to tell, and at 6 pm B Company withdrew without orders to a sunken road just 150 yards from Battalion Headquarters.

At 7 pm, firing began from the exposed rear and left flank of the Black Watch, and the Germans also began to work their way round the right flank. Fearing that his men could not hold out for much longer, Bill Bradford – commanding in the absence of Colonel Honeyman and his second-in-command, Major Dundas – sent the Intelligence Officer, John Moon, on a motorcycle to try and contact brigade for orders. An hour later, having heard nothing, Bradford told the commander of the French troops that he was considering a withdrawal. The Frenchman demurred, saying that his orders were to hold on until dark and then withdraw *before* the Black Watch. As Bradford agonised what to do, and casualties mounted from machine-gun and mortar fire, the enemy continued to make ground, especially on the right flank. This was only halted when a section of carriers was dismounted to cover this danger.

At 9 pm, Bradford agreed to retire 45 minutes later in conjunction with the French, meeting up at the road junction in the rear before making for Gueutteville. In preparation for this, as many wounded as possible were piled into the office truck to be driven across country to a dressing station. Thanks to the determination of their driver, Lance Corporal Farquharson, this truck got through safely. Then, with just minutes to go before the withdrawal, panic set in. Bradford later wrote:

> Just before 2145 hours, one platoon of A Company with its commander withdrew and caused confusion in the remainder of [the company]. Everyone got the idea that the enemy were right on top of us, and it was difficult to keep men at Battalion HQ in their positions ... B Company, I learned later, did not withdraw for some time, as [its commander] was trying to make arrangements for the wounded. As we had no stretchers and only one 8-cwt truck without driver, this was impossible. Wounded

were put on carriers, but I'm afraid many were left. It was awful.[21]

After an exhausting march of over five miles, part of the way under fire, first from the Germans, and later from French troops withdrawing in the opposite direction, Bradford and about 120 survivors of A and B Companies arrived in Gueutteville at 1.30 am. They were still four miles from St Valéry and, after a two hour rest, would not reach the town until well after sun-up.

Shortly after the attack had begun on the St Pierre positions, HQ, C and D Companies near Houdetot were also under pressure from machine-gun and shell fire. They had been joined by the CO, Honeyman, who had found it impossible to return to Battalion Headquarters because enemy armoured cars were blocking his path. With the support of a troop of guns from the 23rd Field Regiment and a Vickers machine-gun manned by the 1st Kensingtons, the Black Watch held on. But orders to withdraw on St Valéry for embarkation never arrived, and at daybreak on 12 June these companies were still holding out, unaware that all flanking troops had left.

The first unit on the eastern perimeter to abandon its positions during the evening of 11 June was the 2/7th Duke of Wellington's. At about 9.45 pm, shortly after the main tank attack had swept through its flimsy defences, the CO, Lieutenant Colonel Taylor, probably assuming that the route to St Valéry had been cut and that there was no time to waste, issued orders for a withdrawal to the beach at nearby Veules-les-Roses. Within minutes, a patrol of German tanks was seen to be advancing on Battalion Headquarters in a sunken road on the edge of the village. In the ensuing confusion, as the defenders dispersed, Colonel Taylor became separated from the main body and was subsequently captured.[22]

The first the 4th Seaforths – holding the perimeter to the south – knew about this withdrawal was when a Duke of Wellington's despatch rider arrived at Battalion HQ at midnight. Shaw-Mackenzie's record of the interview is as follows:

> He was in a state of breakdown and said, 'All the 2/7th DWRs have been killed.' I told him to calm himself and then questioned him. He said that he had been sent from his Bn HQ on a message to one of the companies but had failed to find them. He had been along the whole line and only found some men of the unit dead … He also said that he had failed to find his [Battalion Headquarters] where he had left them. After hearing this story I decided to send him to Bde HQ.[23]

The possibility that 'there were no troops on my left as far as the sea' was 'most disturbing' to Shaw-Mackenzie. But unwilling to do anything about it until he had heard from brigade, he showed remarkable *sang froid* by going back to sleep. Shaw-Mackenzie, like most of his men, had had no proper rest since the Forêt d'Eu on the night of 7/8 June and was exhausted. At 2 am, he was wakened by the arrival of Second Lieutenant Bisset, his liaison officer at Brigade Headquarters, and handed a scrap of paper with an illegible signature. It read: 'Thin out 2130 hrs, abandon positions 2200 hrs. Rdv Rly Stn [rendezvous railway station] St Valéry for embarkation 0200 hrs.' After confirming that it had come from the Brigade Major of 153 Brigade, Bisset was unable to say whether it referred to that night or the following one. To find out which, Shaw-Mackenzie sent his Provost Sergeant back to Brigade Headquarters. In case it was that night, he also sent instructions to his company commanders to report at once, and to leave orders with their second-in-commands to prepare for immediate withdrawal. After what Shaw-Mackenzie described as a 'very short time', the Provost Sergeant returned and said: 'There is only one answer to our message, sir, it is now'. By 3 am, the battalion had formed up and marched out of Yelon, and, despite contacting an enemy patrol near Blosseville and the inconvenience of the first downpour for days, it eventually arrived safely in St Valéry a couple of hours later.[24]

Surprisingly, the 4th Seaforths managed to reach St Valéry ahead of the 5th Gordons, the battalion to its left on the perimeter, despite the fact that the latter got orders to move two hours earlier and had less distance to travel. The time lag was caused by Colonel Clark's over-cautious need to confirm these orders, brought by despatch rider, by sending Second Lieutenant Hughes to Brigade Headquarters. Why he did this is unclear, although it is possible that he wanted to check on a story that General Ihler had surrendered, recounted to him by a French officer shortly before. The net result was that the departure was delayed until 4.30 am by which time it was already light.

The only battalion on the western perimeter to reach St Valéry intact during the night of 11/12 June was the 4th Camerons. Its men would later be grateful for the miscalculation of the 1st Gordons that led to the two battalions swapping positions. Without this, it would have been the Camerons and not the Gordons who faced the horror of the tank attack during the afternoon and evening of the 11th. Instead, the Camerons' positions in front of Néville were untroubled. Finally, at 11.30 pm, a car containing the battalion's liaison officer at brigade, Second Lieutenant McLeod, and the 152 Brigade Intelligence Officer, Captain McCulloch, roared into the village. The message from brigade was for an immediate withdrawal into St Valéry to arrive in time for embarkation at 11 pm! Of course, this was impossible, but steps were taken to move back as quickly as possible. The 4th Camerons was one of the few battalions with its transport still largely intact, and by emptying its trucks of everything but weapons and a little food, it was able to motor all its men straight into St Valéry, arriving sometime after 2 am. The CO, Major Mackintosh-Walker, had gone on ahead in his car with Lieutenant Hunter, leaving Major Stanley Hill in command. Major Bertie MacLeay, commanding HQ Company, later recorded in a diary this unforgettable experience:

> The run to St Valéry ... was macabre in the extreme and reminded one of Dante and his Inferno. [We] passed blazing cottages, chateaux, trucks and loads all of the way ... Normally people would be rushing away from a doomed and blazing town and here we were bringing another 500 men into it. As we reached the town, the glare became brighter and brighter and it was like daylight as we went down the steep street into the upper square. From this square various streets radiated and our instructions were to take the right hand road past the station. The first lot of trucks did this only to find the road impassable with blazing buildings. They turned ... and met the second lot coming in, blocking the street completely.[25]

After a quick conference with the other officers, Major Hill ordered the battalion to dismount and the engines of the trucks were smashed with sledge-hammers and pick-axes. The men were then formed up in the square while Major MacLeay and the Adjutant, Captain Lang, went off to find an alternative route to the harbour.

Considering that the southern perimeter was the weakest held of the three, it was only by good fortune that it remained unscathed during 11 June. The CO of the 1st Lothians, Colonel Ansell, was told during the afternoon that the French cavalry in position a little way to his south would pass through his regiment at 8 pm, while the 1st Lothians would hold on as a rearguard until ordered to withdraw. It was some cause for alarm, then, when hours before time Colonel Ansell, who was on a reconnaissance, spotted a great mass of men half a mile to his front moving towards him:

> It was only four o'clock, so thinking that the Germans must have broken through we hurried back to the regiment. As this mob approached, we saw through glasses their French uniforms – they'd fallen back four hours early. I shall never forget their panic. Officers on motor-bikes, men throwing away weapons or tying white handkerchiefs round the muzzles

of their rifles. For all the world like a herd of frightened cattle, and no stopping them.[26]

The hours ticked by as the men of the 1st Lothians, once again in the front line, strained their eyes to the south for a sign of the attack they thought must come. Eventually, during the early evening, General Fortune himself arrived with their orders. As so often before, they were to act as rearguard for the division and, along with the 7th Norfolks, who were holding the inner perimeter, were scheduled as the last formation to embark. Suspecting that, as the rearguard, his men were unlikely to be able to get away, Colonel Ansell asked Fortune for permission to break his regiment up into small parties after the midnight deadline, because this would give his men the best chance to escape. Fortune agreed, and on hearing of the precipitous French withdrawal asked Ansell to contact the French general concerned and tell him from General Fortune to order his men to stay in position. Ansell immediately set off on this mission in a motorcycle sidecar, and, after endless hold-ups on roads packed with refugees and French soldiers, eventually located the French general's headquarters in an orchard:

> I found him in a long low room overlooking the orchard and that same lovely setting sun. A small man, walking up and down like Felix the Cat. He was in Full Dress, with sword and all his medals. I became very angry as he waved away my questions, saying he did not know where his troops were and now it did not matter, he wished to surrender.[27]

Depressed by this defeatism, Ansell returned to his men to await orders. At last they arrived, setting the time for withdrawal at midnight and the probable hour of embarkation as 4 am. Like all other units of the 51st Division, the Lothians were instructed to destroy all equipment except personal weapons. Tanks, carriers, trucks and wirelesses were smashed, and at the appointed hour the regiment marched off in good order, bristling with Brens, anti-tank rifles and .303s. Despite the dark, the town of St Valéry was soon visible by the tongues of angry flame that rose above it, hinting at an outcome that was unlikely to end with deliverance.

12

The Lucky Few

While the men of the 51st Division were struggling into St Valéry during the night of 11/12 June, Admiral James' armada was doing its best to make the rendezvous. At around 5 pm, when Captain Warren, aboard HMS *Codrington*, received a signal from Captain Tower in Le Havre giving the go-ahead for the evacuation, the armada was strung out a good seven miles north-west of St Valéry.[1] The fact that only 16 vessels had wirelesses out of a total civilian rescue force of 67 merchant ships and 140 smaller boats proved a severe handicap to Warren's efforts to marshal them. This deficiency might not have been so disruptive on a clear day, but the 11th was anything but clear; thick patches of fog drifted across the sea making contact by light signal largely impossible. In this blindness, boats drifted apart and lost touch. HMS *Codrington* and her fellow destroyer HMS *Saladin* were able to instruct a number of vessels to make for St Valéry by loud-hailers, as were some of the boats with which they were in radio contact, but many did not receive instructions until it was too late, and some not at all.

The 'Haven Blue' Flotilla, for example – raised at Newhaven under the command of Lieutenant Dyer, and consisting of nine motor yachts and three fishing boats in the tow of a coastal collier – arrived at St Valéry at 2 pm on 11 June and found no craft in sight. The flotilla then sailed north for two hours, but seeing nothing, and presuming the ships had been withdrawn, returned to Newhaven.

It was not just the lack of communication which caused some boats to return empty-handed. The problem for the men of the 'Haven White' flotilla, one of the earliest to sail during the evening of 9 June, was the accumulation of fatigue caused by the length of time at sea in small vessels. At 6 pm on 11 June, after some near misses by bombing from the air, the exhausted masters of the small boats cut themselves adrift. They only took up the tow again when the naval officer in command agreed to take them back to Newhaven. A similar 'mutiny' occurred later in the larger 'Haven Red' flotilla. Despite losing contact with the rest of the armada, the flotilla commander, Captain Cameron, managed to navigate his three vessels and 14 fishing boats towards St Valéry, where he knew the evacuation was due to take place. As soon as it became obvious that he was intending to make for the town, his men voiced their objections. In his report of the operation, Cameron is clearly sympathetic to their plight:

> We continued on course towards St Valéry for about a couple of hours and as we drew close (the mist having lifted by this time) saw that the whole place was in flames ... but there was still no signs of any other vessels. As we were proceeding at about [2 am] loud cries and whistles and cat calls came from the fishermen in the boats I was towing ... eventually they yelled out that they had no intention of returning to the place they had visited in the afternoon and that they refused to do so. I might point out that these men had had a very gruelling experience. This was their third night on end in open boats and cooking arrangements and accommodation were almost nil, and in addition to the discomforts they had been shelled with us during the afternoon. I felt that to take the *Ocean Sunlight* on and cast the fishermen off would leave me in a very poor position for doing any rescue work ... as the *Ocean Sunlight* drew too much water to do any beach work, and the port of St Valéry was commanded by the battery I have already referred to. I therefore decided to turn round and bring my tow home.[2]

Nevertheless, despite the adverse weather conditions, poor communications and the lack of cooperation shown by some civilian sailors, many boats willing to see the operation through did arrive off St Valéry during the hours of darkness. Among the first were the tug *Fairplay* with nine drifters in tow and two Dutch *schuyts*, commanded by Lieutenant Commander House. At 9 pm, House had made contact with HMS *Saladin* and was instructed by megaphone to make for the narrow front on the west side of St Valéry and to begin embarkation on the signal of a series of white Very lights. Arriving off the town at 12.35 am, House was grateful that the west beach was clear from the glare of burning houses which were mostly on the east side. Soon after this white Very lights were fired from the shore, so House immediately began loading beach parties into his boats at a distance of just 300 yards from the shore. As he did so, the Germans on the cliffs spotted the boats and a heavy fire was opened with mortars and machine-guns. In his report, House, who was in one of the boats, described the situation as 'quite untenable'. Within minutes he had lost four boats, riddled with shot, while the *Fairplay* was damaged. Chastened by the experience, and with no naval ships in the vicinity to issue orders, House set course with his remaining boats for Newhaven and home.[3]

HMS *Saladin*, the destroyer in charge of small craft, was the next to arrive off St Valéry a little before 1 am. Seeing that the town and beach were under fire, and assessing that any evacuation from its beaches and harbour would be suicidal, Captain Armstrong sent the following signal at 1.05 pm to his superior, Captain Warren, on the *Codrington*: 'Have investigated St Valéry which appears full of enemy and beach is under heavy fire, am now moving to Veules. Where are you?'[4] The *Codrington* was, in fact, also in sight of the town and in his report Captain Warren stated that it was clear from Armstrong's signal that St Valéry 'was quite impracticable as a place for evacuation'. Warren could see for himself that 'the place was burning fiercely and a lot of machine-gun and artillery fire was being directed on the beach, also enemy star shell'.[5] It was at this point, shortly after 1 am, that the plan to embark troops at St Valéry was called off and all boats that could be contacted were directed to the quieter beach at Veules-les-Roses, four miles to the east.

* * *

Unaware of the problems and confident that the Navy would arrive during the night, despite the enemy guns on the cliffs, the Divisional Staff had gone ahead with its preparations and by 10.30 pm, a number of troops were already in position in the harbour and on the beaches. After a long hour had dragged by with no sign of the boats, Colonel Roney-Dougal, the staff officer in charge at the seafront, sent a message to this effect back to Divisional Headquarters. After waiting another fruitless hour, Roney-Dougal returned in person to report to General Fortune that in his opinion they would not be coming. Still Fortune did not give up hope and insisted that the men should remain ready to embark a little longer.

At 1.15 am, Lieutenant Commander Elder, waiting anxiously on the seafront with his wireless, sent a signal to the Navy asking when the ships could be 'expected' and pointing out that the situation was 'most critical'. Unbeknown to Elder, the embarkation at St Valéry had already been called off by Captain Warren. No signal informing the 51st Division of this decision was ever sent, and troops remained on or near the beaches under occasional machine-gun and shell fire for another two hours. Finally, at 3 am, fearing the consequences of leaving his men exposed in such positions until dawn which was only an hour and a half away, General Fortune sent Colonel Roney-Dougal to order them to make for the railway station square at the entrance to the town. There they were directed by Colonel Swinburn to woods about half a mile south of the town next to the Cailleville road. Many perimeter troops reaching St Valéry after this time were given similar instructions.

* * *

The first merchant ship of any size to reach Veules-les-Roses was the

Goldfinch, commanded by Lieutenant Thompson. It had been directed there by one of the destroyers and by 2.30 am Thompson was using his lifeboats, manned by three officers and 21 ratings, to pick up soldiers off the beach. In his report of the operation, Thompson shows his admiration for the men he rescued:

> It was a revelation to see men who had been fighting for days without proper food or rest, helping to pull the boats out to the ship, most of them were aboard exhausted when they came aboard. Many were wounded.[6]

By sun-up, the *Goldfinch* had already embarked more than 400 men single-handedly. She had been joined in her work by many other vessels including the merchant ships *Guernsey Queen, Cameo* and *Archangel,* the drifter *Golden Harvest,* the Dutch *schuyt Pascholl,* and the destroyers *Saladin* and *Codrington.* Also present were a number of French and Belgian vessels. Although only a fraction of the original rescue armada reached Veules-les-Roses, the efforts of those who did made up for the small numbers. Much of the credit must go to Commander Chatwin and Sub-Lieutenants Killam and McLernon, the officers in command of the beach party landed by the *Codrington* at 4 am. The two Sub-Lieutenants ensured discipline in the queues that formed, while Chatwin directed the embarkation from his motor boat, preventing boats from leaving before they were fully loaded and then helping to tow them out. Although there was intermittent fire during the early morning, rain and hazy weather reduced its effectiveness and nothing was hit. But at 8.30 am a heavy artillery bombardment was opened against the boats and the beach from both the east and the west. Within half an hour, in which time all the British ships except *Pascholl* had departed, Chatwin ordered the remaining small boats to make for the *Pascholl* while he embarked the naval beach party in his motor boat. Although Chatwin was satisfied that no British troops were still on the shore, he stated in his report that a 'number' of French soldiers 'were left on the beach'.[7]

A total of 1,300 British and 900 French troops were taken off from Veules-les-Rose during the morning of 12 June. An insignificant number when compared to the 24,000 General Fortune had hoped to embark, but a small success nonetheless. Most of the British troops who were rescued had managed to find themselves in the right place at the right time by a combination of resourcefulness and luck. Some had slipped away from their posts without orders, others had made it with the co-operation of their superiors.

By far the biggest number of men rescued from a single unit were 500 or so from the 2/7th Duke of Wellington's Regiment. Once in possession of the order from their ill-fated CO, officers collected small parties together and withdrew under cover of woods to Veules-les-Rose, artillery fire having set alight many of its buildings and making it visible for miles.

The only other unit to escape largely intact from the beaches of Veules-les-Roses was 385 Battery of the 1st Royal Horse Artillery. This battery had begun the war as part of the 97th (Kent Yeomanry) Field Regiment, but had swapped with a battery of the 1st RHA in April because its gun tractors were more mobile and better suited to travel the long distance down to the Saar. Commanded by Major William Mullens – a 31-year-old Kent Territorial who was awarded the DSO for leading this intrepid escape – the battery had been supporting the west perimeter of the bridgehead. The citation for Mullens' decoration states that his battery remained in position until 4 am, holding the enemy back entirely on their own for the last hour. They then marched into St Valéry only to find there were no ships. Along with many other troops in St Valéry, Mullens took his men to high ground to the south of the town and told the junior officers that they could escape individually if they wished. Some time later, an officer who had made his way along the beach from St Valéry to Veules-les-Roses returned on a motorbike with the information that there were boats there. Under fire for much of the way, Mullens then lead his battery the six miles to the beach. On the way, the citations states, they successfully stormed a German-held village blocking their path armed only with revolvers! As a result, Major Mullens and 160 men of his battery, 70 per cent of the total, escaped.[8]

The rest of the British troops who escaped from Veules-les-Roses were a mixed collection of just about every unit in the Highland Division. Most under-represented were members of the Highland infantry rifle companies, the front line soldiers who were holding the perimeter to the last and who had least opportunity to make it to Veules. More typical were men like Driver Alec Bisset of the RASC. Aged 22, Bisset was a member of 527 (Supply) Company and had arrived in St Valéry in his truck during the afternoon of the 11th. After making his way along the beach between St Valéry and Veules-les-Roses, Bissett stopped in a cave full of Frenchmen and fell asleep. At first light he noticed a big shape in the sea outside, and on looking again recognised it as a ship's lifeboat manned by the Navy. Eventually transferred from a trawler to a cross-channel steamer, Bisset made it home.

Some men, like Company Quartermaster Sergeant Jim Smith of the 4th Camerons were desperate enough to try to work their way down the 300 foot cliffs with makeshift ropes. During the evening Smith had been on the cliffs to the east of the town as 152 Brigade Headquarters' trucks were being pushed over to deny them to the enemy. As he recalls, the order 'Every man for himself' was given and a Regimental Sergeant Major said to the men around him; 'If any of you fellows are game to try making a run out of here without actually going by road down into St Valéry, take your rifle slings off and get all the blankets from that truck'. Smith remembers:

> We took out hundreds of blankets from my truck and knotted them all together, interspersed with rifle slings, and tied the end with a double knot onto the front of a three-ton truck. The idea was not so much to get down into St Valéry but to get further away from it up towards Veules-les-Roses. We had no idea if the first rope had hit the bottom and the first few who volunteered to go down didn't know where they were in the dark. Of the first 12 I think about seven were killed. One shouted up, 'We need more length at the bottom.' So we passed more rifle-slings to the boys who were going down and they tied them until eventually they made the ground. Quite a number got down that way, along with me.
>
> It was about three or four o'clock in the morning when we started the trek to Veules-les-Roses. There was a brigade officer, I don't know who he was, and he took charge. The tide was out and we made our way along the beach. There were caves all along, like catacombs, and we just dodged our way in and out of them to avoid fire from the Germans on the cliffs at St Valéry. A little later we saw the light from a ship. We waded out until about chest deep and were picked up by small boats manned by the Navy. I was unloaded onto a destroyer.

Two men who escaped after remaining with their unit on the perimeter to the last were Major Jimmy Dallmeyer and Captain Ronnie Watson, the commander and second-in-command respectively of A Squadron, 1st Lothians. Although ear-marked as the rearguard, by receiving their orders for withdrawal to St Valéry in good time, the men of 1st Lothians had been able to reach the town well before many of the infantry battalions. Just before dawn, once it was learnt that no boats had come in and that all troops had been ordered to woods outside the town, Colonel Ansell gave the order he had discussed with General Fortune the night before – 'Tallyho – Every man for himself'. Most of the officers decided to make for the west. To ease the congestion Dallmeyer and Watson went east, taking three men of their squadron with them. As they moved off the rain began to stream down. Dallmeyer's report reads:

> Our intention was to strike east, find some convenient place to hide during daylight, and at night to try and find a boat on the shore. After walking in ditches and through woods for some 15 minutes we paused to

look at a map ... and found we were heading in the wrong direction. So we turned back, crossed the road and went up the hill on the other side and set our course for a big wood in the distance.

Presently we came upon a French battery which was being shelled, so we altered course to avoid it and to our astonishment found ourselves on the top of the cliffs. About a mile away one ship could just be seen close inshore, but it was impossible to get down as the cliffs overhang. We then set off along the cliffs passing hundreds of abandoned French rifles and equipment. After a time, we sighted some men, so we made for a cornfield and stalked them. They were British and followed us along.[9]

At one point, the expanded party came upon two groups waiting to go down the cliff on ropes, possibly one of which Company Quartermaster Sergeant Jim Smith had used during the night. Judging that this method was 'far too dangerous' and the queue 'far too long', Dallmeyer led his men on. Before long, they could see shapes in the sea which gradually became discernible as ships, lying close inshore off a fishing village. Half a mile later, small boats were visible moving to and fro the shore. They passed more groups trying to take the short route down the cliffs, seven in all, and finally reached Veules-les-Roses and the beach. Here they found five groynes, three allocated to the French and two to the British. While they were waiting in a queue, the French began to fire wildly at some German planes. It occurred to Dallmeyer that 'many were nearer death then than at any other time'. Watson remembers the naval beach party as 'a lot of efficient, burly sailors with revolvers at their side' who gave any queue-bargers 'pretty short shrift'. Eventually, all five of Dallmeyer's party were embarked onto a passenger ship. They were exhausted and Watson could not help noticing with irritation that all the cabins had been taken – by the French.

Many British soldiers arrived at Veules-les-Roses too late to be rescued. One such was Captain Derek Lang, the Adjutant of the 4th Camerons. He was on the seafront at St Valéry at first light and noticed two ships inshore further up the coast. Bumping into his brigadier, Iain Barclay, he suggested trying to reach one of the ships because, if it had a wireless working, he could contact the Navy and find out about embarkation for the Division. Barclay agreed it was worth a try and Lang set off, accompanied by a sergeant major from his battalion. Lang graphically describes the horrors that greeted him on the long trek up the beach in his autobiography, *Return to St Valéry*:

It was harder going than we had expected. We had to keep close in to the rocks to avoid attracting machine-gun fire from the cliff tops. As it was there were places where we could only advance by diving from cover to cover. As we progressed, we came across the bodies of many of our soldiers and Frenchmen who had been caught in the crossfire of the guns. Some lay at the water's edge, washed by the tide. Others were poised in standing or crouching positions against the rocks where they had been shot. They seemed so lifelike that we approached several of them to talk to them only to find their eyes sightless and their bodies rigid in death. These dreadful corpses reminded me vividly of PC Wren's book *Beau Geste*, in which the dead bodies were propped up on the battlements of the Fort of Zinderneuf.

Evidently some of the troops had tried to descend the 300 foot high cliffs on ropes. Few could have succeeded, judging by the smashed bodies lying on the beach while 150 feet above we could see the frayed ends of their broken ropes. Most appalling of all were the wounded. They were everywhere and on our approach called out to us for water or to help them bind up their wounds. There was nothing we could do for them as any delay endangered the success of our mission on which the fate of so many depended.[10]

After an exhausting two hours, made worse as the heat from the sun intensified, Lang and his companion reached the two boats off Veules. The bigger of the two, a French ship named *Citron*, was the furthest off the shore; nearer was a British fishing boat flying the Red Ensign. Both were already packed with men, French and British, and both had run aground and were unable to move. Many more troops sheltered under the rock face, waiting for a break in the firing to try and get aboard. As Lang watched in horror, artillery on the cliffs towards St Valéry opened up on the French boat, first straddling it and then, with the range gauged, smashing shell after shell into its crowded decks. On board was Lance Corporal Tom Potter of the 1st Field Squadron, the engineers of the 1st Armoured Division Support Group. Like Lang, he had set off from St Valéry after spotting the boats, accompanied by two men from his unit, Jock Freeman and Jock McCullum. The day before, McCullum had disobeyed an order and Potter had promised him that he would be court-martialled. Seconds before the shelling began, Potter, who was below deck in the galley, made up his mind to tell McCullum to forget what had happened:

As I went towards him a shell came in exactly where I had been sitting. Jock Freeman was killed and I was knocked out with shrapnel in my backside. In no time Jerry had put in three rounds at the same level and the water was coming in. Jock McCullum came and got me out of there and by the time he got me on deck I had regained consciousness. We got on to the bridge of the ship because it was still above water.

While most of the survivors of the shattered ship swam ashore as best they could, Potter and 15 others, two of whom were badly wounded, stayed hidden on the bridge. With the *Citron* out of action, the guns turned on the British boat. Realising that she could not last long, Lang summoned up enough courage to make a break for her in the hope of finding a wireless set before it was destroyed. As he struggled aboard, he was surprised to find an officer of his battalion – Lieutenant Colin Hunter, the Intelligence Officer – already on deck. From him, Lang discovered that there was no wireless. Shortly after this, Brigadier Barclay appeared, having followed Lang up the beach. As tanks added to the artillery fire, Barclay and Lang manned the boat's two Lewis guns. It was a futile gesture, and seconds later two shells scored a direct hit. Lang was struck on the forehead by shrapnel, and lost consciousness. Barclay was also wounded by a splinter passing through his cheek, the skipper of the boat had had half one leg blown off, while Hunter was hit just above the eye. Hunter recalls:

> Somebody put a field dressing on it and I went down into the hold and lay down. The next thing I remember was Derek's voice saying, 'Colin, are you down there?' I replied, 'Yes'. 'Are you coming up?' he insisted. 'Yes'. I had had a little bit of a rest so I picked up my belt and revolver and strapped it on and thought, 'Last man, last round, here we go!' I went up the ladder and there was a damned big German officer, so I meekly handed over my pistol and my compass. I was furious about this later, I should have hidden it but it was too late. The Germans were damned good. Anyone who looked as if he was wounded was taken care of.

By early afternoon, nearly all the survivors from the two boats had been captured. Only the 16 men hiding on the bridge of the *Citron* remained at large. It was not until 9 pm, after a failed attempt to build some rafts from the wreckage, that these men were finally forced ashore. This was in response to a German ultimatum, shouted through a loudhailer, that they were going to blow what was left of the ship out of the water. The epic saga of Veules-les-Roses was over.

* * *

A lucky few managed to escape from St Valéry itself, despite the non-arrival of the boats. The most spectacular feat was achieved by a subaltern and 18 men of the 7th Norfolks. During the evening of 11 June, Second Lieutenant Jim Walker was with C Company manning part of the inner perimeter in woods on the west of the town, just 400 yards from the tanks of the 7th Panzer Division. All contact had been lost with Battalion Headquarters and, as darkness began to fall, Captain Colley, the company commander, went into St Valéry to ask for orders about evacuation. Failing to find anyone in authority, and horrified by the chaos and fire in the town, he decided to use his own initiative and withdraw his company to the beach.

Using a steep track down to the harbour, which Colley had previously reconnoitred, C company arrived on the west beach in the early hours of 12 June to find no boats but a horde of French and British troops waiting to be embarked. Again Captain Colley took the initiative, suggesting to his platoon commanders that they each try to reach the warships in fishing boats tied up in the inner harbour. Volunteers were called for, and each officer set off with about 18 men. Jim Walker later wrote:

> Making our way cautiously along a stone promenade in a southerly direction, we re-entered ... St Valéry amongst the blazing buildings which made progress rather difficult, and ... proceeded up a stone jetty. We looked over the side of the jetty and saw [two fishing boats] ... Captain Colley and myself each selected a boat. I sent one man aboard, to ascertain if there were any oars on the boats. He reported that there were none. I then ordered the men to look around on the jetty to find some means of propulsion. Four shovels were found and with these we quietly embarked by sliding down the mast of one of the boats.[11]

By this time Captain Colley had got into the adjoining boat with a further 18 men, but the remaining platoon commander refused to have anything to do with the enterprise because he considered it was running away. Problems began when the boats reached the entrance to the outer harbour. A hydraulic bridge barred the way, and, not surprisingly, there was no one manning it and no time to try and raise it. Walker's boat was the smaller of the two and his men managed to get their mast down; Colley's men failed and they had to turn back. As his boat was full, and it was getting light, Walker had no option but to carry on:

> At this point one of the shovels was lost over-board, so we pulled up some of the planks covering the bilge of the boat, and with the aid of these continued down the river seawards. Taking care to keep out of the glare of the burning village we successfully reached the end of the jetty, which at that moment was struck by a shell. We escaped injury but the next moment were surprised by two German soldiers peering at us over the edge of the jetty. Those not paddling levelled their rifles at the enemy, and they not realising that we dare not fire remained quite still until we had proceeded about 50 yards. A burst of machine-gun fire was then directed at us, and although the boat was struck no one was hit.[12]

According to Walker's corporal, Earnest McMath, who was also on the boat, they were then saved by a combination of rain and mist which helped to obscure them from observation as they paddled further out to sea. After taking some time to cover about a mile, several ships were spotted to the north. They were signalled to with the aid of a bicycle lamp, and eventually one, the destroyer HMS *Harvester*, veered off towards the small boat. McMath recalls that just as deliverance was at hand, it seemed it was about to be snatched away:

> They came along beside us and we were about to climb up the scramble nets when a Stuka dive-bomber appeared and they shouted through a megaphone that they would have to leave us to take evasive action. Fortunately, the ship was unharmed from the attack and they came back and picked us up. Once we got on board they took us down to the hold to hammocks and we fell immediately asleep. We were woken with a terrific noise as the guns opened up. Instead of returning immediately to Portsmouth the ship had been ordered to return and shell the French coast.

This bombardment by *Harvester*, opened at about 10 am, was the Navy's sole response to the 51st Division's request, in the form of a signal sent during the morning, for the guns on the cliffs to the west of St Valéry to be suppressed. Two 88mm anti-aircraft guns were knocked out, but most of the guns were untouched. For leading the intrepid escape, Second Lieutenant Jim Walker was Mentioned in Despatches. Sadly Captain Colley, whose initiative had made the escape possible, was killed by shrapnel as he tried to guide his remaining men to the boats at Veules-les-Roses.

The difference between the success and failure of an escape attempt was slim. Compare Second Lieutenant Walker's good fortune to the bad luck that befell some senior officers of the 1st Lothians. At the same time that Major Jimmy Dallmeyer and his party headed east, Colonel Mike Ansell led another group south. Throwing in their lot with Ansell were Major Harry Younger, the former CO, Captain Lord Hopetoun, the future Marquis of Linlithgow, Second Lieutenant Kenneth Spreckley, and Regimental Quartermaster Sergeant Waymark. Ansell recorded:

> We set off in the pouring rain, keeping close to the hedges and trees, and looked for somewhere to lay up and rest till evening ... We came across a farmhouse and climbed into the loft. Had it been fine we would have stayed in the open under a hedge. There was plenty of straw; gratefully we took off most of our sodden clothes, and slept.[13]

As the five fugitives dozed, a party of 1st Gordons, led by a former fighting patrol sergeant, arrived at the farm. These soldiers were told by the French farmer that he had seen some men that he suspected were Germans enter the loft. Without any warning, the Gordons surrounded the loft and opened fire. Ansell was the first casualty:

> A hail of bullets came through the floor and simultaneously the door of the loft flew open and I took the full blast of a Tommy-gun less than ten feet away. We shouted and almost at once it stopped. We then heard voices in French and English below . . .
>
> I'd been hit by the blast through the door, I thought my head had gone, and when it stopped I knew I was blind and my hands were numb. During the next few minutes I believed I'd 'had it'.[14]

Hopetoun, one of only two not hit by the fusillade, was down the ladder in a flash, screaming at his assailants that they had shot their own side. The Gordons' sergeant was in the act of throwing a grenade, realised his mistake in time and chucked it harmlessly to the side before beating a hasty retreat with his men. But the damage had been done. As well as Ansell's terrible injuries, Younger was dead and Spreckley had been shot in the knee. Convinced that he would not survive, Ansell told his comrades to leave him and to tell his wife, Victoria, that he loved her. Hopetoun and Spreckley then set off, the latter badly handicapped by his wounded knee, but neither got far before they were captured. Waymark opted to stay with Ansell, binding his wounds before helping him over a considerable distance to a field dressing station still in operation. Both were taken prisoner.

13

The Last Stand

As dawn approached, General Fortune was working on a plan to secure the heights on both sides of the town. He was convinced that if this could be done, then his men might be able to hold out for one more day and still be embarked the following night. It was with the idea of forming a new perimeter in mind that he had ordered his troops to woods outside the town, from where they would be easier to deploy. While it was still dark, Divisional Headquarters had also been moved to the south edge of St Valéry to be nearer to the main body of troops.

At around 6 am, General Fortune set off to this new location where he hoped to be able to inform his remaining battalion commanders of his new initiative. On the way, he stopped in at General Ihler's headquarters to acquaint the French with his plan. If there was to be any possibility of holding St Valéry with a view to evacuating that night, he told Ihler, it would require the 'recapture of the whole of the cliffs on the west' and 'consolidating the position on the east'. There was 'only one alternative', he concluded, 'surrender'. Ihler made clear his preference by wearily producing the text of a telegram to General Weygand informing him of the surrender of IX Corps. Could General Fortune arrange for it to be sent via London to Weygand, Ihler asked. No, he could not, came the reply, at least not until he had reviewed the situation with his commanders. Fortune then left with the telegram, promising to send it only if and when he decided to capitulate.[1]

About half a mile past the railway station on the road south, General Fortune found his new headquarters, a neat villa facing the church. Inside were some of his senior commanders, including Brigadier Eden, his Commander Royal Artillery, and Brigadier Burney, commanding 153 Brigade. Also present was Captain Victor Campbell, the Brigade Major of 152 Brigade who was standing in for Brigadier Barclay, who had not been seen for some time (he was, of course, making his way up the beach to Veules-les-Roses). With these three men, Fortune discussed the details of his proposed operation using the troops that had already reached St Valéry. It was pointed out to the General that all artillery pieces, tanks and carriers had been rendered useless, and that the infantry available was scarcely that of a brigade. Ignoring this, Fortune outlined his plan. The 5th Gordons and the two companies of the 1st Black Watch would secure the high ground to the east of the town, the 4th Camerons would guard the southern edge, while the 4th Seaforths were given the onerous task of retaking the west cliffs, held by Rommel's tanks.

To provide a measure of assistance for the operation, General Fortune authorised Lieutenant Commander Elder to send a signal to Admiral James at 7.42 am asking for support from naval guns. It read:

> [Waited] all night on beach. Boats arrived too late to allow withdrawal with batteries and MG posts neutralised. Request ships bombard cliff west of harbour and MG posts east of harbour. Faint possibility of withdrawing on this being done, but position very critical.[2]

At about the time that this signal was sent, a message was received from General Ihler asking if his telegram had been despatched. General Fortune quickly sent a staff officer to inform Ihler that preparations were now underway to secure the town and the harbour and that no decision as to surrender would be taken until the outcome of this operation was learnt.

As no one knew exactly where any particular battalion or its commander was, it was some time before all the relevant units were given their tasks. The 4th Camerons were the first to be contacted; a brigade messenger found them in an orchard on the edge of the town and instructed them to defend a sunken road to the south astride the Cailleville road. Although the battalion had destroyed all its Brens and anti-tank rifles the night before, these were now partially replenished from the many abandoned trucks that clogged every road before the new positions were taken up.

A and B Companies of the 1st Black Watch were on the wreckage-strewn road leading into St Valéry when they were found by Captain Victor Campbell with orders to take up a position on high ground above a cemetery, about one and a half miles north-east of the town.

Meanwhile, the 5th Gordons, less B Company which had reached St Valéry, were at Manneville, a mile and a half short of the town. They had been halted there by their CO after he had gone into St Valéry and discovered no ships. The battalion was in orchards at Manneville when Captain Shankley, commanding B Company, reached it at 8 am with a verbal message from Brigadier Burney to clear the enemy off the cliffs north-east of St Valéry. Major Clark detailed A and B Companies to attack, while C and HQ Companies would hold a sunken road facing the German positions.

The 4th Seaforths were the last battalion to receive its instructions.

They were concentrated in woods on the south-east of St Valéry at 8 am when their CO, Major Shaw-Mackenzie, decided to seek out Divisional Headquarters. As he made his way down the road into the town, he could see the first ominous signs of French defeatism: first, a French soldier struggling with a Jock who was trying to take his white flag off him; then another white flag hanging from a church steeple. Opposite the church he noticed two of his company commanders, Captains Baird and Pelham-Burn, talking to General Fortune.

> The General, on seeing me, said, 'Shaw, you're just the man I want. We've got to hold out until tonight when the Navy may come in but we've got to clear the woods on the opposite hillside ... The Black Watch are now going to clear the East side, you clear the West side'. With no map and a horrid feeling that beyond the woods at the top of the valley I should be confronted with enemy tanks, this was indeed a nasty prospect. I suggested sending a strong fighting patrol up to find out what was there, but he would not agree to that. I sent back Baird and Pelham-Burn to get their [companies] and to get [the Adjutant] to send up the other [companies] ... I then went up through a farm and an orchard to a road at the edge of the wood. I decided that the only way for an attack was to make the road the Start Line and to drive through the woods in two waves with fixed bayonets ... but what would happen at the top of the hill where the woods ended I could only guess.[3]

The white flag Shaw-Mackenzie had spotted fluttering from the church steeple had been put there a little after 8 am. Infuriated, General Fortune had sent two staff officers – one of whom was his Intelligence Officer and the future Duke of Argyll, Captain Ian Campbell – to take it down and to arrest whoever was responsible. Within minutes, the staff officers returned with a Moroccan major who told Fortune that General Ihler had given the order to surrender. Showing typical Scottish spirit, Fortune then despatched the same two staff officers to tell Ihler that the Highland Division had no intention of surrendering and would continue to fight, even if the French gave in. Shortly after their departure, a French despatch rider with a white flag arrived with a note signed by General Ihler which he had been ordered to show to everyone. It read: '*Le feu cessera à huit heures*' ('Cease-fire at 8 am').[4] Minutes later, the two staff officers returned with an identical note and a request from Ihler that his telegram to Weygand be despatched. Scornful of this French defeatism and resolved to carry on, General Fortune composed the following signal to the War Office:

> I have been ordered to cease fire as from 0800 hours by Commander IX Corps.

I am in process of trying to clear enemy machine-guns from cliffs overlooking harbour.

A difficult situation exists in St Valéry as all French elements have ceased fire and are hanging out white flags.

I have informed Corps Commander that my policy is that I cannot, repeat not, comply with his orders until I am satisfied that there is a possibility of evacuating by boat any of my division later.[5]

For some reason this signal was not immediately sent. Perhaps General Fortune wanted to wait on the results of his plan before he furnished the War Office with evidence that he had disobeyed a senior officer's order. Certainly he was agonizing over his decision to jeopardise the lives of his men in an operation that had very little chance of success. A witness to these last dramatic moments was Second Lieutenant Andrew Biggar of the Divisional Signals. He had ended up at a military hospital on the seafront during the morning, and, as he was unwounded, he was chosen by the senior officer there to try to find General Fortune to ask for orders. Using a pushbike, he arrived at Divisional Headquarters shortly after Ihler's signed order to surrender had been received. Biggar recalls:

Things were very much astir. Everybody seemed to be popping and whistling about in small circles. I met both the G1 [Swinburn] and the G2 [Major Rennie], but they were much to busy too listen to me. With a boldness which may or may not have been excusable, I made straight for the General. I had to get an answer somehow.

Brigadier Burney was in the General's room and was discussing with him an order received from the French Corps Commander (under whose command we still were) to the effect that we should surrender. The General was gamely hesitating to obey the order and was considering the consequential position.

Just then enemy shells started whizzing over the roof top of the small house we were in. They seemed to come nearer and nearer until it sounded as if they were just missing the chimney pots. With an anguish which I will never forget, the General reluctantly decided that he had little option but to obey the orders and he said: 'Tell somebody to hoist that bloody white flag on the church tower.' It was the most dramatic moment I had ever experienced ... The General instructed me to take the news to Colonel Hunter at the Hospital and to tell him to march all fit men up to Divisional Headquarters in a smarter manner than they had ever marched before.[6]

It was a few minutes before ten. Staff officers hurried out to try and prevent the attack on the heights. The first wave of the 4th Seaforths had set off, and Shaw-Mackenzie was forming up the second to follow when Brigadier Eden rushed up waving his arms, shouting that the Division had surrendered. Almost simultaneously, as if the sceptical Seaforths needed confirmation, a bugle could be heard sounding the 'cease-fire'. Leaving his Adjutant, 'RAAS' Macrae, to collect the battalion together, a shattered Shaw-Mackenzie tramped down to Divisional Headquarters. He could not bring himself to believe the awful news until he had heard it from the horse's mouth:

> Here I found the General who said, 'Shaw, I have decided to surrender, there was nothing more to be done and I have done it for sentimental reasons to save useless loss of life'. He was very broken up and my own feelings could not be described. Since taking over command nine days before we had been through much. The [battalion] which for five years I had worked so hard for had proved itself in battle and after heavy losses on 4 June had made five withdrawals, four of which had been when in close contact with the enemy. On 10 June, they had again acquitted themselves with honour in the all day battle at Arques-la-Bataille and now all was over. It did not bear thinking about and I had hoped that I should take them home and re-form them under happier circumstances.[7]

When Major Thomas Rennie, Fortune's G2, reached the two companies of the 1st Black Watch with orders to cease-fire, their positions near the cemetery were being shelled by mortars and a tank attack was just developing on their left flank. Bill Bradford's first reaction was one of disbelief; but Rennie was a Black Watch officer he knew well, and there was no doubt that the order was genuine. As the news spread, battle-hardened troops began to cry. The mortar detachment was the last to hear, and continued firing at an enemy tank for some time before it was silenced.

News of the surrender arrived not a minute too soon for the 5th Gordons also. Minutes earlier, D Company had been overrun and captured by tanks that had moved up under the cover of French soldiers carrying white flags. The sound of the bugle reached the troops on the sunken road as 12 tanks were advancing ominously towards them. Second Lieutenant Don Ritchie had only seconds earlier been ordered by Major Clark to support the advance:

> I was completely overcome by emotion. Tears rolled down my cheeks. I was keyed up to attack this bloody ridge and then the reversal. I'll never forget Platoon Sergeant Herbie Forsyth giving me a wallop on the back and a bottle of brandy to swig from and saying, 'It's not your fault, Sir.' It was a terrible thing, and we were completely unprepared. I didn't have anything at all, so I started off for my carrier to get my small pack when

I met this bloody German *Feldwebel* who tried to stop me. But I wasn't going to be stopped, and when he shouted at me I tried to explain what I was going to do. Then this Oxford-educated German officer arrived and said, 'What seems to be the trouble?' I explained and he told the *Feldwebel* to leave me alone. Very civilised. When I got my pack I suddenly felt very tired.

They quickly segregated the men from the officers and we were marched off. When we got to a crossroads there was a crowd of French officers in their best uniforms with their suitcases. Ready. The buggers could have disappeared into the countryside, but there they were – waiting! On the march the French villagers gave them hell.

As they were in the least danger, the 4th Camerons were the last of the four battalions to be told of the surrender. After his dash up to the 4th Seaforths, Brigadier Eden then made his way to the sunken road being held by the Camerons. In the absence of Major Mackintosh-Walker, who was trying to escape from Veules-les-Roses, Major Hill was in command. On hearing the news he said to Eden: 'May individual units fight on'. 'No', Eden replied, 'the General considers that would only lead to unnecessary slaughter.' As the word spread, the adrenalin of battle ceased to flow, and the mental and physical exhaustion of men who had been in almost constant action for over a month returned. Individuals collapsed to the ground, some to cry in frustration and shame. Company Quartermaster Sergeant Gregor Macdonald aptly sums up the feelings of many Highland soldiers that day:

> To say we were shocked would be an under-statement; as infantry soldiers we had at some time imagined ourselves wounded or even killed, but now our only thought was the humiliation of the Highland Division surrendering.

At about the time General Fortune gave the order to surrender, General Rommel was following his tanks on foot down the narrow, winding roads into the western quarter of the town. Accompanied by Colonel Rothenburg, his tank regiment commander, Rommel walked up the side of the harbour until he could see a large number of British and French soldiers standing amidst the smouldering rubble of the eastern quarter. Despite entreaties for these men to lay down their weapons, Rommel recalled that 'it was some minutes before the British could bring themselves to it'. When, at last, they did, German infantry crossed the narrow footbridge to round them up. Rommel followed. Soon more troops were pouring into the market square to surrender, among them General Ihler. Rommel's record of this historic encounter is as follows:

When I asked the General what division he commanded, he replied in broken German: 'No division. I command IX Corps.'

The General declared himself ready to accept my demand for the immediate capitulation of his force. He added, however, that he would not have been standing there if his force had had any ammunition left.[8]

Back at Fortune's Headquarters, the signal informing the War Office of the French surrender was at last despatched. Before sending it, and on his own initiative, the operator brought the signal up to date by adding the words: 'I have now ordered cease-fire. 1030 hrs'. The wireless set was then destroyed, along with all codes, ciphers and documents. As this was being done a German officer drove up in a tank and walked into the villa as casually as if he had come for lunch. He told General Fortune that he was required in the town square, and soon after they left, accompanied by Colonel Swinburn.

In the square, Fortune was directed to a group of generals that included Rommel, Ihler and three of his divisional commanders. The one missing was General Berniquet, commanding the 5th Light Cavalry Division. He had been hit by machine-gun bullets outside Ihler's headquarters the night before and had since died of his wounds. After formally accepting Fortune's surrender, Rommel, true to his chivalrous nature, asked the British general if he would do him the honour of sharing his lunch. Although famished, Fortune still had enough pride to refuse by saying he would have something in his own mess. Of course, there was next to nothing left, and he would later regret this obstinacy. As a mark of his respect for the Highland Division and the stand it had made, Rommel allowed Fortune to retain his batman, a particular favour as officers were normally separated from their men. That night Rommel wrote of the surrender in his diary: 'A particular joy for us was the inclusion [among the divisional commanders] of General Fortune, commander of the British 51st Division'.[9]

Not every unit of the Highland Division was in a position to hear about General Fortune's capitulation, and at least two fought on long after 10 am. One of these was the remnants of the three companies of the 1st Black Watch stranded near Houdetot. No orders to withdraw to the coast had arrived the night before, and by morning these men were surrounded by units of the German 5th Panzer and 2nd Motorised Divisions, who vastly outnumbered them. Even without the disparity in numbers, the position was hardly a favourable one; some 200 men holding an open field, the only cover being provided by a fringe of ivy-covered banks and trees. One side of the field backed onto a wood, while a road ran along its base.

After a quiet night in which persistent rain was the only discomfort, the German attack opened at 7 am with a heavy bombardment of shell and mortar fire which sent great fountains of earth and grass into the air. When Colonel Honeyman ordered the artillery Forward Observation Officer to ask for counter-battery fire, the reply came back that the telephone line had been severed (in any case the gunners had long since withdrawn). Soon tanks began to circle the position, pounding it with their guns but unwilling to risk crossing the high embankment, and small groups of infantry tried to advance. In response, the coolness of the Black Watch Regulars was evident as they repulsed any intrusion with measured rifle and Bren fire.

At times the battle resembled the desperate defence of Rorke's Drift, where in 1879 a company of South Wales Borderers had managed to repel 4,000 Zulu warriors by shifting men to whichever point on the perimeter the pressure of attack was the strongest. But this unequal struggle was against a better equipped foe, and inexorably the battle began to take its toll: casualties mounted up as ammunition ran out. Tragically, Captain Neil Grant-Duff, commanding C Company, was killed one hour after the surrender at St Valéry, as he led his men from one point to another in an attempt to stave off an attack. His father had also been killed in action in the First World War, commanding the same battalion.

By noon it was clear to Colonel Honeyman that the game was up. The small detachment of French cavalrymen, who had fought so well since joining the Black Watch the day before, had just surrendered. Food, water and ammunition were all but finished, and any withdrawal of the fit men across open country was out of the question. Standing next to Honeyman as he hesitated to give the order to surrender was Second Lieutenant Angus Irwin. His Carrier Platoon had performed heroics during the defence by collecting the wounded from the perimeter and shielding them with their vehicles. According to Irwin, it was a last, heavy attack put in by the Germans that made Honeyman's decision for him.

> As the final attack was coming in, Colonel Honeyman was standing near me and said, 'I never thought this would happen. Certainly not that I would ever have to chuck the can in but I'm afraid we're going to have to give up to save lives because we're completely surrounded.' He then sent some runners to give the order to cease-fire.

At St Sylvain, the three companies of the 2nd Seaforths were mostly left in peace during the morning and early afternoon of 12 June. Sniping and the odd burst from a Tommy-gun were the only signs that the surrounding Germans were still in place. Patrols were sent out at intervals, but no clashes took place. There was even a small cause for cheer when a flight of Hurricane fighters, the first seen for days, circled over the village, causing its defenders to tear up sheets and make an 'HD' sign in the hope that they would be identified. This optimism was dampened in the afternoon when large groups of what appeared to be prisoners were spotted through field glasses on the edge of the cliffs above St Valéry.

The absence of confirmation, though, made speculation about a surrender academic, and soon the defenders were concentrating again on the business at hand. First four German vehicles raced through the village, taking the Seaforths by surprise and emerging the other side unscathed. Then a tank advanced towards their positions down the road from the rear of the village. This time the defenders were prepared and it was put out of action with an anti-tank rifle, its crew escaping into an orchard opposite.

Tiring of this obstinate defence, the besieging Germans played their trump card. Company Quartermaster Sergeant 'Gracie' Fields of HQ Company, who had been captured earlier that day while trying to get through to St Valéry, was sent into St Sylvain on a tank to deliver an ultimatum. 'Surrender, or you'll be blown to bits', he told Major Grant. When asked what had happened to the rest of the 51st Division, Fields could not say for sure but he had seen German infantry, machine-guns and tanks on the outskirts of St Valéry. Before making a decision, Grant again decided to consult his officers and they were immediately called to a conference in the farm cottage that was serving as a headquarters. One man who was present, the Adjutant Philip Mitford, later wrote an account of this meeting:

> Major Grant made a moving address which brought tears to the eyes of many: he explained the situation and reminded us of the glorious traditions of our regiment. The alternatives were: One: fight it out in our present position. Two: attempt a mass break-out in daylight. Three: try and hold our position until nightfall and then attempt an escape in small parties leaving the wounded to surrender. Four: surrender. Opinions were freely given. There was little need for a vote. It was decided to carry on the fight from our present position.[10]

Only one officer had put forward the case for surrender: Second Lieutenant Richard Broad, the second-in-command of C Company. A 28-year-old stockbroker from Kent, Broad had joined the Seaforths as a

Supplementary Reserve Officer and was therefore in two senses an outsider and a man with less sense of regimental history than his fellow officers. In response to the assertion that no Seaforth battalion had ever surrendered, and that it would be a disgrace to do so, Broad questioned whether it would be fair to ask the men to sacrifice their lives for the sake of regimental honour. In his eyes they should surrender, while any men who wished to try to escape should be allowed to do so. The rest of the officers did not agree, swayed by the sentiments of men like Captain Ian Hobkirk, the son of a general, who asserted that he would not be able to face his family again if they surrendered and that he would rather die fighting.

The decision taken, the officers left to inform their men. But as they did so, a number of unarmed Jocks were seen carrying some of the wounded towards the Germans. A German car had driven up while the officers were in the conference, and its occupants had informed these soldiers that everyone in St Valéry had surrendered and that a cease-fire was official. Furious at this breach of discipline, Major Grant immediately ordered the battalion to 'Stand-to!' At this crucial juncture, John Keil, the Regimental Sergeant Major, stepped in. Keil had performed heroically during the battle, organising the anti-tank gunners and personally leading numerous patrols. But he was aware of the reality of the situation, and along with several other senior NCOs, he went to make a deputation to Major Grant. The situation was 'hopeless', he told Grant. The men were 'utterly exhausted after 12 days of continuous marching and digging without proper food or rest', with 'heavy fighting on eight of these days'. Because of this and the many casualties suffered, the majority of the men were 'incapable of offering any resistance'. Like Broad, he suggested that surrender was the only practical option, while those who wished to escape could do so.

With the suffering of his men and the hopelessness of their position laid before him by a man as respected as John Keil, Grant changed his mind. Volunteers were called for to break out in small parties, preferably led by an officer, while the rest of the battalion would surrender. Soon after this decision was taken, Padre McCutcheon marched out with the wounded, carried by the fit men who wanted to surrender. Most of the rest preferred to wait for dusk to make a break. One such was the Adjutant, Philip Mitford:

> I went with [Second Lieutenant] John DuPree, my mate, Corporal Spears, from the Orderly Room, and a few bandsmen – there were eight of us. I was badly wounded in the arm and leg and I could hardly walk, but the arm didn't worry me and I was bloody well going to go. We set off for the

sea which we could see. It was a most gorgeous evening – the last thing
we wanted – and we were in a cornfield. The corn was getting fairly ripe
and as we moved through it, it rustled. There was also a moon and the
next thing we saw was a German tank disgorging a whole lot of people.
I think they must have heard us rustling through the corn because they
just came straight towards us. When they were about ten yards away we
decided it was all up and surrendered. I was put inside a tank, bleeding
like hell, with a bandsman and the rest were on the outside. The German
sentry inside was playing Russian roulette with a revolver and it went off
straight through the foot of the bandsman! However, after that, we were
looked after fairly well.[11]

Second Lieutenant Colin Mackenzie, despite his wounds, also joined
an escape party. It included six Jocks and his former company
commander, Major Paul Nason, who by this time was exhausted and
incapable of command. Unlike Mitford and many others, Mackenzie's
group was lucky enough to reach the coast. There they came across
another group of Seaforths who were trying to get down the cliff, some
of whom were killed in the attempt. Seeing the futility of this method,
they carried on and eventually found a path leading down to the beach
guarded by two German sentries. This pair departed when they realised
they were outnumbered, allowing the escapers to reach the shore. After
walking for a while to the west, away from St Valéry, they collapsed in an
exhausted heap, sleeping where they fell. It was during this slumber that
they were captured by some German troops combing the beach, alerted
by the startled sentries.

Unlike most of his fellow officers, Richard Broad decided to go inland
rather than make for the coast on the grounds that failure to find a boat
would mean inevitable capture. After taking a compass bearing for a
point on the Seine, he left heading south, accompanied by a sergeant
from his company and five Jocks. A short while after leaving the village,
this small band was augmented by one other – Private George Dodd.
Being a D Company man, Dodd was amongst strangers at the end. After
overhearing a group of reservists, men who had done their time and
who he looked up to, saying they were giving up, he had decided to
strike out on his own. Like Broad, Dodd also decided to head south, and
it was by pure luck that he spotted a man he recognised from the
recruits' course, Private Frank Drayton, at the back of Broad's group as
it crawled in single-file through the corn. When Dodds made his
presence known, Broad, suspecting he was a Fifth-Columnist, drew his
revolver. Luckily, Drayton was able to confirm that he was a genuine
Seaforth. The group had expanded to eight.

Thus began one of the most remarkable escapes of the Second World

War, led by the only unwounded officer of the 1940 2nd Seaforths to avoid capture. Walking by night and hiding by day, Broad and his men reached the Seine at Duclair on 19 June, crossing the following day in a boat lent by a local schoolmaster. Helped by numerous other sympathisers, including the English Mother Superior of the convent at Honfleur and the Prefect of Police in Calvados, who was also head of the fledgling resistance, the men were hidden until February 1941 when they were moved to Marseilles via Paris. Within days, seven of the men had been arrested by the Vichy authorities and sent to the notorious Fort St Hyppolyte near Nimes. Broad, who had evaded capture, soon managed to wangle the release of six of them; Private Osborne, who had been wounded by German sentries while crossing the line between occupied and Vichy France, had to be left in hospital. The remaining seven crossed the Spanish frontier on 16 February, only to be arrested again on arrival in Barcelona by Spanish Police.

After languishing for two months in Franco's notorious political prisons, Figeuras and Miranda, in indescribably appalling conditions, they were released with the assistance of the British Embassy in Madrid. Two weeks later, they were repatriated by boat via Gibraltar, arriving at Liverpool on 15 May, 1941. Thanks largely to Richard Broad's determination and resource, 'Snow White and the Seven Dwarfs', as they were known by the French resistance, were the single largest group from the Highland Division to return home through France and Spain. For this incredible feat, Broad was awarded the Military Cross.

14

Sacrificed for Nothing

The long, hot day of 12 June was the start of a five year hell for the men of the 51st (Highland) Division, spent in German prison camps of varying unpleasantness. In his history of the war, Churchill attributed the capitulation to the 'gross mismanagement' of the French. He continued:

> I was vexed that the French had not allowed our division to retire on Rouen in good time, but had kept it waiting until it could neither reach Havre nor retreat southward, and thus forced it to surrender with their own troops.[1]

Admiral Sir William James, the man who so nearly snatched the Highlanders from the jaws of the German encirclement, also criticised the French in a report to the Admiralty dated 13 June, 1940. He wrote:

> Before any definite orders were received, and whilst the French authorities were still hesitating to order evacuation, air attacks drove our sea forces some miles off the coast and then fog descended on them. The necessary elements for success, either early orders or clear weather, were thus missing . . .
>   I do not, however, consider that any great number would in any case have been evacuated from the St Valéry area. On 10th June enemy batteries fired on our ships. By 9.30 on 11th June the enemy were machine-gunning our ships off St Valéry, and by noon they had guns in position . . . to dominate the beaches and later to dominate that part of the town in which our troops were crowded.[2]

James' second point is the more relevant. By 11 June it was already too late to save the Division. Up until the afternoon of 10 June, when Rommel's troops reached the coast, it would have been possible for the 51st Division to have used all its transport to motor to Le Havre and safety. But given that General Fortune was technically under the orders of the French, and had neither the authority nor the wish to abandon the remainder of IX Corps, the last opportunity for the majority of the corps to escape was 9 June.

On hearing that its route of withdrawal south of the Seine had been cut at Rouen, Fortune, who had taken over as *de facto* corps commander, should have made for the beaches and harbour of Dieppe. He did not partly because he was unaware that the harbour was still usable, partly because he felt that to do so would have favoured his own troops who were nearer the coast then than the French, and partly because he had not received permission to do so from the French High Command. Instead, Weygand had instructed IX Corps to retire over the Seine by using the ferries below Rouen. This order was clearly impossible to carry out, and Fortune was offered a way round it by the contradictory message from Admiral Platon which stated that he had been ordered to prepare an evacuation from Le Havre 'if necessary'. At that stage, a withdrawal to this well-equipped and largely-intact port must have seemed to Fortune as his only hope of saving the Highland Division without causing his Government far-reaching political repercussions.

Contrary to Churchill's history, a large share of the responsibility for the disaster must be borne by him, the British Government and its High Command who allowed the 51st Division to remain under French command despite many warnings from the senior British general in France that it was in grave danger. By 8 June, General Marshall-Cornwall was so concerned about the fate of the 51st Division that he was prepared to suggest that it should operate independently. Churchill was never likely to listen to this advice while French armies were still fighting because he was convinced that it would be used by the French as an excuse to break the terms of their agreement with Britain that neither would seek an armistice without the permission of the other. The French had already shown their aptitude for blaming others for the disasters of the campaign; the most recent manifestation being their condemnation of the British unwillingness to throw all their fighters into the battle.

By leaving the 51st Division in France after Dunkirk to fight in an unequal battle that could not be won, the British Government showed it was prepared to risk losing it for political ends. The determination to stick by this policy of appearing to support the French through thick and thin is clearly illustrated by the War Office's instruction to the Admiralty during the evening of 8 June to block Dieppe, its failure to inform General Fortune about the possibility of using Dieppe on 9 June, its insistence as late as 11 June that he must obey Weygand's absurd order to retire over the Seine by ferry, and finally its refusal to allow the Navy to begin the evacuation from St Valéry without French permission. But could these facts be interpreted in an even more cynical light: namely that the British Government deliberately sacrificed the 51st Division as a symbol of Allied unity which would silence French complaints that the British had abandoned them? It is not out of the question.

Certainly, as Churchill implies, the British Government cannot shoulder the blame for the military incompetence that culminated in St Valéry. After all it was the French High Command's inflexible strategy of insisting that there should be no retreat from the line of the River Somme, and later the River Bresle, that lost crucial days and allowed the swiftly advancing panzer divisions time to get behind IX Corps. This policy was never meant as a long-term strategy to prolong the war; it was a short-term means of recouping French military pride before the inevitable fall of France. A fall that Paul Reynaud, the French premier, had predicted to Churchill as early as 26 May.

Even without a deliberate policy to sacrifice the 51st Division, the decision to leave it in a position of grave danger from which its survival was unlikely could only have been justifiable if there had ever been a realistic chance of keeping France in the war. Yet most of the signals Churchill was getting from the French political and military leaders from 26 May onwards were to the effect that defeat was inevitable and that it would be followed by an armistice. Certainly, this is what General Alan Brooke expected to happen, and that is why he was so horrified at the prospect of trying to reform the BEF in France. When he finally did arrive to take up his unwanted appointment on 12 June, too late to save the 51st Division, his fears were already close to being realised. Two days later, Weygand told him that the French Army was 'no longer capable of organised resistance'. Despite sending a record of this conversation to the War Office in the shape of a telegram on 14 June, it took two more days and some very straight talking before Brooke was able to wring from Churchill permission to re-embark the recently arrived 52nd (Lowland) Division. Three days later, the new French Government headed by Marshal Pétain began negotiations for an armistice with Germany. It was only on hearing this news that the British Government finally allowed Brooke to embark with the last of his men.

Perhaps the last word should go to two officers of the Highland Division. Major Wattie McCulloch of the 1st Lothians wrote the following in his prison camp:

> At this time France was on the verge of collapse and every effort was being made to keep her 'in the war'. It was no doubt thought that the desertion by the Division at this point of its French comrades would be fatal to the negotiations. One is forced to conclude, therefore, that it was deliberately sacrificed as a political pawn. Whether this sacrifice was worth while is not for me to say. In the light of after events, it seems not.[3]

The Duke of Argyll – Captain Ian Campbell in 1940, Fortune's Intelligence Officer – speaking many years later, agreed:

> It has always been abundantly clear to me that no Division has ever been more uselessly sacrificed. It could have been got away a good week before but the powers that be – and owing I think to very faulty information – had come to the conclusion that there was a capacity for resistance in France which was not actually there.[4]

Epilogue

The soldiers of the 51st (Highland) Division paid a heavy price for the miscalculations of their Government. More than 10,000 were taken prisoner at St Valéry, including the members of all three Regular Highland battalions. The 1st Battalion, The Gordon Highlanders, had also been captured intact in the opening year of the First World War at Le Cateau. With the 1,000 or so taken on the Somme and in the Saar, a total of over 11,000 soldiers of the Division marched into captivity.

Fatal casualties among the Highland infantry alone were over 1,000 with more than four times that number wounded. Balanced against these casualty figures should be the 1,300 rescued from Veules-les-Roses and the 4,000 evacuated from Le Havre over the nights 11/12 and 12/13 June as part of Ark Force.

Hardest hit by the surrender of the Division were the small Highland communities from which the majority of its members were drawn. Many had lost the flower of their manhood at a stroke, some never to return, others not for five years. The families of those killed, missing and taken prisoner would not receive confirmation of their fate for months. Yet, out of the ashes of this disaster a new 51st Division rose like a Phoenix, made up from the duplicate battalions of the original formation, and destined to emulate and even outdo the deeds of its First World War forbear.

A small softening of the blow from the losses was provided by the return of numerous escaped prisoners. By the end of June 1941, 290 British Army prisoners-of-war had escaped and returned to Britain; an incredible 134 of this number, almost half the total, were members of the 51st (Highland) Division.[1] Pride of place among the Division's escapers must go to Commander RF Elkins, the Naval Liaison Officer and Captain Leslie Hulls MC, the Intelligence Officer on the staff of 153 Brigade. After just three days in captivity, these men climbed through the wire of a prisoner-of-war transit camp near Breteuil. Using Elkins' pocket compass and Hulls' fluent French, and assisted by a sympathiser they met in Rouen, the pair made their way by foot and by cycle to the Atlantic coast. After a number of failed attempts to arrange for passage on a boat, they finally managed to steal one from the tiny fishing village of Lion-sur-Mer during the early hours of 24 June. Utilising Commander Elkins' navigational abilities to the full, they managed to sail this 18-foot vessel to Britain, arriving at Hayling Island, near Portsmouth, at 1 pm on Tuesday, 25 June, the first of the prisoners taken at St Valéry to arrive home.

Hulls' feat – for which he was awarded a Bar to his Military Cross – is even more remarkable given his age, over 50, and the fact that he had escaped from a Turkish prison camp in 1918, after being captured earlier that year while serving in an armoured car brigade attached to the Russian Army. He is reputed to be the only British officer to have escaped from captivity in both world wars.[2]

Next to return, in similarly spectacular fashion, were two privates, Hugh Oliver and Neil Campbell, from the 4th Camerons. On the first day of the march to Germany, Oliver, a member of the Carrier Platoon, decided to escape but was unable to find a comrade from HQ Company willing to risk crossing the Channel with him. It only occurred to him later that the reaction was caused by a fear of the sea. It was not surprising, then, that Campbell, the man who did agree to join him, was from the isle of South Uist and had worked as a fisherman.

That same day, on the pretence of getting some water, they dodged out of the line of march into a small copse of trees. Still wearing their battle dress – two black French berets their only form of disguise! – Oliver and Campbell reached the coast about five miles north-west of St Valéry after walking for three nights. To recoup their strength, they lay up in an abandoned house for a few days, living on nothing but rice pudding, made from a large tin of rice they had found and milk from a nearby cow.

Eventually they reached St Valéry, and after a close call when some Germans entered the abandoned house they were sleeping in, they took refuge in the brushwood on the slopes above the town. They did not have to endure this discomfort for long. Spotting a likely-looking 20-foot sailing boat on the edge of the inner harbour, Oliver and Campbell spent the next few nights scavenging food for their voyage and waiting for a suitable tide. At last, at 1 am on 3 July, they set off up the harbour in the boat, using the tide as propulsion. Even a noisy collision with the closed lock-gates to the outer harbour could not deter the two escapers. Although they had temporarily to abandon their attempt, tying up to some nearby boats and staying under cover during the day, the following night they were able to work their way through an opening between the gates and the main wall of the harbour.

Once through, they rowed like the devil until they had cleared the mouth of the harbour, hearing the shouts of a German sentry as they did so. But no pursuit followed, and after 16 hours at sea, with Campbell navigating by the stars and the sail gradually being reduced by wear to only three feet, they were picked up by the minesweeper HMS *Dalmatia*. Forced to spend two nights aboard because of bad weather, they finally landed at Portsmouth on Sunday, 7 July. For this incredible effort, achieved without the assistance of any third party, they were both awarded the Military Medal.[3]

There were many, many other notable escapers. Major Thomas Rennie, Fortune's deputy chief of staff, and Major Ronnie Mackintosh-Walker MC, commanding the 4th Camerons at St Valéry, slipped from a column of officer prisoners as it neared Lille on 21 June. After discovering the Channel coast was guarded, they headed south, buying two bicycles on the way. The River Loire was crossed near Amboise on 8 July, and Marseilles reached 10 days later. There they borrowed 10,000 francs from the American Consul, obtained visas for Spain and Portugal, and took a train to Cerbère on the Spanish border. On the evening of 25 July, they crossed the hills on foot and entered Spain. From there they took the train to Lisbon, and finally arrived home by plane. Mackintosh-Walker later became a brigadier, while Rennie outdid him by rising to the rank of major general in 1944, commanding the reformed 51st Division. Both were later killed in action; Rennie at the head of his beloved division during the crossing of the River Rhine in March 1945.[4]

Captain Bill Bradford, the Adjutant of the 1st Black Watch, left the prisoner-of-war column near Billy-Berclin on 19 June. He had originally been asked by Rennie and Mackintosh-Walker if he would like to try his luck with them, but had said 'No' because he thought they were too old and he would have more chance with someone younger! His initial choice of companion, Second Lieutenant David Campbell, the intrepid fighting patrol commander who had won an MC in the Saar, refused to go, on the grounds that it was too dangerous!

Travelling by bicycle he reached the Pyrenees in July but was arrested by the Vichy French as he tried cross to Spain. He languished in Montferran concentration camp until 17 October when he was transferred to Fort St Jean, the old Foreign Legion barracks in Marseilles that was being used to detain escaped prisoners-of-war, many of whom were from the 51st Division. Luckily, the officers were free to move about the port and, on 28 October, Bradford stowed aboard a ship to Algiers.

Arrested by the Vichy authorities in the port of Oran as he looked for a passage to Gibraltar, Bradford was returned to Algiers where he spent six weeks recovering from illness. Then followed the disappointment of being passed for repatriation by a medical board, only for the ruling to be cancelled by the French. As he began to despair of ever reaching home, he was approached by a Jew who had just bought a 15-foot sailing yacht. Would Bradford help him and an accomplice, a communist, sail to Gibraltar? Although not one of this unlikely trio had had any sailing experience, Bradford agreed.

They set out on 13 June, 1941, almost a year to the day since his capture, with Bradford navigating by the light of the Cueta lighthouse. After an epic week-long voyage of over 500 miles, during which water often had to be bailed out as fast as it poured in, the battered vessel was spotted by a Royal Navy patrol boat a few miles off Gibraltar. Suspecting the boat might be Spanish, Bradford decided to smarten himself up by putting on a tie, despite his tatty beard and rotting clothes. He was relieved to discover it was British, and was much amused when an immaculately dressed naval lieutenant came alongside in a launch and asked, 'Permission to come aboard, Sir?' Bradford finally arrived in Glasgow by ship on 11 July, 1941.[5]

For his escape he was made an MBE. He later joined the 5th Black Watch in the reformed 51st Division, commanding the battalion from July 1944 to the end of the war. To add to his MBE, he won an MC during the North African campaign, and a DSO and Bar following the Normandy landings. He retired as a brigadier.

Captain Derek Lang, the Adjutant of the 4th Camerons, who so nearly got away at Veules-les-Roses and was wounded in the process, was more successful during the march to Germany. Hidden by sympathisers in Lille and Paris, he was eventually smuggled into Vichy France and made his way to Marseilles. On 16 November, after one aborted attempt, Lang paid to be hidden on a boat bound for Beirut, arriving there in five days. In the early hours of 24 November, he crossed into Palestine and was back in Britain by January 1941.[6]

In addition to the MC for his escape, Lang won a DSO in the North African campaign with the 5th Camerons, a battalion he later commanded. After the war he was knighted and rose to the rank of lieutenant general as GOC Scottish Command.

Perhaps the most romantic escape story involves Private Arthur Fraser of the 4th Camerons. After dodging from the line of march with the help of a French woman and her young son, he was taken home with them to the nearby mining town of Auchell. When this family began to show unease the next day, as posters appeared warning inhabitants that anyone sheltering British prisoners would be shot, Fraser decided to leave. Before he had a chance to do so, he was visited by a 20-year old woman with the very un-French name of Helen Macleod. Her father, a Highlander from Dunbeath, called Mackay Macleod, had met and married a French girl while serving as a sergeant in the First World War.

Fraser was taken in by the Macleods and remained with them for more than a year, during which time 19 other servicemen passed through their house. In August 1941, an escape organisation in nearby Roubaix arranged for all the British in the area to be moved south, and Fraser was in the last group to go. It was led by an Englishman called Paul Cole, a shady character who was reputed to have deserted from the British Army at Dunkirk, and who later betrayed much of the escape network to the Germans. Fortunately for Fraser, his group got through to unoccupied France safely.

After successfully crossing the Pyrénées, Fraser was arrested and spent three months in Spanish prisons before the British Embassy secured his release. Back in Britain by January 1942, he was commissioned in the Seaforth Highlanders and served with a West African regiment in Burma. Demobilised as a Captain in 1946, he kept his promise to return to visit the Macleods.

Much had happened in the meanwhile. Soon after Fraser's departure, the Macleods had been betrayed by a British soldier. Mackay was sent to a concentration camp in Germany, never to return. Madame Fernande Macleod spent the remainder of the war in a French prison, and was later rewarded for her family's sacrifice in 1961 when General de Gaulle made her a *Chevalier* of France's most prestigious order, the *Légion d'Honneur*. Helen was jailed for a year. In the Spring of 1947, Helen returned Fraser's visit and within four months they were married.

Other successful escapers included Lieutenant Colin Hunter and Company Quartermaster Sergeant Gregor Macdonald of the 4th Camerons. Hunter, wounded at Veules-les-Roses, was sent to a French military hospital in Doullens. While recuperating, he was encouraged to put an advertisement into the French newspaper *Le Matin* mentioning who and where he was. Amazingly, a reply arrived from Kitty Bonnefous, a middle-aged Englishwoman who worked for the Red Cross. On her third visit, Bonnefous smuggled Hunter out in the boot of her car and back to her flat in Paris. With the help of her estranged French husband, who was in the wine trade, Hunter made it into unoccupied France and down to Marseilles where he briefly met up with Lang. There Hunter was sent before a medical board to determine whether his injuries merited repatriation. Although by this time his eyesight was back to normal, Hunter was lucky enough to be tested by a pro-de Gaulle occulist who wrote out a false report confirming his partial blindness. On 18 January, 1941, he arrived at Gourock by boat.

The fate of Kitty Bonnefous makes a sad post script to Colin Hunter's escape. Shortly after he left Paris, Bonnefous was arrested by the Gestapo. Under torture, her fingernails were removed one by one in an unsuccessful attempt to force her to betray her accomplices. Finally, she was sent to a concentration camp in Germany, where she languished until 1945. Unfortunately, the camp was in the Russian Zone and her 'liberation' resulted in her being forced into a Russian Army brothel. Six months later she arrived back in Paris, weighing just five stone. Her incredible courage was subsequently recognised when she was awarded the MBE and the *Croix de Guerre* by the British and French Governments respectively.

Company Quartermaster Sergeant Macdonald escaped from the line of march on 18 June with his great friend Private John MacGlynn. They headed south but were recaptured near Amiens. Undeterred, they escaped again from a German farm in which they were being housed for the night and jumped a train heading west. Forced to leave the train prematurely at a station near the Dutch–Belgian border, because guards began to check the wagons, they re-crossed into France on foot.

They had to endure many more close shaves, including crossing the River Yonne, a tributary of the Seine, in a small coracle rowed by a priest, and in the company of a German officer and a sergeant. Macdonald even had the nerve to play his role as an oarsman to the full by asking the officer for ten francs as payment! Although Macdonald accidentally parted company with MacGlynn soon after this, he found out later that MacGlynn had arrived safely back in Britain in October 1940. Macdonald's own route home took him to Marseilles, where for a time he took charge of the new internees at Fort St Jean. Shortly before Christmas, with the help of the Reverend Donald Caskie, the Scottish minister who was working with the French underground to smuggle Allied airmen to safety and who became known as the 'Tartan Pimpernel', Macdonald was guided over the Pyrénées into Spain. Like so many others, he was arrested and spent some time at Franco's pleasure in various Spanish prisons. His release was finally secured by the British Embassy, and on 23 February, 1941, he arrived by boat at Gourock.

* * *

For those who were not bold enough or lucky enough to escape, 12 June was the start of five long years behind the wire. First there was the long march into captivity. Covering at least 16 miles a day, the huge POW columns took 16 days to reach the railhead at Hulst, in Holland. During this time, food was virtually non-existent and the prisoners had to survive off hand-outs from the French and Belgian villagers and raw vegetables from the fields they passed. The men slept mostly in fields with no cover. Many collapsed through hunger and exhaustion, some were shot as they tried to leave the column in search of sustenance.

From Hulst, the troops were taken in open railway wagons to Valsoorden, where they embarked for a voyage that would take them down the Rhine into Germany. The officers were crammed into a Rhine steamer; the men faced far worse conditions below deck in barges. At Wesel, a town on the Rhine a little way north of Cologne, the prisoners were disembarked and sent by train to various prison camps: the officers to *Oflags*, the men to *Stalags*; the main difference being that under the terms of the Geneva Convention the men were required to work, a euphemism that for some came to mean forced labour in the salt mines in Poland.

Many felt frustration and guilt that other men were 'doing their bit' while they idly sat out the war. It was perhaps worst of all for the Regular troops, the career soldiers whose greatest opportunities for glory and advancement come during war. While they languished, others were winning medals and rapid promotion. For these reasons, and because it was a soldier's duty to do so, escape attempts were commonplace.

Though he was not able to escape, it is good to be able to record that Harry Swinburn, the supremely professional and indefatigable GSO I of the Division, upon whose skill and efforts so much rested throughout the Division's operations and moves, returned after his release to resume his career and retired as a major general. This book owes much to his beautifully prepared diary of the campaign, written in his POW camp, and packed with accurate detail.

Getting out of a prison camp was one thing, reaching Britain quite another. One man who succeeded was Second Lieutenant Chandos Blair, the ex-fighting patrol officer of the 2nd Seaforths. He got away from a camp in southern Germany by absconding from a working party, and took eight days to walk the 75 miles to Switzerland. At Berne, the British Military Attaché provided him with money which he used to acquire a passport and genuine French and Spanish visas. With these he was able to travel to Madrid, arriving in January 1942. Before the month was out, he was back in Britain, the first Army officer from a prisoner of war camp to make it. His reward: an MC. Like Derek Lang, he was knighted and ended up as GOC Scottish Command with the rank of lieutenant general.[7]

Two out of the next five Army officers to emulate Blair's feat were from the Highland Division. Second Lieutenant Peter Douglas of the 8th Argylls, who escaped a day after Blair, and Second Lieutenant Angus Rowan-Hamilton of the 1st Black Watch who broke out ten weeks later.

It was not only the escapers who returned to Britain before the end of the war. In October 1943, an exchange of seriously wounded POWs took place between Britain and Germany, two years after it was originally scheduled. Among the repatriated members of the Highland Division were Colonel Mike Ansell, Corporal John Stevenson and Troop Sergeant Major Jimmy Hogarth, all of the 1st Lothians. Hogarth had finally been captured, strapped to a stretcher, on the beach between St Valéry and Veules-les-Roses.

* * *

On 2 September 1944, a four year debt was finally repaid when the reformed 51st (Highland) Division – fresh from successes in North Africa, Italy and Normandy – liberated St Valéry. This signal honour had been granted by Field Marshal Bernard Montgomery who deliberately changed the layout of his forces to make it possible. At the head of the leading battalion to march into the town that day was Lieutenant Colonel Derek Lang, commanding the 5th Camerons. Also present during this emotional occasion was Lieutenant Colonel Bill Bradford, commanding the 5th Black Watch, who laid the wreath at the memorial service for the men who had died in 1940.

During the advance on St Valéry, Major General Thomas Rennie had addressed his troops, reminding them of the fate of the original Highland Division:

> That magnificent Division was sacrificed to keep the French in the war. True to Highland tradition, [it] remained to the last with the remnants of our French Allies, although it was within its capacity to withdraw and embark at Le Havre.[8]

The day after the liberation of St Valéry, following a stirring rendition of 'Retreat' by the massed bands of the Division outside the château at Cailleville, Major General Thomas Rennie again addressed his men:

> That Highland Division was Scotland's pride; and its loss, and with it the magnificent men drawn from practically every town, village and croft in Scotland, was a great blow ... It has been our task to avenge the fate of our less fortunate comrades and that we have nearly accomplished ... We have lived up to the great traditions of the Fifty-First and of Scotland.[9]

Bibliography

PUBLISHED WORK

Ansell, Colonel Sir Michael, *Soldier On* (Peter Davies, 1973)

Avon, Earl, *The Eden Memoirs: The Reckoning* (Cassell, 1965)

Barclay, Brigadier CN, *The History of the Royal Northumberland Fusiliers in the Second World War* (William Clowes & Sons, 1952)

Baudouin, Paul, *The Private Diaries* (Eyre & Spottiswoode, 1948)

Bell, PMH, *The Origins of the Second World War in Europe* (Longman, 1986)

Bewsher, Major FW, *The History of the 51st (Highland) Division – 1914–18* (Blackwood, 1921)

Bryant, Arthur, *The Turn of the Tide 1939–43: A Study based on the Diaries and Autobiographical Notes of Field Marshal The Viscount Alanbrooke* (Grafton, 1986)

Cameron, Captain Ian C, *History of the Argyll & Sutherland Highlanders 7th Battalion 1939–45* (Thomas Nelson & Sons, 1947)

Chapman, Guy, *Why France Collapsed* (Cassell, 1968)

Churchill, Winston S, *The Second World War: Volume II – Their Finest Hour* (Cassell, 1959)

Collier, Richard, *1940: The World in Flames* (Hamish Hamilton, 1979)

Colville, John, *The Fringes of Power – Downing Street Diaries 1939–55* (Hodder & Stoughton, 1985)

Davidson, Major H, *History and Services of the 78th Highlanders – 1793–1881*: Volume I (Johnston, 1901)

Douglas, Roy, *New Alliances 1940–41* (Macmillan, 1982)

Ellis, Major LF, *The War in France and Flanders, 1939–40* (HMSO, 1953)

Fergusson, Bernard, *The Black Watch and the King's Enemies* (Collins, 1950)

Fraser, David, *And We Shall Shock Them: The British Army in the Second World War* (Hodder & Stoughton, 1983)

Gilbert, Martin, *Finest Hour: Winston S Churchill 1939–41* (Minerva, 1989)

Glover, Michael, *The Fight for the Channel Ports* (Leo Cooper, 1985)

Goutard, Colonel A, *Battle of France 1940* (Frederick Muller, 1958)

Grant, Roderick, *The 51st Highland Division at War* (Ian Allen, 1977)

Guderian, General Heinz, *Panzer Leader* (Michael Joseph, 1952)

Harpur, Major BCV, *'The Kensingtons' – Princess Louise's Kensington Regiment (Second World War)* (ROC Association, 1952)

Harris, John, *Dunkirk: The Storms of War* (David & Charles, 1980)

Horne, Alistair, *To Lose a Battle* (Macmillan, 1969)

251

Hull, Cordell, *The Memoirs of Cordell Hull* – Volume I (Hodder & Stoughton, 1948)

Ismay, General The Lord, *The Memoirs of General The Lord Ismay* (Heinemann, 1960)

James, Admiral Sir William, *The Portsmouth Letters* (Macmillan, 1946)

James, Admiral Sir William, *The Sky Was Always Blue* (Methuen, 1951)

Karslake, Basil, *1940 The Last Act: The Story of the British Forces in France Aftrer Dunkirk* (Leo Cooper, 1979)

Kemp, Colonel JC, *The History of the Royal Scots Fusiliers – 1915–1959* (Glasgow University Press, 1963)

Kemp, Lieutenant Commander PK, RN, *History of the Royal Norfolk Regiment 1919–1951 – Volume III* (Soman-Wherry Press, 1953)

Lang, Derek, *Return to St Valéry* (Leo Cooper, 1974)

Linklater, Eric, *The Highland Division* (HMSO, 1942)

Malcolm, AD, *The History of the 8th Argylls – 1939–1947* (Thomas Nelson & Sons, 1949)

Miles, Captain Wilfrid, *The Life of a Regiment: The History of the Gordon Highlanders Volume V 1914–45* (Frederick Warne, 1980)

Moore, William, *The Long Way Round: An Escape through Occupied France* (Leo Cooper, 1986)

Pratt, Paul, W, *The Highland Regiments – Tigers in Tartan* (Impulse, 1971)

Rankin, Eric, *A Chaplain's Diary 1939–40* (privately published, 1978)

Reoch, Ernest, *The St Valéry Story* (privately published, 1965)

Reynaud, Paul, *In the Thick of the Fight 1939–1945* (Cassell, 1955)

Rommel, Field Marshal Erwin, *The Rommel Papers* (edited by BH Liddell Hart; Collins, 1953)

Roskill, Captain SW, RN, *The War at Sea: 1939–45, Volume I – The Defensive* (HMSO, 1954)

Salmond, JB, *History of the 51st Highland Division 1939–45* (William Blackwood & Sons, 1953)

Spears, Major General EL, *Assignment to Catastrophe: Volume I – Prelude to Dunkirk July 1939–May 1940* (Heinemann, 1954)

Spears, Major General EL, *Assignment to Catastrophe: Volume II – The Fall of France June 1940* (Heinemann, 1954)

Stockman, Jim, *Seaforth Highlanders 1939–45: A Fighting Soldier Remembers* (Crecy, 1987)

Sym, Colonel John, *Seaforth Highlanders* (Gale & Polden, 1962)

Taylor, AJP, *The Origins of the Second World War* (Hamish Hamilton, 1961)

Weygand, Commandant Jacques, *The Role of General Weygand – Conversations with his Son* (Eyre & Spottiswoode, 1948)

Weygand, Maxime, *Recalled to Service – The Memoirs of General Maxime Weygand* (Heinemann, 1952)

Woods, Rex, *A Talent to Survive: The Wartime Exploits of Lieutenant Colonel Richard Broad* (William Kimber, 1982)

UNPUBLISHED SOURCES

Barker, Brigadier CN, MC MBE, *Wielding the Sword*
Biggar, Second Lieutenant WA, MC, *Personal Account*
Bowring, Lieutenant TA, *An Account of his Experiences*
Bradford, Brigadier Bill, DSO MC MBE, *Diary*
Bruce, Major GW, *Movements of 5th Gordons from Mobilisation to Capture*
Buchanan, Lieutenant Colonel EP, MC, *Report: 30 May–5 June*
Buchanan-Smith, Lieutenant Colonel AD, *Handwritten Statement*
Christie, Major RN, *Narrative of the 5th Gordons, 1939–40*
East Surrey Regiment St Valéry Association, *France 1940*
Elkins, Commander RF, RN, *Secret Report*
Fullerton, Second Lieutenant C, *Handwritten Statement on Events May–June 1940*
Geddes, Captain GA, *War Diary*
Grant, Major JM, *Diary*
Halkett, Sir PA, *My Military Life – Volume I*
Hewitt, Captain EPA, *Report: 5 June*
Hogarth, Troop Sergeant Major JM, DCM, *Personal Account*
Honeyman, Lieutenant Colonel GEB, DSO, *Operations in France 24 May–12 June*
Logan, Captain J, *Report: 30 May–5 June*
Macdonald, Captain GG, MC, *A Letter to Janette*
MacLeay, Major WA, *Diary*
Malcolm, Lieutenant John, *Diary*
McCulloch, Major W, *War Diary: August 1939 to June 1940*
Mitford, Second Lieutenant PC, MBE, *Diary*
Moore, Second Lieutenant P, *Report: 30 May–5 June*
Murray, Major TPD, MBE, *History of the 4th Black Watch 1939–1945*
Murray, Lieutenant Colonel TPE, OBE, *51st (Highland) Divisional Signals' War Diary – August 1939–April 1945*
Powell, Second Lieutenant RL, MC, *Report: 5 June*
Shaw-Mackenzie, Major CJ, MBE, *Diary*
Smith, Private FG, *Diary*
Swinburn, Lieutenant Colonel HR, MC, *History of the 51st Division – 26 May to 12 June 1940*
Tarbat, Major The Viscount, MC, *Diary*
Walker, Major HJ, DSO, *Account of Events*
Young, Major RM, *Report: 30 May–7 June*

Chapter Notes and Sources

ABBREVIATIONS: ARCHIVES AND UNPUBLISHED DOCUMENTS

The Public Record Office, Kew, London: PRO
Army records (WO); Cabinet Records (CAB); Prime Minister's Papers (PREM); Foreign Office Records (FO); Admiralty Records (ADM)

The Imperial War Museum, London: IMP
Department of Documents

Regimental Museums: REG
The Black Watch, Balhousie Castle, Perth (BW); The Argyll & Sutherland Highlanders, Stirling Castle, Stirling (A&SH); The Queen's Own Highlanders, Fort George, Inverness (QOH); The Gordon Highlanders, Viewfield Terrace, Aberdeen (GH)

The Scottish United Services Museum: SUS
Edinburgh Castle, Edinburgh

CHAPTER NOTES

CHAPTER ONE *No Heroes Welcome*
1. PMH Bell, *The Origins of the Second World War in Europe* (Longman, 1986), pp 117–8
2. David Fraser, *And We Shall Shock Them – The British Army in the Second World War* (Hodder & Stoughton, 1983), pp 10–11
3. Captain GG Macdonald, *A Letter to Janette*, unpublished memoirs, pp 5–6
4. Major LF Ellis, *The War in France and Flanders, 1939–40*, (HMSO, 1953), The Official History, pp 11–12
5. *Lord Gort's Despatches – 1939–40 France & Belgium*, CAB 120 247, PRO
6. Corporal J Cairns, 'A Trip to France', *The Thin Red Line*, Autumn 1991
7. Letter from Major General Fortune to Lieutenant General Adam, 51st Division General Staff War Diary, WO 167 314, PRO

CHAPTER TWO *The Saar*

1. *Instructions on Patrolling*, 27 April 1940, General Staff War Diary, WO 167 315, PRO
2. Major JM Grant, *Diary of Events – 1940*, written in POW camp, QOH, REG
3. Sergeant JA Mackenzie, 'Forty Years Ago – With the 78th to St Valéry', Part III, *The Queen's Own Highlander*, Summer 1980
4. Colonel Sir Mike Ansell, *Soldier On* (Peter Davies, 1973), p 63
5. Eric Rankin, *A Chaplain's Diary* 1939–40 (R & R Clark, Edinburgh, 1978)
6. Major W McCulloch, *War Diary: August 1939 to June 1940*, personal account written in POW camp, SUS

CHAPTER THREE *Blitzkrieg*

1. General Gamelin, *Special Order of the Day*, 10 May 1940, 1st Black Watch War Diary, WO 167 710, PRO
2. *GOC 51 Division Directive*, 11 May 1940, 1st Lothians War Diary, WO 167 455, PRO
3. Second Lieutenant AS Chambers, *Report of Action: 11 May 1940, ibid*
4. Letter from Lieutenant Colonel R Macpherson to Bernard Fergusson, 18 Dec 1947, NRA 153, BW, REG
5. Lieutenant GG Howie, *Report of Action: 13 May 1940*, 1st Black Watch War Diary, WO 167 710, PRO
6. Second Lieutenant JRP Moon, *ibid*
7. Captain GP Campbell-Preston, *ibid*
8. Lieutenant JR Johnston, *Report of Action: 13 May 1940*, 1st Lothians War Diary, WO 167 455, PRO
9. Captain BC Bradford, *Diary*, personal account written up from notes made during the campaign
10. Captain Campbell-Preston, *op cit*
11. Second Lieutenant Moon, *op cit*
12. Sergeant S Newman, *Report of Action: 13 May 1940*, 4th Black Watch War Diary, WO 167 711, PRO
13. Citation for the award of the Military Medal to Sergeant S Newman, *ibid*
14. Platoon Sergeant Major McLaughlan, *Report of Action: 13 May 1940, ibid*
15. Captain RC Thomson, *ibid*
16. Second Lieutenant DR Elder, *ibid*
17. Second Lieutenant C Millar, *ibid*
18. *Ibid*
19. Citation for the award of the Distinguished Conduct Medal to Company Quartermaster Sergeant S Taylor, *ibid*
20. Letter from Major General Fortune to Brigadier Burney, 14 May 1940, *ibid*
21. Lieutenant Colonel AD Buchanan-Smith, Handwritten Statement, GH, REG

CHAPTER FOUR *'We Have Lost the Battle!'*
1. WS Churchill, *The Second World War: Volume II – Their Finest Hour* (Cassell, 1959), pp 38–9
2. *BEF Gallantry Awards, 1940*, London Gazette, Friday 5 July, WO 373 Reel 8 (microfilm), PRO
3. 7th Argylls' War Diary, 18 May, WO 167 704, PRO
4. General Condé, *General Order No 27*, 8th Argylls' War Diary, WO 167 705, PRO
5. Lieutenant Colonel HR Swinburn, MC, *History of the 51st Division – 26 May to 12 June 1940*, unpublished diary of campaign written in POW camp
6. Paul Reynaud, *In the Thick of the Fight 1930–1945* (Cassell, 1955) p 382
7. Minutes of the War Committee, 25 May 1940, Appendix VII, *Recalled to Service – The Memoirs of General Maxime Weygand* (Heinemann, 1952) pp 428–435
8. Major General EL Spears, Assignment to Catastrophe: Volume I – *Prelude to Dunkirk July 1939–May 1940* (Heinemann, 1954) p 173
9. *Ibid*, pp 180–1
10. *Ibid*, pp 188–9
11. *Ibid*, pp 206–7, 223–4
12. Confidential Annex, Minutes of the War Cabinet, No 140 of 1940, folios 146–53, CAB 65 13, PRO
13. Reynaud, *op cit*, p 405
14. Chiefs of Staff Paper No 168, 27 May 1940, CAB 80 11, PRO
15. John Colville, *The Fringes of Power – Downing Street Diaries 1939–55* (Hodder & Stoughton, 1985), p 141
16. Spears, *op cit*, p 293
17. Minutes of the 13th Supreme War Council Meeting, 31 May 1940, CAB 99 3, PRO
18. Spears, *op cit*, p 313–15
19. *Ibid*, p 319

CHAPTER FIVE *The Somme*
1. Lieutenant Colonel Swinburn, *op cit*
2. *Ibid*
3. Memo from Major General Dewing to General Dill, *Policy for British Forces remaining in France*, 31 May 1940, WO 106 1717, PRO
4. Arthur Bryant, *The Turn of the Tide 1939–43: A Study based on the Diaries and Autobiographical Notes of Field Marshal The Viscount Alanbrooke* (Grafton, 1986), pp 159–60
5. Lieutenant Colonel Swinburn, *op cit*
6. *Ibid*
7. *Ibid*
8. *Ibid*
9. Sergeant JA Mackenzie, 'Forty Years Ago', Part IV, *The Queen's Own Highlander*, Winter 1980

10. Major CJ Shaw-Mackenzie, *Diary of Events: 1940*, written in POW camp, QOH, REG
11. *Ibid*

CHAPTER SIX *The Highlanders Attack*
1. Major Grant, *op cit*; Sergeant Mackenzie, op cit
2. Roderick Grant, *The 51st Highland Division at War* (Ian Allen, 1977), pp 20–21
3. Major The Viscount Tarbat, *Diary of Events: 1940*, written in POW Camp, QOH, REG
4. *Ibid*
5. Major Shaw-Mackenzie, *op cit*
6. *Ibid*
7. *Ibid*
8. *Ibid*
9. Company Quartermaster Sergeant Macdonald, *op cit*, p 12
10. *Ibid*, p 13
11. Major WA MacLeay, *Diary of Events: 1940*, written in POW camp, QOH, REG
12. Brigadier CN Barker, MBE, MC, *Wielding the Sword*, Memoirs
13. Lieutenant Colonel Swinburn, *op cit*
14. Copies of the telegrams in the *Minutes of the War Cabinet*, 2 June, 6.30 pm, 10 Downing St, CAB 65 7, PRO
15. *Confidential Annex to War Cabinet Minutes*, 152nd of 1940, Folios 229–30, 2 June, 6.30 pm, CAB 65 13, PRO
16. Colville, *op cit*, p 146
17. *Confidential Annex to War Cabinet Minutes*, 154th of 1940, 4 June, 11.30 am, CAB 65 13, PRO
18. Paul Baudouin, *The Private Diaries* (Eyre & Spottiswoode, 1948), p 76
19. *Foreign Relations of the United States Diplomatic Papers 1940: Volume I – General* (US Government Printing Office, 1959)
20. Lieutenant General JH Marshall-Cornwall, *Report of Operations of the BEF in France – June 1940*, WO 216 116, PRO

CHAPTER SEVEN *'Operation Red'*
1. *Order of Battle of the German Army for the French Campaign of 1940*, WO 106 290, PRO
2. Army Group B War Diary, quoted in Ellis, *op cit* p 274
3. Second Lieutenant P Moore, *Report: 13 Platoon, 30 May–5 June*, A&SH, REG
4. Second Lieutenant RL Powell, *Report: 1 Section Carrier Platoon in support C Company on 5 June*, A&SH, REG
5. Second Lieutenant Moore, *op cit*
6. Captain EPA Hewitt, *Report: C Company on 5 June*, A&SH, REG

7. Major RM Young, *Report: D Company, 30 May–7 June*, A&SH, REG
8. Captain J Logan, *Report: B Company, 30 May–5 June*, A&SH, REG
9. Lieutenant Colonel EP Buchanan, MC, *Report: 7th Argylls, 30 May–5 June*, A&SH, REG
10. *Ibid*
11. Lieutenant Colonel R Macpherson, *op cit*
12. Lieutenant Colonel Buchanan, *op cit*
13. 7th Argylls' War Diary, 5 June, WO 167 704, PRO
14. Corporal J Cairns, *op cit*
15. Major Young, *op cit*
16. *Ibid*
17. Captain JD Inglis, *Account of the action in which he was captured: 5–7 June*, written for the Regimental History by George Malcolm
18. *Ibid*
19. Major LM Campbell, *Report on Move by A & B Companies: 5–8 June*, 8th Argylls' War Diary, WO 167 705,PRO
20. Captain J Taylor, *History of B Company in withdrawal of Battalion from the Somme*, A&SH, REG
21. Major Campbell, *op cit*
22. *Ibid*

CHAPTER EIGHT *Withdrawal to the Bresle*

1. R Ogilvie, 'A Platoon Commander with the BEF, 1940', *The Tiger and Sphinx*, 1990
2. *Ibid*
3. Letter from Second Lieutenant Slater to Major WA MacLeay, found in latter's *Diary*, *op cit*
4. Major MacLeay, *op cit*
5. Major CJY Dallmeyer, *Report of Action 5 June*, 1st Lothians' War Diary, WO167 455, PRO
6. *Ibid*
7. *Ibid*
8. Major McCulloch, *op cit*
9. Sergeant Mackenzie, *op cit*
10. Lieutenant General Marshall-Cornwall, *op cit*
11. *Ibid*
12. *Ibid*
13. Major General EL Spears, *Assignment to Catastrophe: Volume II – The Fall of France June 1940* (Heinemann, 1954), pp 74–6

CHAPTER NINE *The Sickle Stroke*

1. Field Marshal Erwin Rommel, *The Rommel Papers*, edited by BH Liddell Hart (Arrow, 1987), pp 46–9
2. German XV Corps War Diary, 6 June, quoted in Ellis, *op cit*, p 276

3. Lieutenant Colonel Swinburn, *op cit*
4. Second Lieutenant AJ Redfern, Abridged Report, *France 1940*, East Surrey Regiment St Valéry Association, pp 17–18
5. Lieutenant General Marshall-Cornwall, *op cit*
6. Reynaud, *op cit*, p 472
7. Lieutenant General Marshall-Cornwall, *op cit*
8. *Cipher Telegrams relating to the evacuation of the 51st Division*, WO 106 1619, PRO
9. War Office to Howard-Vyse, 4.25 pm, 8 June, *ibid*
10. *Conclusions of Defence Committee*, 8 June, PREM 3 188 1, PRO
11. *Ibid*
12. War Office to Admiralty, 11.55 pm, 8 June, *Telegrams relating to the evacuation of the 51st Division, op cit*
13. Lieutenant Colonel Macpherson, *op cit*
14. Admiral Sir W James, *Operation Cycle – Reports*, ADM 179 158, PRO
15. Commander RF Elkins, RN, *Secret Report written on return to Britain at end of June 1940 – Part I*, found in the papers of Colonel LR Hulls MC, IMP

CHAPTER TEN *The Net Closes*

1. Lieutenant Colonel Swinburn, *op cit*
2. *Ibid*
3. Lieutenant Colonel Swinburn, 51st Division General Staff War Diary, 9 June, WO 167 314, PRO
4. Admiralty War Diary, 9 June, ADM 199 2206, PRO
5. *Daily Summary of Naval Events – April–June 1940*, ADM 199 1959, PRO
6. Le Havre Garrison War Diary, 9 June, WO 167 314, PRO
7. Lieutenant General Marshall-Cornwall, *op cit*
8. Lieutenant Colonel Swinburn, *History, op cit*
9. *Cipher Telegrams relating to the evacuation of the 51st Division, op cit*
10. *Ibid*
11. Major Parsons, *Report*, Le Havre Garrison War Diary, WO 167 314, PRO
12. Lieutenant Colonel Swinburn, *History, op cit*
13. *Cipher telegrams relating to the evacuation of the 51st Division, op cit*
14. *Ibid*
15. Lieutenant Colonel Swinburn, *History, op cit*
16. Admiralty War Diary, 10 June, *op cit*
17. *Prime Minister's Office – 1940 France* (Western Front Ops), PREM 3 188 3, PRO
18. Admiral Sir William James, *The Sky Was Always Blue* (Methuen, 1951) p 211
19. *Ibid*
20. Admiral James, *Operation Cycle – Reports, op cit*
21. Admiral James, *The Sky Was Always Blue, op cit*, pp 211–12
22. Admiral James, *Operation Cycle – Reports, op cit*
23. *The Rommel Papers, op cit*, pp 59–60

CHAPTER ELEVEN *St Valéry*
1. Lieutenant Colonel Swinburn, *History, op cit*
2. Sergeant Mackenzie, *op cit*
3. Major McCulloch, *op cit*
4. *Cipher Telegrams relating to the evacuation of the 51st Division, op cit*
5. Quoted in Ellis, *op cit,* p 288
6. *Cipher Telegrams relating to the evacuation of the 51st Division, op cit*
7. Lieutenant Colonel Swinburn, *History, op cit*
8. *Cipher Telegrams relating to the evacuation of the 51st Division, op cit*
9. Lieutenant Hemans, *Operation Cycle – Reports, op cit,* PRO; Commander Elkins, *op cit*
10. Major Grant, *op cit*
11. Sergeant Mackenzie, *op cit*
12. Major Grant, *op cit*
13. R Ogilvie, *op cit*
14. *Ibid*
15. Commander Elkins, *op cit*
16. *Ibid*
17. *The Rommel Papers, op cit,* p 63
18. *Evacuation from St Valéry and Area – June 1940,* WO 106 1608, PRO
19. *Cipher Telegrams relating to the evacuation of the 51st Division, op cit*
20. Major Shaw-Mackenzie, *op cit*
21. Captain Bradford, *op cit*
22. 2/7th Duke of Wellington's War Diary, 11–12 June 1940, WO 167 737, PRO
23. Major Shaw-Mackenzie, *op cit*
24. *Ibid*
25. Major MacLeay, *op cit*
26. Colonel Ansell, *op cit,* p 71
27. *Ibid,* p 72

CHAPTER TWELVE *The Lucky Few*
1. Captain Cameron, *Operation Cycle – Reports,* ADM 179 158, PRO
2. *Ibid*
3. Lieutenant Commander House, *Ibid*
4. *Cipher Telegrams relating to the evacuation of the 51st Division, op cit*
5. Captain Warren, *Operation Cycle – Reports, op cit*
6. Lieutenant Thompson, *ibid*
7. Commander Chatwin, *ibid*
8. London Gazette, 18 Oct, *BEF Gallantry Awards – 1940,* WO 373 Reel 8 (microfilm), PRO
9. Major Dallmeyer, *Report 11/12 June,* 1st Lothians' War Diary, WO 167 455, PRO
10. Derek Lang, *Return to St Valéry* (Leo Cooper, 1974), p 33

11. Second Lieutenant HJ Walker, *Account of Events*
12. *Ibid*
13. Colonel Ansell, *op cit*, p 73
14. *Ibid*, pp 73–4

CHAPTER THIRTEEN *The Last Stand*
1. Lieutenant Colonel Swinburn, *op cit*
2. Admiralty War Diary, 12 June, *op cit*
3. Major Shaw-Mackenzie, *op cit*
4. Lieutenant Colonel Swinburn, *op cit*
5. Signal from 51st Division to War Office, *Cipher Telegrams relating to the evacuation of the 51st Division, op cit*
6. Second Lieutenant WA Biggar, *Personal Account*
7. Major Shaw-Mackenzie, *op cit*
8. *The Rommel Papers, op cit*, p 65
9. *Ibid*
10. Second Lieutenant PC Mitford, *Diary of Events*, written in POW Camp
11. *Ibid*

CHAPTER FOURTEEN *Sacrificed for Nothing*
1   Churchill, *op cit*, p 134
2. Admiral James, Message to Admiralty explaining failure to rescue 51st Division, *Evacuation from St Valéry and Area – June 1940, op cit*
3. Major McCulloch, *op cit*
4. Duke of Argyll, quoted in Ernest Reoch's *The St Valéry Story* (privately published, 1965) p 22

EPILOGUE
1. *Reports of Escapes of Prisoners of War (German Hands) – Volume 7*, WO 208 3304, PRO
2. *Reports of Escapes – Volume 1*, WO 208 3298, PRO
3. *Ibid*
4. *Ibid*
5. *Reports of Escapes – Volume 7, op cit*
6. *Reports of Escapes – Volume 4*, WO 208 3301, PRO; *Return to St Valéry, op cit*, pp 37–177
7. Sir Martin Lindsay, *Escapers All*, British Army Review No. 54, Dec 1976
8. Major General T Rennie, quoted in the *Inverness Courier*, Tuesday, 12 June, 1990
9. *Ibid*

Glossary
(As applicable in 1940–41)

AA & QMG	*Assistant Adjutant and Quartermaster General:* principal administrative officer of the division.
Adjt	*Adjutant:* personal staff officer to the Commanding Officer of a major unit. Responsible for the day-to-day administration of the battalion and the co-ordination and distribution of the CO's orders.
ADMS	*Assistant Director of Army Medical Services:* senior medical officer (colonel) of the division and overall command of all medical support.
ADOS	*Assistant Director of Ordnance Services:* (lieutenant colonel): Senior Ordnance officer within the division and responsible for holding, issue and repair of all vehicles, weapons and equipment, technical stores and clothing. Co-ordinates workshop activities including recovery.
Bde	*Brigade:* principal tactical formation within the division. An infantry brigade will normally have three rifle battalions together with supporting arms and services – RA, RE, R Signals, RAOC, RASC and RAMC
Bn	*Battalion:* the basic infantry unit. Four rifle companies and headquarters company which includes such heavy weapons as mortars.
BM	*Brigade Major:* the operations officer and senior staff officer of a brigade.
CO	*Commanding Officer:* of a battalion or regiment.
Corps	Major tactical formation consisting of two or more divisions. Commanded by a lieutenant general. Two or more corps constitute an army.
CQMS	*Company Quartermaster Sergeant:* administers and issues all stores, clothing, equipment and rations for his company.
CRA	*Commander Royal Artillery:* senior artillery officer within the division. Responsible for the control and co-ordination of all fire support (brigadier).
CSM	*Company Sergeant Major:* Warrant Officer Class II and senior soldier in his company below commissioned rank.
DCM	*Distinguished Conduct Medal:* after the Victoria Cross, the highest

gallantry award available to soldiers below commissioned rank. Usually, but by no means invariably, awarded to sergeants and above.

Div   *Division (infantry):* in 1939–40 a troop formation of three infantry brigades, a divisional reconnaissance regiment, three field artillery regiments, an anti-tank regiment and major units of supporting arms and services. About 16,000 men. (See Appendix 2.) Commanded by a major general.

DSO   *Distinguished Service Order:* after the Victoria Cross, the highest award for gallantry and leadership available to officers. Normally, but by no means invariably, awarded to officers of field rank (major and above).

FOO   *Forward Observation Officer:* normally a captain or subaltern. Directs artillery fire from an observation post in the forward area.

GHQ   *General Headquarters:* headquarters of the Commander-in-Chief (Lord Gort).

GOC   *General Officer Commanding:* a division (major general) (eg. General Fortune).

GSO   *General Staff Officer:* concerned with operations, intelligence, training and the co-ordination of all staff work within the formation concerned. Within Divisional Headquarters, GSO I = Principal Staff Officer, GSO II (Operations and co-ordination of Staff Duties), GSO III (Operations), GSO III (Intelligence) and GSO III (Training).

HE   *High Explosive.*

IO   *Intelligence Officer:* within the battalion, commands the Intelligence Section.

KIA   *Killed in Action.*

MC   *Military Cross:* officer's gallantry award, normally for those below field rank.

MM   *Military Medal:* gallantry award for those below commissioned rank.

MG   *Machine-gun:* LMG – light MG (eg. Bren gun); MMG – medium MG (Vickers .303); HMG – Heavy MG (Vickers .50) (within the division found on light tanks only).

MO   *Medical Officer.*

OR   *Other Rank:* blanket term for all below commissioned rank.

POW   *Prisoner-of-War.*

PSM   *Platoon Sergeant Major:* Warrant Officer Class III. Commanded a platoon due to the shortage of officer platoon commanders. (The rank was discontinued after the campaign in France.)

RAF   *Royal Air Force.*

RAMC   *Royal Army Medical Corps.*

RAOC   *Royal Army Ordnance Corps:* (see ADOS).

RAP	*Regimental Aid Post:* normal battle location for battalion MO and his staff.
RASC	*Royal Army Service Corps:* responsible for transporting all forms of supplies to units within the division, particularly ammunition, rations and petroleum products.
RQMS	*Regimental Quartermaster Sergeant:* Warrant Officer Class II. Senior member of the Quartermaster's staff and senior Warrant Officer in the battalion after the RSM.
RSM	*Regimental Sergeant Major:* Warrant Officer Class I.
SAA	*Small Arms Ammunition:* for pistols, rifles and machine-guns.
SC	*Staff Captain:* administrative officer of a brigade. At divisional level – Staff Captain (A) – personnel and discipline; Staff Captain (Q) – co-ordination of logistics and supply.
SO	*Signals Officer:* responsible for all line and radio communications within the battalion or regiment. Commands battalion Signal Platoon.
SSM	*Squadron Sergeant Major:* Royal Armoured Corps equivalent of CSM.
TO	*Transport Officer:* commands battalion transport section.
TSM	Armoured equivalent of PSM.
VC	*Victoria Cross:* the supreme award for gallantry. Awarded to all ranks.

Appendix 1

Author's Note of Appreciation

I would like to express my special gratitude to the following members of the original 51st (Highland) Division without whose assistance this book could not have been written.

The Black Watch
1st Battalion: Brigadier BC Bradford DSO, MBE, MC; Private J Brennan; Private A Brierley; Lieutenant Colonel FJ Burnaby-Atkins; Brigadier ADH Irwin DSO, MC; Major RN Jardine-Paterson
4th Battalion: Private J McLuskey; Major GH Pilcher MC, TD

The Seaforth Highlanders
2nd Battalion: Private GW Dodd; Private N Hill; Major CD Mackenzie MC; Lieutenant Colonel PC Mitford MBE
4th Battalion: Sergeant WG Mackintosh; Private D Maclennan; Private W Miller; Captain JE Young

The Gordon Highlanders
1st Battalion: Brigadier CN Barker MBE, MC; Captain B Brooke MC; Private T Copland; Lance Corporal T Denholm; Major JIR Dunlop; Major B Hay; Major R Ogilvie; Captain JWP Rhodes-Stampa MC
5th Battalion: Private T Anderson; Captain HMcR Gall-Gray MC; Private DJ Mackinnon; Lance Corporal G MacLennan; Captain GF Raeburn; Sergeant JG Rainnie; Captain AD Ritchie MC; Private R Shand

The Queen's Own Cameron Highlanders
4th Battalion: Private A Allen; Captain AC Fraser; Private A Grant; Major C Hunter; Lieutenant General Sir Derek Lang KCB, DSO, MC, DL; Captain GG MacDonald MC, CdeG, TD; Private T Macdonald; Corporal W Macdonald; Private H Oliver MM; Company Quartermaster Sergeant D Pirrie; Private AJ Russell; Company Quartermaster Sergeant J Smith

The Argyll & Sutherland Highlanders
7th Battalion: Captain JEM Atkinson; Captain DH Macalister Hall;

Captain CG Mackie TD, DL; Major JV Parnell; Private H Pert
8th Battalion: Professor James Campbell; Major T Campbell-Preston;
Captain HBI Cheape; Private D Smith; Major AP Stewart-Bam

The Lothians' & Border Yeomanry
1st Regiment: Sergeant J Allan; Colonel Sir Michael Ansell DSO; Sheriff
HW Ford; Troop Sergeant Major JM Hogarth DCM; Trooper WA
Hogg; Corporal J Stevenson; Captain R Watson MC

The Royal Northumberland Fusiliers
7th Battalion: Fusiliers A Black; TS Brewis; G Carter and J Charters

The Royal Norfolk Regiment
7th Battalion: Privates LG Aldous; HJ Bugden; D Clarke and G Goffin;
Captain Sir Paul Hawkins TD; Privates H Jermy and VW Kent;
Corporal E McMath; Major HJ Walker DSO

The East Surrey Regiment
2/6th Battalion: Privates B Bampton; C Bobart; M Cross and SCJ Payner;
Major J Redfern MC, TD; Captain N Tannock TD

The Royal Artillery
51st Anti-tank Regiment: Gunner GN McLellan

The Royal Engineers
1st Field Squadron: Lance Corporal T Potter

The Royal Corps of Signals
51st Division Signals Regiment: Captain WA Biggar CBE, MC; Captain RT
Ellis; Signalman J Fenwick

The Royal Army Ordnance Corps
No 2 Recovery Section: Private KJ Epps
Light Aid Detachment: Private JG Bryden

The Royal Army Service Corps
525 (Ammunition) Company: Private J Armstrong
526 (Petrol) Company: Private D Duffield; Driver J Lawson
527 (Supply) Company: Driver MA Bisset

The Royal Army Medical Corps
152 Field Ambulance: Private A Anderson

The Royal Navy
Chatham Barracks: George Fletcher

Appendix 2

51st (Highland) Division
(Order of Battle 1940–41)

GOC: Major General VM Fortune DSO

152nd Brigade (Brigadier HWV Stewart DSO)
2nd Bn, The Seaforth Highlanders (Lieutenant Colonel IC Barclay MBE)
4th Bn, The Seaforth Highlanders (Lieutenant Colonel H Houldsworth MC)
4th Bn, The Queen's Own Cameron Highlanders (Lieutenant Colonel The Earl of Cawdor)

153rd Brigade (Brigadier GT Burney MC)
1st Bn, The Gordon Highlanders (Lieutenant Colonel H Wright MBE, MC)
4th Bn, The Black Watch (Lieutenant Colonel RC Macpherson)
5th Bn, The Gordon Highlanders (Lieutenant Colonel AD Buchanan-Smith OBE)

154th Brigade (Brigadier ACL Stanley-Clarke DSO)
1st Bn, The Black Watch (Lieutenant Colonel GEB Honeyman)
7th Bn, The Argyll & Sutherland Highlanders (Lieutenant Colonel EP Buchanan MC)
8th Bn, The Argyll & Sutherland Highlanders (Lieutenant Colonel DJ Grant MC)

Divisional Armoured Reconnaissance Regiment
1st Lothians & Border Yeomanry (Lieutenant Colonel MP Ansell)

Divisional Artillery (CRA – Brigadier HCH Eden MC)
17th Field Regiment RA (Lieutenant Colonel LGRF Hamilton-Bell MC)
23rd Field Regiment RA (Lieutenant Colonel LF Garrat DSO, MC)
75th Field Regiment RA (Lieutenant Colonel GT Nugee DSO, MC)
51st Anti-tank Regiment RA (Lieutenant Colonel EK Page)

Royal Engineers (CRE – Lieutenant Colonel HM Smail TD)
26th Field Company RE (Major WH Blagdon)
236th Field Company RE (Major JP Jeffrey)
237th Field Company RE (Major JJD McInnes)
239th Field Park Company RE (Captain EM Munro)

Divisional Signals (CSO – Lieutenant Colonel TPE Murray)
51st Divisional Signal Regiment

Royal Army Medical Corps (ADMS – Lieutenant Colonel DP Levack)
152nd Field Ambulance (Lieutenant Colonel WEA Buchanan)
153rd Field Ambulance (Lieutenant Colonel JC Mackay MC)

154th Field Ambulance (Lieutenant Colonel JC Adam)
No 13 Field Hygiene Section

Royal Army Service Corps (CRÁSC – Lieutenant Colonel T Harris-Hunter)
525th (Ammunition) Company
526th (Petrol) Company
527th (Supply) Company

Royal Army Ordnance Corps (ADOS – Lieutenant Colonel AA Roth OBE)

Divisional Provost Company (Military Police)

Divisional Postal Unit RE

Attached Troops
1st Regiment Royal Horse Artillery
51st Medium Regiment RA
213th Army Field Company RE
1st Bn, Princess Louise's Kensington Regiment (Machine-guns)
7th Bn, The Royal Northumberland Fusiliers (Machine-guns)
6th Bn, The Royal Scots Fusiliers (Pioneers)
7th Bn, The Royal Norfolk Regiment (Pioneers)
Additional units of RASC and RAOC

ARK FORCE (formed 9 June 1940) (Brigadier ACL Stanley-Clarke DSO)
'A' Brigade (from Beauman Division) (Brigadier MA Green)
4th Bn, The Border Regiment
5th Bn, The Sherwood Foresters
4th Bn, The Royal East Kent Regiment (The Buffs)

154th Brigade (A/Brigadier DJ Grant MC)
4th Bn, The Black Watch
7th/8th Bn, The Argyll & Sutherland Highlanders
6th Bn, The Royal Scots Fusiliers (Pioneers)

Royal Artillery
17th Field Regiment RA
75th Field Regiment RA
204 Anti-tank Battery (from 51st Anti-tank Regiment RA)

Royal Engineers
236th Field Company RE
237th Field Company RE
239th Field Park Company RE
213th Army Field Company RE

154th Field Ambulance

Detachments from 525, 526 and 527 Companies RASC

Index

wins a DCM 34
Taylor, Lieutenant Colonel 210
Territorial Army 2, 4
Thom, Second Lieutenant RG 85
Thomas, Second Lieutenant 108
Thomson, Captain RC ('Chick') 24, 33, 160
Thompson, Lieutenant (RN) 217
Thorburn-Brown, Second Lieutenant Addie 134, death of 135–6
Thornton, Sergeant, wins a DCM 145
Threlfall, Major JM, death of 82–3
Tiergarten 17
Tighe, Second Lieutenant, death of 136
Tilloy 109, 110
Toeufles 61, 127, 128
Tôtes 161, 170, 173
Tourbières 77, 130, 133
Tower, Captain (RN) 182, 187, 206, 214
Tress, Captain PHM 111
Trois Mesnils, Les 71, 72, 84, 85
Tully 111
Turcan, Captain Pat 175–7, 178
Tweedie, Captain 130–2

Upton, Squadron Sergeant Major Alfie 4, 175
Usher, Captain Harry 130, 131–2

Valines 106, 107
Valsoorden 248
Varennes, River 45, 161
Vautier, General 63, 65, 84
Verdun 45
Vernon 94
Veules-les-Roses 185, 207, 208, 216–22, 224
Veulettes 174, 178, 182, 183
Villers, Bois de 69, 71, 72, 75; Château de 82; -sur-Mareuil 62, 64, 66, 69, 75, 76, 89, 128–9, 132
Villerwald Wood 43
Vismes-au-Val 128, 136, 137
Vuillemin, General 90

Watson, Captain Ronnie, escape of 219–20
Watson, Company Quartermaster Sergeant 99
Waldweisstroff 13, 15, 26
Waldwisse 24

Walker, Second Lieutenant Jim, escape of 222–4
Walsh, Lance Corporal 84, death of 128–9
Wanderer, HMS 164
Warren, Captain (RN) 182, 206, 214, 216
Waymark, Regimental Quartermaster Sergeant 224
Webb, Captain JL 117, 120, 121, wins an MC 122
Wesel 248
Weygand, General Maxime 93
    replaces Gamelin as C-in-C 47
    Gort disobeys his order 47, 49
    first considers peace 48
    pessimism 48, 50
    and demand for British fighters 90
    accuses Churchill of a double game 92–3
    'no retreat' 137, 151
    and hostility to British 148, 156, 157
    and conference at Tenth Army HQ 155–6
    and withdrawal of IX Corps over Seine 161, 180, 239
    army 'no longer capable of resistance' 240
Whayman, Sergeant 117
Will, Private, death of 88
Williams, Major 207
Wilson, Lance Corporal 'Ginger', wins an MM 116
Winkelmerter Wood 26, 28
Woignarue 118
Woincourt 113, 136, 137, 138
Wolschler Wood, Grand 33–6; Petit 33–4
Wright, Lieutenant Colonel Harry 125, 127, 198, 199
Wright, Trooper 175, 176

Yelon 187, 207, 211
Yonne, River 247
Yonval 61, 64, 84
Young, Captain JE ('Bim') 71, 172
Young, Major RM 98–100, 111, 112–14, 115
Younger, Major (originally Lieutenant Colonel) Harry 21, death of 224–5
Younger, Major Ossie 106, wins MC 109
Yvetot 172
Yzengremer 113, 116, 137, 138

Zailleux 65